Epic Events

EPIC EVENTS

Classics and the Politics of Time in the United States since 9/11

Sasha-Mae Eccleston

Yale
UNIVERSITY PRESS
NEW HAVEN & LONDON

Published with assistance from the Kingsley Trust Association Publication Fund
established by the Scroll and Key Society of Yale College.
Published with assistance from the Louis Stern Memorial Fund.

Yale University Press books may be purchased in quantity for educational, business, or promotional use. For information, please e-mail sales.press@yale.edu (U.S. office) or sales@yaleup.co.uk (U.K. office).

Printed in the United States of America.

Library of Congress Control Number: 2024938772

ISBN 978-0-300-26341-1 (hardcover : alk. paper)

A catalogue record for this book is available from the British Library.

This paper meets the requirements of ANSI/NISO Z39.48-1992
(Permanence of Paper).

10 9 8 7 6 5 4 3 2 1

Page 235 constitutes a continuation of this page.

1:07–1:17

For all my aunties

Contents

Acknowledgments

THIS BOOK, LIKE ALL THE BEST LABORS, GREW WITH AND OUT of the help of so many.

I completed a considerable portion of the manuscript on research leave as a Ford Foundation Postdoctoral Fellow. Thanks too to the Office of the Dean of the Faculty at Brown University and to Justine Brown for her administrative brilliance during the pandemic.

Before I knew exactly what this project was, I benefited from stimulating conversations with Marques Redd, Joel Rygorsky, Michael McGee, Kyla Tompkins, Jodi Valentine, Zhiru Ng, Hentyle Yapp, and John Varga. Kathy McCarthy, Graham Oliver, Joe Pucci, David Konstan, Steve Kidd, Johanna Hanink, and Françoise Hamlin listened encouragingly as I began sketching its contours. Audiences at Wake Forest University and Haverford College greased important wheels of thought.

Allowing me to voice frustrations, restoring perspective, and laughing from our collective belly, Reginald Blockett, Christin Fort, and Mekeila Cook act as a ballast against the more lethal forces of academe and its anti-Blackness. Thanks, also, to our original leader, Carla Guerrón Montero.

Another round of applause to Reginald Blockett for organizing cowriting sessions that sustained my work during the first wave of the pandemic—and to all the other scholars whose nonjudgmental support invigorated long hours at the keyboard, especially Brian McGowan for the opera medley. I am grateful to Patricia Akhimie and Anastasia Bailey for letting me join them and for regular check-ins with Sarika Chandra.

I discovered fairly early on in graduate school that writing in the company of Monica Huerta—on campus, near mooing cows, or in the Outer Banks—always leads to magic. *Grazie* to that other one, Dan-El Padilla Peralta, for (almost) always having that PDF I need and indulging stray thoughts about FDR. Liz Young deserves a medal for listening to me analyze the same poetry collections for six years. And for never doubting that I had worthwhile things to say about them.

No one has more consistently yearned for this book longer than Yekaterina Ildeykina: спасибо. Alicia Bonaparte and Dora Ivanišević have buoyed me with their fierce, fierce friendship.

After years of grief and disillusioning antagonism, I found in Joy Howard a compassionate and intellectually dexterous coach. Likewise, it has been incredibly restorative to have such an easygoing, grounding, and fun editor at Yale University Press in Heather Gold.

Always and in all ways, I am grateful for Armando García and Collette Eccleston.

In a world that continues to tell Black women that our lives don't matter, that we must accommodate others above all else, that we deserve nothing, that our pain isn't real, and that our accomplishments are not ours, I acknowledge myself. For digging deep and getting soft. For listening well and laughing loudly. For showing up, for singing, and for never losing sight of due North.

I thank myself.

Epic Events

Timelessness, An Introduction

ON A WALL INSIDE THE NATIONAL SEPTEMBER 11 MUSEUM, A quotation attributed to the Roman poet Virgil cuts a staid path through a dynamic field of blue. The words, "No Day Shall Erase You from the Memory of Time," have been excerpted from Virgil's epic poem, *Aeneid,* and translated into formal English. Museum visitors encounter this line of poetry as they descend the staircase leading from the museum's ground floor down into the impressively cavernous subterranean corridor that is Memorial Hall. These words meaningfully echo "never forget," the phrase that gained patriotic currency right after the 2001 terror attacks and continues to circulate, thanks, in part, to social media hashtags around the anniversary of the attacks and, in part, to being engraved on keepsakes for sale at the museum gift shop.[1] Here—in entirely capitalized letters, in a traditional font, and matching the wall's neutral color tone while standing out due to their metallic sheen—the epic excerpt assures the attacks' victims that the events of one single day will not consign them to eternal oblivion. Instead, acts of remembrance—including the museum's institutionalization of their memory—will grant them immortality as recompense for the way their lives ended.

Described as "a monument to human dignity, courage, and sacrifice," the complex, which includes a museum, a glade, and twin memorial water features on the site where the Twin Towers once stood, seeks to "honor the nearly 3,000 people killed in the terrorist attacks of September 11, 2001 and February 26, 1993, recognize the courage of those who survived, and salute those who risked their lives to help others." As "the country's principal institution for examining the attacks of September 11, 2001 and documenting their continuing impact and significance," the museum houses an

Fig. 1. Installation composed of *Trying to Remember the Color of the Sky on That September Morning* by Spencer Finch and translated excerpt from Virgil's *Aeneid.* Credit: 9/11 Memorial & Museum, Photograph by Jin S. Lee.

array of materials in its collection of "monumental and authentic artifacts."[2] It displays some of these materials in permanent exhibitions, highlights others in temporary installations, and incorporates still others in design elements located throughout the building. A host of devices help visitors make coherent sense of this array and curate an experience in line with the institution's stated mission. Continuing to glorify the World Trade Center's Twin Towers as objects to be mourned as much as the human victims of the attacks, the museum repeatedly makes the buildings part of a story about the long struggle against "radical Islamist" violence and thereby establishes the 1993 truck bombing of the World Trade Center as the smaller scale, less catastrophic precursor of the 2001 attacks. Audio and video installations complement more tangible objects and convey the scale of the Towers and the horror of escaping them as they collapsed, or of attempting to recover people from the rubble.

Interacting with these elements of the museum stokes fear and grief—as stories and images of pain, suffering, and death must. But the museum's ostensible preoccupation with time serves numerous affective, historical, and political purposes.[3] Installations that prominently display dates and clock-times reframe the inconceivable in more familiar and accessible terms. Such is the case, generally, with using "9/11" as a shorthand for the various events that occurred as part of the attacks. Calendrical dates depend on standardized methods of measuring time (chronometrics) and temporal norms. They help social groups cohere because they facilitate necessary social activities like conversation and group planning. Furthermore, when unthinkable, unspeakable, and, especially, unforeseen events occur, chronology's perceived objectivity communicates a sense of certitude and control that offers stability and comfort, however illusorily, as salves for fear and grief. Narrating the countless harrowing experiences from a day's events that caught most of those in the United States entirely unaware speaks to the chaos and upheaval the terrorists managed to create. Chronology, in contrast, speaks to the maintenance of order, to the legitimacy and continuation of those shared norms and methods.

The epic excerpt posted on the wall of Memorial Hall encapsulates the approach to time that the memorial complex authorizes: properly harnessing time, putting it under the control of the state, enables the state to protect the memories of the deceased, to govern the lives of its citizens, and, going further, to ensure the *pax Americana*, if not American *imperium*, worldwide.[4] This messaging about time begins with the museum's first installation. Named for the date, "September 11, 2001" pairs an audio-video track with a wall-length map. In the background, visitors hear voices of interviewees recounting how they learned that the attacks were happening. Panels hanging from the rafters display excerpts from these stories in time with the audio track. Each speaker begins narrating their experience by identifying their geographical location. Eventually, though, these individual narratives will overlap, each voice converging into the others. Staggered along the length of the hallway, as Amy Sodaro noticed, the individual panels function similarly. The locations they display will eventually constitute a crude world map. On the wall to the left, a black, static map that covers the geographical space extending from America's mid-Atlantic seaboard to the Midwest bears little cartographic information. Rather than state names or capitals, the map locates the airports involved in the attacks, includes the flight paths of the aircrafts weaponized by hijackers, and incorporates timestamps of the collisions in emboldened silver letters. Filling in the otherwise empty cartographic space, two paragraphs pick up the collective and affective threads of the chronological gestures mentioned above. The paragraphs give a standardized narrative of the four hijackings, establish the day's singularity via quantities ("single largest loss of life resulting from foreign attacks," "single greatest loss of life of rescue personnel"), and, finally, in keeping with the audio, describe 9/11 as an event of global significance—despite the Eastern Standard timestamps as a poignant reminder of locality. From that point onward, in the museum and likewise on its website, chronological devices like timelines and timestamps continue to contribute to the transformation of collected memories into collective or social memory.[5]

Public criticism of the quotation's inclusion in the museum has neglected time as a matter of politics, although it has always acknowledged the politics involved in this consummate site of memory. The need for a commemorative structure on the site of the Twin Towers was identified not long after the plane crashes caused their collapse. Amid the chaos and aftermath of large-scale events that garner national and international attention, designing commemorative structures always entails fraught decision-making. Decisions about the whos, whats, and hows of remembrance coexist with and derive from power struggles over who has the authority to decide these matters. The museum and memorial complex as it exists today emerged from years of negotiations about finances, logistics, responsibilities, and design, between a variety of stakeholders. Some, like New York governor George Pataki or the representatives of the New York Port Authority, wielded official power in these discussions. Survivors and the families of the victims leveraged power on the more symbolic part of the spectrum. By the time the planning commission released initial renderings for the museum and memorial complex to the public in 2011, these stakeholders had already reached enough of a consensus to commit resources toward obtaining permits and breaking ground.[6] Because one of the renderings showed the epic excerpt appearing alone on Memorial Hall's bare concrete wall, drawing the gazes of visitors upward and across otherwise empty space, the public interest seemed to privilege a new group of stakeholders: those who had proven expertise in Virgil's poem had to contend with how others understood the line and what they wanted it to accomplish at the site. Knowledgeable about an epic from the ancient Roman world but less enfranchised in realms of traditional political power, these new stakeholders could access the symbolic authority that European antiquity has continuously enjoyed in American culture to influence a contemporary structure of immense significance. The *New York Times* published an op-ed by translator Caroline Alexander, an article that included the perspectives of the museum representatives and several classicists, and a panel-style blog post on the debate as part of its ongoing coverage of the impact of 9/11.

In the article and op-ed, citing the quote's poetic context explained worries that it inappropriately memorialized the victims of the terror attacks. Many critics pointed out that, according to the goals of the museum, the "you" must refer to the casualties of the attacks.[7] In the epic poem, however, the pronoun refers to the Trojan assailants of a nighttime raid, Nisus and Euryalus, a pair of lovers who die waging war against Italic communities after one of them indulges his bloodlust and greed for war spoils (*Aen.* 9.354). According to the prevailing interpretation of the poem, narrating their final moments seeks to remind the audience of their deaths *and* the vices that caused them—not just of their love for one another: the episode warns those who lay claim to this mythological past (Romans descend from the Trojans in the poem) about the violent ends of greed and the unsavory origins of imperial conquest. Comparing the victims of the terror attacks to Nisus and Euryalus undermines their claim to heroic innocence and runs the risk of associating them with blameworthy behavior, instead. The World Trade Center's association with global finance only furthered these problematic comparisons. Understood this way, Caroline Alexander observed that the quote offers "neither instruction [to onlookers] nor solace [to the deceased]."[8]

Even as she appeared to brush these concerns aside, the museum director, Alice Greenwald, underscored an important nuance in the debate: the words mattered less as a poetic excerpt than they did as an aphorism, a valuable and timeless bit of wisdom. Faced with the problem of the quote's original poetic and sociopolitical circumstances, Greenwald reported that the committee did not choose these words because of "the classic story" from which they were taken. It thought they spoke to the idea of a single day being unable to thwart the long-lasting power of memory motivated by love, and so suited "the museum's overall commemorative context." Yet, when *The New York Times* "asked a few classicists to share their thoughts about the appropriateness of this quotation" for the newspaper's blog "City Room," the selected experts grappled with the consequences of the quote's origins in a "classic" text just as much as with the poem's story.[9] For Helen Morales, the line's provocation of memories about those who commit atrocious acts of violence could have been just as productively ironic in its contemporary context as it was in its original poetic context. But Morales also acknowledged that

Virgil could have been chosen just to fulfill the role of the "rent-a-quote Latin author" in the museum. Shadi Bartsch-Zimmer conceded that the imputed nobility of the quote and Virgil's cultural authority could have influenced the committee's selection as well. In that case, the committee's "willingness to accept noble sentiments without looking at their origin" would represent a troubling passivity, one Bartsch-Zimmer wagered was antithetical to American culture. Llewelyn Morgan emphasized that his authority as an expert on Virgil does not exist in a vacuum in this debate or, frankly, in others about how ancient Roman material ought to be used. Attempting to avoid the gatekeeping that leads academics to "snootily" pass judgments, he toed a more practical line: "you don't deploy a Virgilian tag in the first place unless you want to lend things some kind of dignity, and the citation does make the viewer assess the words as Virgil's . . . Ninety-nine-point-nine percent of people won't read [the excerpt] in context, and there's no reason why they should, but they might respond to the rhetorical move of citing an ancient author, the significance and timelessness of the sentiment that implies."

Adding a temporal dimension to his fellow classicists' observations about Virgil as a status symbol, Morgan made a point worth clarifying further than the blog format allowed. The timelessness the quote was made to traffic in was less a matter of acknowledging its having been valued and thus preserved throughout the ages and more a matter of its having been stripped of its age, deriving value from its belonging to no particular time period at all. Encouraging visitors to pore over the *Aeneid* or to carry out a comparative analysis of imperialist regimes was outside of the excerpt's brief; encouraging them to classicize the attacks and the Twin Towers, to use their importance as a standard and scale against which other events, regardless of time, would be compared, fell squarely within its parameters. Unburdened of sociocultural specificity and yet laden with significance, the quote was meant to, as John Levi Barnard put it, "perform the function the idea of 'the classics' has always performed" in American history—to grant the undertakings of the relatively new nation legitimacy, solemnity, and majesty, and consequently to stir up a yearning to belong and feelings of awe.[10] The expertise of the classicists invited to weigh in on the design emplotted the excerpt into a particular space and time, and thus conflicted with the timelessness of the museum's double-pronged classicizing (classicizing both the ancient Roman poem as aphorism and the attacks as something of transcendent significance).

Once the institution opened its doors to visitors, the quote looked different than it had appeared in the renderings. Most obviously, the line of poetry sat in the center of a commissioned artwork, Spencer Finch's *Trying to Remember the Color of the Sky on That September Morning*—the dynamic field of blue mentioned above—and so contributes to a larger assemblage dedicated to the concept of commemoration. More subtly, the word *Aeneid* no longer accompanied Virgil's name on the line beneath the excerpt. Instead, the epic's markedly un-English title only appears on museum labels located throughout the space, the same labels that identify Virgil as a poet from ancient Rome.

Minimizing the poem's title skirts the issues raised in earlier debates without overtly gesturing at them. Museum labels near the piece, however, bear traces of a more aggressive approach. They omit further information about the poem's narrative or about its political contexts, explain that the excerpt "suggests the transformative potential of remembrance," and then pivot to details about its individual letters being manufactured of steel salvaged from the former World Trade Center. Shifting focus from Virgil to the transformative process of forging "wounded, remnant steel" allows the museum to sidestep the problems flagged by initial debates and to claim that it—by way of the blacksmith Tom Joyce—had already fulfilled the quote's promise on behalf of the buildings and the human beings memorialized there. Moreover, by describing the steel letters in terms of their "hope" and "beauty," the labels convey information that seeks to guide the viewers' emotional and aesthetic responses to them. Responding to earlier controversies with attempts to direct how visitors both think and feel about the quote and, through it, about the larger significance of the 9/11 attacks, they function both as informational devices and as tools of institutional control.

Still, posting the quote within Spencer Finch's mosaic productively complicates memory's perdurance and brings to the fore the issues that can arise when time remains incompletely harnessed or straitjacketed. The 2,983 slips of paper in assorted shades of blue that make up Finch's mosaic refer to events that took place years apart.[11] Because a fountain and plaque for the victims of the February 1993 truck bombing had been installed on site in 1995, above the location of the explosion, the collapse of the Towers in 2001 also destroyed the memorial to this earlier act of violence. The number 2,983 represents the sum of the 2,977 people who died on 9/11 and the 6 official casualties of that earlier attack. To memorialize 9/11—the

September morning mentioned in the artwork's title—therefore entails acknowledging how unexpected and uncontrollable events threaten to disrupt if not destroy our monuments to remembrance. Attempts to memorialize are imperfect and precarious. Things that seem to come "out of the blue" can and will still happen.

As with the epic excerpt, the labels for Finch's mosaic share details about its manufacture—Finch painted each slip by hand with watercolors—before interpreting the work for visitors. After pointing out the nearly 3,000 slips and the same number of shades of blue, the labels explain how the work probes the relationship between "common reference" (for instance, blue as a concept) and "individual perception" (for example, where one person sees cobalt, another sees navy). It comes just short of treating "Trying to Remember the Color of That September Morning" as a visual representation of the national motto, *e pluribus unum* (a phrase, if excerpted from a Latin poem of uncertain authorship, then missing a crucial word, *color*), or even of the post-9/11 affirmation, "united we stand." Rather than highlighting how the mosaic recognizes the reality of the nation's claims to remember completely, the labels sustain the normative discourse of American liberalism.

Although both the line of epic and the mosaic speak to the idea of permanence, the assemblage they create juxtaposes the value the excerpt places on persistence and the value the mosaic places on ephemerality. Because the variety of colors in the mosaic creates the effect of movement, Finch's artwork effectively recalls the dynamism of the sky visitors left behind to enter the museum—remarkably, at this moment of descent—and of the "clear, blue sky" over lower Manhattan that Tuesday morning in 2001 before smoke, ash, and debris became all that anyone could see. The artwork gestures toward memory's ability to overcome the absence that death causes and that the passage of time worsens, ideas in keeping with the interpretation that influenced the committee's selection of text and its placement on the wall before a repository for unidentified and unclaimed remains.[12] But "trying," the first word in the artwork's title, acknowledges the effort involved in curating memory—if not also the possibility of failing to remember completely or accurately—and thus echoes the line that precedes the quoted excerpt (*nulla dies umquam memori vos eximet aevo, Aen.* 9.447) where Virgil qualifies the immortality he promises Nisus and Euryalus: "if my verse can achieve anything" (*si quid mea carmina possunt,* 446). Because each of the mosaic's uniquely colored slips pays heed to an individual person as well as to a shade of blue, the piece's form complements its acknowledgment of this struggle. Just as the mosaic produces an image through the subtle nuances and differences of its individual pieces, so too with recollecting the victims: the difficulty of recalling in detail the play of light and shadow that colors the heavens at any given moment equals that of faithfully recalling an individual's idiosyncratic way of being once they are gone. Appreciating the rich subtlety and vibrancy that accumulates over a single day honors the fullness of each individual human life. The line from the *Aeneid,* excerpted and appropriated in the way it has been, attempts to limit the power of a single day in order to endow collective memory with the ability to endure forever.

One approach is no more valid than the other. In fact, in keeping with the messaging established by the Bush administration, the institution treats the events of September 11, 2001, as both powerful enough to "change the world forever" and yet not powerful enough to thwart the will of the United States. Because such messaging can accommodate either of the approaches to timelessness noted above, there is greater onus on the viewer to notice the dimensions that each installation adds to the cultural work of timelessness in the space.

This discussion has thus far paid attention especially to temporal rhetoric—how people and things make arguments about using time—at one site in order to make aspects of critical time studies more accessible. It remains important, however, to recognize that chronopolitics, that is, a politics of time, involves considerably more than making persuasive arguments or literary tropes. Time is fundamental to human and creaturely existence. It plays a role in, determines, or conditions every aspect of our lived experience even as it challenges our attempts to define or describe it without recourse to spatial metaphors.[13] This elusiveness, however frustrating, renders time an especially productive analytic because attending to it can uncover previously underexamined threads of our existence as individuals, as social beings, and as inhabitants of this planet, and therefore afford new forms of resistance and redress.

The design elements in Memorial Hall and their relationship to strategies that begin with the very first installation scratch the surface of a full chronopolitical study of the museum. An analysis of time and the museum could consider, for example, its role in the historicization of 9/11 and the War on Terror or the relationship between its proposed lesson plans, student practices, and human development. Further, such an analysis could examine how, as a tourist site, it has been embedded within one of the largest cities in the world (timed entry, tour bus schedules, public transportation options, peak or slow visitation periods); how designs ignored or acknowledged climate change; or how it shapes a visitor's experience of time (the duration of guided versus self-guided tours, the length of interactions with exhibits, the time spent in the museum, and its impact on time spent in the gift shop). A chronopolitical analysis could consider any or all of the above with an eye to the circulation of power, in its numerous forms, rather than to the multiplicity of temporalities alone.[14] And because it is just one site, such an analysis could contribute to a much larger chronopolitical study of the contemporary United States.

Periods marked by instability have their own chronopolitical dynamics. A discourse of national unity prevailed after the 2001 attacks: homogenizing temporal experience attempted to facilitate a mode of national belonging capable of both transcending politics and drumming up support for certain military, legislative, and diplomatic actions. As with other discourses that create and reinforce false universals, this one obfuscated how experiences of time have always varied considerably within the nation and thus avoided inconsistencies, failures, and injustices. Time organizes, regulates, and differentially shapes life outcomes.[15] It genders, racializes, sexualizes, classes, disables, and otherwise hierarchizes people, as individuals and as parts of larger populations. If citizenship is both a formal legal status *and* a relationship between strangers who have learned to *feel* intimately that they belong to a group, then it has temporal and not just spatial components.[16] By factoring in social practices and relationships, time configures access to the rights, protections, and privileges associated with citizenship as both a legal and an affective state according to various intersecting structures of difference.

Tempus Quo

"We are here in the middle hour of our grief."[17] With those words, President George W. Bush began his address before those who had gathered to participate in a special midday service at the Washington National Cathedral on September 14, 2001. Just one day before, the office of the president issued a proclamation declaring that Friday would be a "National Day of Prayer and Remembrance for the Victims of the Terrorist Attacks on September 11, 2001."[18] In formulaic language befitting the solemnity of the occasion,

President Bush called on the "authority vested in [him] by the Constitution and laws of the United States" to endow that Friday with this particular significance. The text of the proclamation specified how Americans and their allies could spend the noon hour on Friday honoring those who had died and comforting one another. Given the president's quoting of the Bible in the proclamation itself, it isn't surprising that it asks faith-based institutions to mark the National Day of Prayer and Remembrance with the ringing of bells, services, and other activities. Recognizing that Friday noon would find many Americans in the middle of their workday, the nation's leader also asked employers to give their employees leave to attend such services during their lunch hour. By asking for the consent of employers across the country, Bush revealed their authority over the way many American adults "spend" their time and how much of American social life depends on obeisance to capitalist norms and power relations. Synchronizing the American people on this Friday midday would have been practically impossible without the cooperation of those who enforced the standard American workweek. Employers became just as necessary to the alteration of the weekly rhythms as the faith-based institutions whose noontime bells would signal that the moment had arrived for a collective outpouring of grief.

On the one hand, the president's ability to control the calendar dovetailed with his desire to (re-)set behavioral standards in accordance with it: participating in the National Day of Prayer and Remembrance fomented affective belonging within the nation at the same time as it demonstrated the Bush administration wresting power over time back from those who perpetrated the attacks. Identifying this noon as the "middle hour of grief" initially confronted an undeniable reality: the events that had taken place just three days before had not yet sunk in for many, and, in addition to the thousands officially declared dead, the search for the missing still continued. For several paragraphs, President Bush cast himself as a mere representative of a sympathetic nation by referring to a shared sense of "sorrow." He thus picked up elements of the occasion's liturgical and religious context established by the preceding remarks of several religious leaders. Halfway through, the president departed from delivering a message in line with the emotional and religious consensus, and moved to offering one about historical significance and human-made rather than divinely delivered justice.[19] The president paired recognition that Americans did not yet "have the distance of history" with history making a "clear" demand of the American people "to answer these attacks and rid the world of evil." Sharing sorrow no longer meant preventing families of victims from experiencing isolation; it created a "kinship" that necessitated that people also share "a steadfast resolve to prevail against our enemies." Bush echoed President Franklin Delano Roosevelt (FDR) when he declared the attacks in New York City, Virginia, and over Pennsylvania as acts of war. He then lamented that such "conflict [began] on the timing and terms of others," but promised that "it will end in a way, and at an hour, of our choosing," building toward a comparison between what would become the War on Terror and World War II.

The rhetoric of kinship leads to a kairological call to action, the nation's shared qualitative sense of the moment and the decision that ought to follow it: "the commitment of our fathers is now the calling of our time." Seeking to apply the power he already used over the nation's citizens to punish the nation's enemies, the president framed the already inevitable war as a way to put the United States back in control of time, as, he suggested, it had been ordained to be all along. And this was the opportune moment. Indeed, when he announced the War on Terror in the speech before a Joint Session of Congress on September 20, 2001, President Bush reiterated the point he made at the National Cathedral: "This country will define our times, not be defined by them."[20]

On the other hand, because this Friday deviated from weekday norms, the president's remarks about temporal control also evinced the nostalgic idealization of the pre-9/11 status quo in the United States. His handling of this occasion and others during his eight years in office reflected a widely felt desire to return to normalcy, since the attacks had put American society and even time itself "out of joint."[21] Those who designed and perpetrated the attacks wanted them to be violent, deadly, and disruptive. And by all measures they were. At the three sites, across the nation, and beyond, their actions created emergency situations that interrupted and superseded everyday routines for a period of time. The televisual circumstances of the attacks also meant that many Americans watched them live as they happened, unsure what exactly was occurring and when or where it would all come to an end. During the day, the quick cascade of hypermediated events rendered updates from the Bush administration untimely when members of the administration were not hidden from view or otherwise absent. Weaponizing fear as well as the planes they hijacked, the terrorists thus managed to provoke real uncertainty about aspects of life that many—but certainly not all—Americans had been trained to take for granted when imagining the collective present, past, and future: assumptions of American invulnerability, geopolitical supremacy, societal stability, and national progress felt increasingly precarious or patently untrue. The evening of September 11 the president and his administration attempted to recover control of the narrative of the attacks by summarizing what had happened, explaining its causes, and promising to protect America's citizens.[22] Mixing recognition of the thousands of people wounded and killed in the attacks with pride in American selflessness and heroism, the president reassured Americans that the terrorists had not actually succeeded in interrupting the government, weakening the American economy, or stifling the military. A vision of Americans "from all walks of life unit[ing] in our resolve for peace and justice" proclaimed that the (imagined) foundations of the social order remained intact as well.

From a chronopolitical standpoint, that, of course, was the rub. Ours was not a perfect democratic society before the collapse of the Towers or the crash of United Flight 93 in Shanksville. The binary of "us versus them" that pervaded so much of the Bush administration's post-9/11 rhetoric favored moralizing and plainspoken decisiveness in order to excoriate the nation's "enemies." Neither it nor the brand of jingoism it sanctioned left much room for complex analysis, dissent, or geopolitical self-examination. Instead, the nation assured itself that it had been and remained a bastion of freedom and democracy, coopting the innocence of the day's casualties for itself as an exceptional geopolitical actor.[23] The reality was far from exceptional: like other societies, the institutions, systems, and structures that constituted America's social order (re-)produced a society rife with injustice and inequality. As a result, there were many Americans for whom a return to normalcy meant they were more likely to have shorter-than-average life expectancies, to be adultified or infantilized, to experience frequent discrimination and harassment, to "do time," or to constantly live with the kinds of insecurity that mainstream discourse associated with the spectacular circumstances of the attacks. If the status quo and the power relations that established it had not truly changed, the temporal order—the aggregate of timeframes that societal systems, structures, and institutions establish as normative according to explicit and implicit means—had not changed either. During periods of perceived upheaval, appeals to the former social and temporal orders attempt to conjure a feeling of belonging, well-being, and stability. But for those disenfranchised by established orders, the continuation of prior norms and social relations reinstates a flow of power that has structured their disadvantage, reminding them of the ways that they viscerally know their personal identities and national identities do not mesh well and of the penalties that accrue as a result.[24] It becomes impossible for them to forget that they had always been out of joint with the dominant culture's way of inhabiting, measuring, or even conceptualizing time.

A society's dominant culture can weaponize the *tempus quo,* or temporal order, by denying coevalness to those it considers deviant, radically different, or as "Other." As work in critical time studies across various academic fields has demonstrated, the dominant culture's institutions, structures, and systems will dismiss these Others as allochronistic, living in or belonging to a different time, rather than accepting the plurality of ways people think about and live in time within the same historical period. Charges of allochronism can come freighted with spatial or developmental and evolutionary assumptions: "primitive" people occupy a "there" and "then." Readers of colonialist travel literature or science fiction may be familiar with this conceit whereby long-distance journeys that put different cultures in contact with one another involve time travel: travelers pit their assumed present against that of the populations native to the lands they visit.[25] After 9/11, the Bush administration and mainstream American media outlets frequently Orientalized Arab people and Islamic nation-states as barbaric and incompatible with modernity and progress: such allochronism associated their transformation from geopolitical objects into geopolitical actors with catastrophic danger, if not the end of history itself.[26] Allochronistic thinking also informs how regional, cultural, and ethnic differences within the boundaries of a country or a society are understood: it is not uncommon in the United States to hear, for example, dismissals of the Deep South as being "stuck in the past" or "backward," or to encounter the invisibilization of Indigenous people as "of the past" or extinct.[27] Such understandings can come with ready-made laments and longings for that past rather than the range of feelings that motivate future-facing action in the present.

Privileging, for example, Silicon Valley or a gentrified neighborhood as "the future" signals how allochronistic thinking veils racial, ethnic, and class-based violence against communities under the guise of innovation and the feeling of optimism.[28] The gentrification of the future consigns preexisting residents to a troublesome past overdue for a renaissance. Such temporal framing can facilitate the disavowal of societal injustice insofar as those who have been instantly reassigned to a "there" and "then" cannot make effective claims for redress in the "here" and "now" where they are imagined to no longer reside. We need not think so abstractly about temporal disenfranchisement, though. Deadlines, expiration dates, minimum ages, and statutes of limitations determine how people participate in and think about social institutions, such as the law. Neoliberal thinking especially makes it so that the problems of temporal others remain theirs to fix, not just at the level of communities but also individually. Criticisms of an alternate, counter-, or sub-"culture" in this vein take no account of the historical and structural reasons that brought these differences from or problems with the dominant culture into being. They therefore delegitimize or even villainize attempts to bring about radical change, associating such change with upheaval, insecurity, and even terror.

Because the Bush administration's attempt to regain control of time often gave primary place to the future in its discussions of national security and global peace, one could consider it the dominant timeframe of the post-9/11 security state.[29] The Bush doctrine prioritized preemptive military action overseas in order to, as the 2002 National Security Strategy states, "prevent [terrorists] from doing harm against our people and our country."[30] To be freed from the collective experience of terror that the nation experienced on 9/11 meant limiting the capacity of others to do harm, not just foiling their actual plans to do so: or as President Bush told a graduating class of the US Military Academy, "if we wait for threats to fully materialize, we will have waited too long."[31] Domestically, the newly created Department of Homeland Security focused on preparedness. Both preemption and preparedness depend on the idea that taking proper action in the present can eliminate the discomfort and danger of not knowing. Previous foreign policy strategies that prioritized diplomatic solutions over military action, Cold War–era military tactics, and domestic safety procedures had looked to the future as well. However, the post-9/11 approach to the future worked according to a different calculus of risk than before.[32] Analyses of this approach have emphasized how the Bush doctrine's futurity actually involved several other temporalities in practice: it extended the duration of the state of exception, allowing for unilateral decision-making by the executive branch of the US government, and legitimized a similar geopolitical stance; it gave itself an out from the oversight of deadlines, expiration dates, and budgets because a future always remains to be prepared for. Logics of preemption and preparedness also favor speed—the ability to perceive an emerging risk, to communicate that risk instantaneously, and to take decisive actions against it turns a split second into an opportunity for safety rather than a guarantee of destruction—and thus fit exceedingly well within global capitalist systems, such as the military-industrial complex.[33] Preferring speedy decisiveness over meaningful deliberation also meant, among other things, curtailing how democracies work, despite the pretenses of a war effort trying to effect humanitarian peace by spreading democracy worldwide.[34] And decisions made in times of crisis could be strategically enforced long after the crisis had been resolved, falling out of sync with term limits or making wartime and peacetime indistinguishable.

The decades since the attacks and since the Bush administration left office have seen the proliferation of debates about the plurality of collective temporalities and hierarchical citizenship, bringing the politics of time into the mainstream of the so-called "culture wars." Nikole Hannah-Jones and the other contributors to *The New York Times Magazine*'s 1619 Project echoed a critique of anniversaries made nearly two centuries ago by Frederick Douglass in "What to the Slave is the Fourth of July?" By positing the year enslaved Africans purchased by Jamestown colonists touched down in Virginia as a foundational date, they made 1776, the year that the white male land- and slave-owners at the Continental Congress signed a Declaration of Independence and the year that is traditionally celebrated as when the United States of America came into existence, a belated milestone. Memorializing it on the federal calendar replays the consequent conceptual error annually on July 4.[35] The slogan "Make America Great Again" installed President Trump in a timeline of Republican leaders by echoing President Reagan's campaign slogan and offered a route back into a golden age of the party by extolling the virtues of that age and faith in the power structures that underlay it. Stoking the fires of white supremacist resentment, the Trump administration responded to the 1619 Project with its own patriotic curriculum that defends the propriety and accuracy of the 1776 founding date. The organization "Time's Up" attempted to leverage the momentum of Tarana Burke's #MeToo viral hashtag to tackle gender-based discrimination and sexual harassment in the workplace.[36] The global coronavirus pandemic disrupted capitalist schedules and production timelines; confounded the workweek, the weekend, and holidays along socioeconomic lines; spread more quickly than government agencies could handle efficiently; lasted longer than many expected; and made planning for the future both emotionally exhausting and logistically challenging. The varied responses to the novel coronavirus taxed American institutions; revealed how limited and limiting our post-9/11 conceptualizations of security, peace, and preparedness had been; and underscored the vast inequities that structure American society and the world beyond. Although the COVID-19 pandemic overtook 9/11 as an unforeseen, era-defining national tragedy in terms of casualties, the coronavirus, the pandemic's microscopic and misunderstood agent, has not sustained the same hold on the national(ized) psyche as the 2001 attacks did. Nevertheless, its effects cannot be ignored. Whereas the United States framed itself as ideally suited to lead the defense of democracy and free markets after 9/11, this attack's adaptive microscopic agent calls into question the ability and suitability of this or any single nation to combat the next wave of global crises.

When disasters scale upward to the level of global or planetary catastrophe, retreating to well-entrenched universalisms, including those about time, might seem justified. Climate change has awakened nonexperts to the idea of planetarity via geological and ecological time, and cast the notion of any recognizable future on Earth in doubt at the same time as increasingly sophisticated technologies expand our knowledge of deep space and afford our "witnessing" of foundational cosmological events. Although climate change does affect everyone on the planet, it does not affect everyone identically at the same time. Given the geopolitical imbalances in which nations and communities are currently situated, everyone on Earth will not be given equal access to scarce resources and solutions developed to mitigate the various crises that accompany climate change at the same time. The coronavirus pandemic demonstrated that. Instead of false universals, the combination of our widening knowledge about our planet, other planets, and outer space and the coronavirus pandemic encourages us to think about the *differential* impact these crises and the advances that can mitigate them have upon individuals, communities, and whole societies based upon preexisting relations of power.[37] They demand that human beings recognize those relations of power and organize across difference so as to effectively stem the tide of impending disaster rather than pretend that such differences do not exist.

Epic Events

This book delves into an archive of texts that engage ancient Greek and Roman material (including speeches, op-eds, novels, poems, plays, artworks, museums, and memorials) in order to disaggregate lived experiences of time that discourses of national unity homogenize. The ancient Greeks and Romans can be strategically deployed to classicize, lending an event, object, or practice "transcultural and transhistorical value" in exchange for cultural specificity.[38] But classicization is messy work. It's not just the survival of anything over millennia that ought not to be taken for granted. A host of processes, contingencies, and power struggles turn the fact that ancient Greek and Roman civilizations chronologically precede the nation's founding into a license to derive standards from them, a responsibility to preserve their artifacts, a will to render them as a possession-in-common, and, consequently, the endorsement of—if not material rewards for—imitating, re-creating, and alluding to them. The smooth veneers of an unstinting tradition, utopian universals, and timelessness hide these processes and contingencies with varying levels of success: while deploying classical timelessness may seek to depoliticize an event, object, or practice and attempt to determine what they mean and how they feel, as with the National September 11 Museum and Memorial's inclusion of Virgil's *Aeneid,* such attempts belie the unanimity and consensus they aim to project. Other attempts to engage ancient Greek and Roman material emphasize these paradoxes, parody their status, and/or attempt to recover what has been disavowed. In addition to explaining how the ancient Greeks and Romans have been enlisted to structure and maintain the temporal order, this project explains that they have been used to confront how time differentially structures the experience and exercise of membership in the national community.

The assortment of communities, sociopolitical formations, cultures, dialects, and so on that merely seem neatly encapsulated by the term "ancient Greece and Rome" do not, in and of themselves, have an endemic purchase on time and cannot act as a Rosetta Stone for the politics of time of all peoples everywhere. These cultures have been a constant resource for various nation-building projects since the settler colonialists who arrived on this portion of the continent declared themselves an independent political entity and destroyed the new nation's connection to the Indigenous peoples who had previously inhabited this land: many of the elite Europeans who colonized this continent and founded new countries on it had been habituated to think about themselves as the inheritors of an ancient Mediterranean past through education and social customs, and they continued negotiating their present through that relationship to that past. From state seals with Latin mottos and Corinthian columns on plantation houses to speeches televised from the Senate floor and popular entertainment, the ancient Greeks and Romans have enjoyed a cultural visibility and authority that has been coterminous with the nation.[39] This authority and the norms it is used to buttress have been routinely and persistently contested however. As research in classical reception studies has demonstrated, ancient Greek and Roman material has been among the many resources reappropriated by those seeking to rectify societal injustice and to thereby challenge the limits imposed upon them. This material from the ancient Mediterranean, more immediately recognizable than time and often conspicuously employed to bid for status, can therefore register the effects of temporal control instead of simply ratifying fictions of temporal transcendence. Heeding the various power struggles involved in the creation, maintenance, and defense of the ancient Greek and Roman stuff as "*the* classics" draws attention to it as another of the many fictions sustaining the normative order.[40]

To some extent, conducting research in classics has always meant treating the ancient Greeks and Romans as historically and geographically bound civilizations with cultural particularities rather than as avatars of civilization writ large.[41] Classics has grappled with the classicism that underwrites its name ever more seriously in recent decades, with some departments changing their name accordingly.[42] During this time, the subfield of classical reception studies has grown in the number of its practitioners and in its importance. Pathbreaking work in this subfield has introduced new areas of interest and methodologies to the discipline and kept a set of practitioners in classics who would not have found a secure foothold within it otherwise. The university, the museum, and other institutions have, in this same period, had to reckon with their relationship to racialized and other forms of injustice, both as a matter of changing mores and as a result of demographic changes that threaten their financial survival. But in the United States, academic disciplines historically have not communicated what their research entails clearly to the nonacademics who constitute the vast majority of the general public. Siloing research behind institutional and paywalls has only made it harder for nonacademics to understand the variety of academic labor and to assess its outcomes. It is not surprising, then, that classicism and the work of the classics can so widely diverge, that discrepancies should arise between what research in the field about the ancient Greeks and Romans reveals or at least argues and how the ancient Greeks and Romans continue to be perceived by the general public.

However, the field cannot completely externalize the problems caused and indexed by classicizing its objects of study as the misperception of those outside of it alone. It has, explicitly and implicitly, profited from this misperception, trafficking in classicization in order to market itself, to attract students, to secure funding, and, therefore, to perpetuate itself. For a long time, reception studies had documented how—despite the classicized ancient Greeks and Romans circulating via projects of imperialism, elitism, Eurocentrism, and white supremacy amid temporally and geographically distant cultures—they had also been enlisted in political struggles against oppression. But, on the whole, the fact that these struggles had happened, historically, did not directly impact the way the discipline functioned in the present; even worse, such research could more readily function as an apology for the discipline's contribution to and courting of classicism. The subfield has until quite recently been considered less rigorous than some others and has enjoyed less intradisciplinary prestige—which, within the field's political economy, especially exacerbated gendered and racialized exclusion.[43] The new strand of reception studies and other disciplinary subfields whose political orientation might be fruitfully gathered under the rubric of critical classical studies does not approach the relationship of the classics to the aforementioned projects of imperialism, elitism, Eurocentrism, patriarchy, and white supremacy as things of only historical interest or that affected every other social institution, system, or structure in the present except the academic discipline itself.[44] Attentive to how these projects continue to differentially structure lived experience, it also critiques how they have influenced the way the discipline currently operates.

One can find a considerable amount of research on time within the field of classics. It has been especially common in analyses of literary texts that skew toward and deeply engage narratological methods.[45] Work in the field of contemporary critical time studies often notes how global capitalism has dictated the measurement and standardization of time in order to facilitate the transport of goods and supplies. In premodern fields, numerous articles and book-length studies have devoted attention to parsing the stakes and conceptualization of time underwriting ancient chronometrics. Scholarship in classics abounds on ancient horology and timekeeping devices, like sundials, water clocks, and the Roman calendar (*fasti*). In the case of the ancient Roman calendar, research has uncovered practical details about its appearance, paratextual aspects in situ, or still extant examples, and has described how it functions as a technology of *Romanitas* (Roman identity) and imperialist propaganda as well as a tool for commercial, religious, and juridical life in the city of Rome itself. Focusing on politics in the traditional sense, that is, as decisions made by the elite and political actors, these studies tend to eschew analyses of the "private dimensions of Roman time." In *Caesar's Calendar,* for example, Denis Feeney explains how Romans emplotted themselves in historical time to legitimize and to naturalize their imperial ambitions, clarifying the ways that territorial expansion forced the Romans to synchronize the histories of different communities and why the Romans did not universalize their calendar.[46] Once dismissed as little more than a versified almanac, Ovid's etiological poem based on the calendar, *Fasti,* has long been redeemed as a complex work that blends generic innovation and appropriation with cultural commentary.[47] Maurizio Bettini's *Anthropology and Roman Culture* analyzes the ways that Romans spatialized time, especially with regard to the language and social practices that involved aristocratic genealogies. On the ancient Greek side, Alex Purves centers much of *Space and Time in Ancient Greek Narrative* upon "advances in the practical and spatial arts" of mapmaking and frequently addresses how texts negotiate the way they are experienced in time.[48] *Narratives of Time and Gender in Antiquity* explores how concepts of time help construct and emphasize gender difference in ancient Greek and Roman cultures. In the volume's introduction, editors Esther Eidinow and Lisa Maurizio rightfully observe how "gendered conceptions of time . . . have simply become unremarked elements of [the Western imagination's] mental furniture."[49] Recent work on anachronism has further explored the multiplicity of times that constitute the presents and pasts in ancient texts, and work on time continues to be forthcoming.[50]

Nevertheless, the cultural politics of time has not been thoroughly theorized or studied as part of a thrust toward a critical classical studies. Most recently, the Postclassicisms Collective has "set untimeliness against the time line of classicism" in its debut book, *Postclassicisms.* The chapter "Time" sets out how reconsiderations of "philosophies of time . . . historical self-consciousness. . . . the complexity of how a subject is situated in historical space . . . and the way narrative form encodes temporal models" can help "redraft classicism's temporalities." Querying classicism's role in creating genealogical relationships between past and present and the narratives that different regimes of classicism use to sustain and to actualize those relationships, the collective favors cultivating "untimeliness" for the purpose of "unsettling any sense of 'being of one's time' " without reverting to a "longing for an unattainable but desirable past."[51] Cultivating untimeliness stems from an acknowledgment of the temporal complexity of the present and a refusal to choose sides in the battle between continuity and rupture or disjuncture that classicism can set up. The collective's argument thus gestures toward many of the issues already flagged about time's ability to conjure certain affects and kinships that can run afoul of what has been accepted as self-evident. But its citational and intellectual politics don't seem to depart significantly from the disciplinary mainstream. As Johanna Hanink indicated in her review of the book, by pursuing these issues about time, value, and so on through Eurocentric intellectual history, the collective misses an opportunity to dive deeply into the lived experiences and knowledge traditions that have been marginalized within academe and society and thereby to put postclassical critique into practice.[52] It is one thing to encourage readers to "unsettle any sense of being of one's time" so that they can question the hierarchized value placed on the present and/or the past. It is another thing to question who gets to settle into what times as their own in the first place.

This book takes up that question directly. *Epic Events* analyzes how authors and artists have drawn on the temporalities operating within ancient Greek and Roman material to critique the *tempus quo* of the contemporary United States. The ancient material included in this study is not limited to epic poetry or to any single genre understood as uniquely applicable to American crisis (for example, tragedy): the ancient Greek word *epos* more generally meant "utterance" or "word," and its archaic semantics included speech's function as a "social bonding mechanism."[53] The title of this book thus alludes to the fact that the contemporary texts analyzed within it capture the dynamics of the national conversation about events whose differential impact on the constituent communities of the United States prompted reflection on the nation's self-image. The rewards that these texts have earned for engaging ancient Greek and Roman material (contracts, production, marketing support, mainstream critical or commercial success, prizes) warrant further consideration in another project. This book's interest remains in the fact that, despite their success, the temporal critique of these texts has not been thoroughly discussed or considered as a facet of their reception of ancient Greek and Roman material. This oversight has the effect of continuing to promulgate fictions about classical timelessness and, often, to satisfy a market for diversity, within and beyond the academic field of classics, but it does little to address the hierarchies of American citizenship.

Epic Events sets out to complement the valuable work that has already been done in classics on the relationships between time, gender, nationhood, and empire, and to deepen the investment of critical classical studies in lived experience, embodied knowledge, and contemporary sociopolitics, particularly when racial, ethnic, economic, sexualized, and gendered injustice meet. Each chapter analyzes the temporal critique of one or more contemporary literary texts that adapt, allude, or otherwise respond to ancient Greek and Roman material, with supplementary texts providing historical and cultural context where appropriate. In addition to engaging with classics and classical reception studies, this book sustains dialogue with work from other fields, including English, comparative literature, and American studies: methodologies from classical philology (close reading, rhetorical analysis) feed into and off of theoretical interventions from critical time studies, critical theories of race, critical refugee studies, critical finance studies, queer of color critique, sonic studies, performance studies, environmental humanities, and so on. In order to make those interventions accessible to classicists and the project accessible to an even wider readership, highly specialized jargon has been avoided where possible and defined where necessary.

With regard to the contemporary texts, when I began this project, I had anticipated that World War II would play an important role in defining American society's ideal of itself and its ideal role on the geopolitical stage. I did not predict just how important a touchstone the Vietnam War would be for so many of the authors I selected, so that it had a classical status of its own. A significant amount of attention has been paid to thinking about how the authors, artists, and public figures quoted herein select ancient Greek and Roman intertexts to weigh the impact that the classical status of these more recent events makes upon citizenship. Analyses of the ancient texts prioritize the complications of comparison rather than strict analogue. Likewise, attention has been devoted to understanding how a contemporary author or artist has adapted the ancient texts to critique the

American temporal order and how the ancient texts relate to their own, contemporary temporal order: because of different ideologies, societal structures, and historical circumstances, the chronopolitics of the ancient text may not be identical to that of the contemporary text, and they need not be in order to yield effective comparisons.

Throughout the book, flagging conceptual, ideological, sociological, and historical linkages between the events and texts covered along the way intends to disrupt chronology's primacy and to signal the interwoven complexities of the sociopolitical fabric. Each chapter takes its name from a single temporality. But that temporality acts more as a gateway toward identifying the always multiple temporalities involved in the maintenance of the normative order than as a standalone term: each chapter explains how social practices, roles, systems, institutions, and structures *coordinate* time(s) in particular ways in order to better understand the rights, protections, and privileges that time allows or prohibits communities and social groups from exercising. In this way, what could be characterized as "private dimensions of time," including how time conjures the individually embodied *feeling* of national belonging, have very nonprivate, collective, and public ramifications. This is especially evident in the multiple chapters that uncover how the various temporalities that make up the domestic sphere reproduce or challenge the social order.[54] It also means that focusing on texts from the last twenty years does not intend to definitively periodize them: reconsidering the period immediately following September 11, 2001, and crises that reflect critically on the American response to the attacks does not attempt to mark them as a wholly singular set of events in the history of American social life or as the origin of certain social problems.[55] In the case of climate change, the policies and practices that are rendering Earth increasingly uninhabitable predated the 2001 attacks. So did the structural anti-Black racism, anti-Asian discrimination, white supremacist yearnings, and gender-based harassment that animate the other movements that have dominated public discussion in recent years. Returning to an event that drove national discourse for years and continues to influence American life acknowledges the ways that the practical circumstances of the attacks, the geopolitical relationships involved, and the US government's response—especially, but not exclusively, the Bush administration's interest in temporal control and recourse to, if not enforcement of, a virulent form of patriotism—intensified trends linking a politics of time to particular practices and feelings of citizenship. Doing so intends to kindle a desire for a fuller power chronography, to use Sarah Sharma's evocative term, of the United States and to provoke readers to follow the trends identified herein in other contexts.[56]

Given the changing investment of classics in diversity and the field's constant pursuit of relevance to contemporary American culture and, most importantly, to those racialized students whose enrollment in courses, programs, and schools sustains the study of the ancient Greeks and Romans, this book is a product of its times. In the United States, Canada, and the United Kingdom, especially, the field of classics is currently reckoning with how it reproduces societal structures, systems, and norms that run the gamut from problematic to deadly. By attending to contemporary chronopolitics with an unapologetic interest in racialized communities and in theories and methodologies that center these communities, *Epic Events* asks about belonging in the United States at the same time as it pushes the boundaries of what people and knowledge belong in the discipline of classics as it currently exists.

CHAPTER 1

Instants and Replays

ERIC FISCHL'S SCULPTURE *TUMBLING WOMAN* STOOD, FOR A limited time, in the lower concourse of Manhattan's Rockefeller Plaza. Unveiled in 2002, on the first anniversary of the September 11 attacks, the artwork suspends a nude female figure in a state of vulnerability, either free-falling through the air or, as the position of the neck against the sculpture's pedestal also suggests, making awkward, potentially dangerous contact with the ground. An artist in various mediums, Fischl actually began taking photos of a woman tumbling on the floor a year before 9/11.[1] He repurposed that preparatory work after losing a friend in the World Trade Center attacks. The details of this repurposing vary, but in one interview Fischl claims he hoped *Tumbling Woman* would serve as a reminder of his experience of the day's events: "I, like most of the world, watched the tragedy unfold on television. . . . [W]atching this nightmare unfold all day long . . . and just feeling myself spin out of control with all, you know, the mind going crazy, the emotions going crazy with all of the feelings that were being caused by this terrifying thing. And so, it was in that moment of feeling myself spin out of control that I knew that the only way back would be to create something that created a kind of solid anchoring construct, something that would articulate the feelings that would try to reconnect me to it."[2]

Fischl's work had spurred debate before. His sculptural tribute to Black tennis trailblazer Arthur Ashe confused tennis stars and visitors alike once revealed at the USTA Billie Jean King National Tennis Center in 2000. The nude figure, straining as if in mid-serve, did not resemble Ashe, and even if the statue fit the "athletic classical image of physicality and heroism," professional athletes in the United States do not compete in the

Fig. 2. Eric Fischl's *Tumbling Woman* (2002) on display as part of "Rendering the Unthinkable: Artists Respond to 9/11," a retrospective exhibition at the 9/11 Memorial Museum, on September 1, 2016. Spencer Platt / "First Major Exhibition at 9/11 Memorial and Museum to Open" via Getty Images.

nude.[3] Some wondered if it meant (and failed) to portray Ashe himself, and what it—either as a representation of the man or, less directly, his spirit—communicated about the legend's place in American sporting history, or if the nudity was appropriate to a venue open to visitors of all ages.[4] Despite this public response, it met the criteria that Ashe's widow, Jeanne, had set for the USTA's commission, and consequently the sculpture remains in place to this day. In contrast, the uproar surrounding *Tumbling Woman* marked it for removal from Rockefeller Plaza within one week of installation.

Tumbling Woman is bumpy, rather than chiseled, in a relatively realistic style, and of a smaller scale than the classically inspired statues that stood nearby it. To its west, a statue of Prometheus seems to glide effortlessly through the air, the fire in his hand a contrast to the ice of the rink he decorates. An excerpt from Aeschylus in granite tells viewers that that gift of fire "Hath Proved to Mortals a Means to Mighty Ends." Not too far away Atlas holds aloft the globe of the world, the Titan's defined muscles attesting to the strength required for such a feat. *Tumbling Woman* does not depict a male figure from ancient Greek myth that links mortal ingenuity to a feat of immortality, yet it may be no less classically resonant. Most obviously influenced by the classicisms of Auguste Rodin and Aristide Maillol,

Tumbling Woman, in its so-called "ashen state," also reminded one art historian, Randall Van Schepen, of the victims of the eruption of Mount Vesuvius in 79 CE.[5] Murals from Pompeii had inspired some of Fischl's prior work. But Van Schepen noted how the lumpiness of *Tumbling Woman* and the fact that it preserves someone in a moment of vulnerability recalled the archaeological site's casted bodies. Long after the flesh of the volcano's casualties had decomposed, plaster re-created their bodies, hauntingly posed, out of what had become a void, communicating aspects of their last harrowing moments.[6] Moreover, the toxic debris that circulated in the air after the Twin Towers collapsed recalls the mix of ash, rock, and gas that spewed from Vesuvius. As that mix covered (and destroyed) everything for miles, the debris from the collapsed buildings likewise caked those who were in Lower Manhattan the morning of the attacks. Photos captured these ashen survivors stunned, weeping, and/or searching for safety. Like those photos and the casts, Fischl's sculpture evokes the disconcerting suspension of humans somewhere between life and death.

Popular among tourists and as backdrops to public (and publicly televised) events, Rockefeller Plaza's other classical sculptures have been made to support various narratives about American thriving. They have symbolized the triumph of commerce, nationhood, and philanthropy. But face to face with *Tumbling Woman*—a singular, nude yet not sexualized female form—viewers had to confront vulnerability, not triumph, and could not seek solace in projections of institutional power. Some early viewers of the casted "pitiable remains" at Pompeii thought "they had too much of the horror of death about them" to be considered beautiful.[7] *Tumbling Woman* elicited reactions in this vein. Reminding viewers of the shock of 9/11, especially those who jumped from the Twin Towers in order to escape the fire engulfing the structures, Fischl's sculpture, as one viewer quoted in *The New York Times* put it, had failed to "dignify" the deaths of the attacks' victims in New York City.[8]

Conjuring unwieldy feelings and thoughts, Fischl's attempt to represent his experience of September 11, 2001, resulted in the creation of a powerful countermonument.[9] Because the sculpture "forced viewers to consider the panic and desperation of some of the WTC victims in their final moments" in a more strikingly personalized manner, perhaps, than the photograph of *Falling Man* that ensconces the individual, seemingly resigned and equanimous, figure against a large-scale grid of steel and glass, Fischl leveraged

Fig. 3. Plaster casts at Pompeii re-create the body shapes of the victims buried by ash from the eruption of Vesuvius in 79 CE. Michael Harris / Alamy Stock Photo.

the body's mediated presence in ways that ran afoul of the quickly accepted convention.[10] Powerful forces soon shaped the discourse around what to remember about 9/11 and, just as important, what to forget, despite, or perhaps precisely because, of the hypermediated nature of the events: the news media had agreed to scrub truly gruesome images from their incessant coverage of the attacks. They did not reuse footage or photography where those who had jumped to their deaths could be seen. They were careful to avoid showing any of the dead at all. Instead, they broadcast images of the Towers either ablaze, collapsing, or in a state of ruin, attaching any sense of destruction and vulnerability to the buildings themselves; as Fischl said in a 2005 interview, "The weird thing is that [the falling people were] the only bodies that we saw. It was amazing how fast that experience—3,000 people dead—all we're talking about is the buildings. All we're talking about is the architecture."[11] The print news industry, the television news industry, the city of New York, and the federal government all leveraged the World Trade Center's absence in the name of nationalism and, soon afterward, of the War on Terror. Fischl's sculpture managed to emphasize that, despite all this coordinated forgetting, viewers of the original broadcasts could not completely unwitness what they saw, unknow what had taken place, or unfeel what they experienced.

Tumbling Woman has experienced a considerable reappraisal since its removal from Rockefeller Plaza. Fischl has sculpted other versions of it in different sizes and from different materials, like acrylic. Prominent galleries, national museums, and even foreign government buildings have exhibited the sculpture, as an important artwork for the ongoing memorialization of the attacks. In 2016, the September 11 Memorial and Museum included Fischl in the exhibition "Rendering the Unthinkable: Artists Respond to 9/11." The exhibition webpage sanitizes the controversy that erupted around the statue as "public dialogue." It defends Fischl's "heartfelt desire to bring people together after the tragedy"—emphasizing the sentimentality of the piece and its creator rather than, for example, the challenge of its aesthetics. Its headlining image obscures precisely those aspects of the statue that once upset viewers (nudity, point of impact), even as it portrays Fischl interacting with the statue as he had hoped others would, taking the figure's extended hand as an invitation to connect. Fischl's inclusion in the exhibition even impelled the journalist whose original column in the *New York Post* helped mobilize the furor over the sculpture, Andrea Peyser, to declare that the time had come to reconsider what Fischl had been up to.[12]

In the decades since 9/11, the media landscape has continued to change and to shift. Each change and shift opens up questions about the news media's relationship to the government and the industry's ability to contribute to a healthy, functional democracy instead of an imperial war machine or merely global capitalism. For many people, 9/11 awakened a yearning for a deeper, sustained sense of connectivity and an awareness of the possibilities for collective political action that the then current and still emerging media landscape afforded them. Those who disapproved of the media's collusion with the Bush administration criticized its exploitation of the body as a site of affective response and connection for commercial ends rather than in dutiful service to any democratic prerogative. Its ability to conjure a feeling of connectedness to others might lead to a unity emptied of true political significance. Stifling the formation of well-informed communities of dissent as well as healthy, productive debate between communities, the industry crafts the image of unity or civilization but leaves the underlying desires for it unsated and the possibilities of it underexplored.

I am here less interested in Fischl's sculpture or the built structures that commemorate the attacks—the monuments and memorials. Rather, I take the statue's open hand as an invitation to consider how allusions to ancient Greek and Roman material register the body's troublesome place in the post-9/11 sensorium and what we could consider the body's countermonumental potential. As a work whose dynamic with multiple classicisms troubled acceptable ways of representing, remembering, and engaging the body, the fate of *Tumbling Woman* inspires this chapter's study of a set of classically engaged texts that reflect on the bodily experience of watching the attacks, rewatching them, and, to a lesser extent, watching the subsequent War on Terror unfold on television and in print.[13] Some employ traceable allusions to specific Greco-Roman literary works to reconfigure normative conceptions of domesticity. Others do so to confront readily understood public identities and spaces, if not also how those identities and space comprise a commodified, politically inert public. Some ironize and parody the faux transparency of public sentiment. Others defiantly lean into emotional complexity and its relationship to political action. They all attempt to articulate concerns about an affective experience, that is, the troublesome sensations *individually and collectively* perceived on 9/11, that nationalist narratives and memorials could not completely resolve, including those about American exceptionalism, innocence, and trauma. Their work reveals time as an important material in the struggle to afford political dissent from the state's control over feelings, emotions, thoughts, movements, and behaviors in the wake of 9/11.

The term "countermonumental" refers to temporalities that contest the temporal frameworks with which an event and its memory have been enshrined as historical, that open up an event whose commemoration dominant institutions have foreclosed to alternative interpretations and affective responses, and that afford dissenting responses in different spheres of political action. Thinking of temporality as a route to understanding the affective regulation that accompanies the politics of public, collective memory, I mean to take up aspects of Lauren Berlant's "national sentimentality" ("historically the sentimental intervention has tended to involve mobilizing a fantasy scene of collective desire and identification that endures within the [sociopolitical] contingencies of the everyday," but "compartmentalize[s] the fundamentally psychically felt social ambivalences so that a sense of potentiality can be experienced enduringly . . . and even utopianly") and Dana Luciano's Nietzschean- and Foucauldian-inflected research on countermonumentalism, a perspective that "resists the monumental vision of the national public as a . . . simultaneous totality, merged within the unanimity of automatic response."[14] James E. Young has written extensively on the relationship between memory and monuments; both Randall Van Schepen, whose work on Fischl I have quoted, and Dana Luciano draw on his theories to perform their respective analyses. Young used the term "countermonumental" to identify trends in the memorializing representation of catastrophic events after the twentieth century's multiple world wars and the long-lasting effect of modernist "hostility." Therefore, while he has influenced the critique of modernisms running through this chapter, Young's work shapes the arguments about affect and conformity less directly.

Watching 9/11

Because the Bush administration controlled the post-9/11 narrative so thoroughly—pushing its message of national(ist) unity, summoning righteous anger on behalf of a nation of innocents, and promising retaliation against America's enemies with vehemence—it can be difficult to recall that during most of that Tuesday its representatives were absent from public view. Famously, we do have footage of President Bush receiving first word that the United States was being attacked, because he received the news during a photo opportunity at a Florida elementary school. Having decided to continue with the established protocol for the school visit, President Bush would first address the attacks on the World Trade Center at 9:30 that morning, within 30 minutes of the South Tower collision. From behind a podium bedecked with the seal of his office, he declared the "apparent terrorist attack" on the World Trade Center a national tragedy and pledged to find the "folks" responsible.

As stalwart a response as it may have been at the time, continuous video from the sites of the attacks meant that the transmission of images far outstripped the pace of reliable data or standardized information, let alone substantial analysis of the events taking place. CNN started broadcasting a live feed of the South Tower of the World Trade Center within minutes of the first collision. Other networks, like NBC, interrupted their regularly scheduled programming with an unplanned commercial break in order to secure footage. Having pivoted to coverage of this event, many networks coupled this video with interviews of eyewitnesses to try to understand what exactly had happened. Journalists were still working on the *story* about an event that had, presumably, come to an end. But as footage of the World Trade Center continued playing onscreen, the morning shows and news programs that had switched to covering this developing story ended up broadcasting a second crash live before their viewers on air and in studio. Less than an hour after the president's appearance at that podium, both towers of the World Trade Center and a portion of the Pentagon would be seen to collapse on air, and the foiled attack on the Capitol would result in a plane crash in a Shanksville, Pennsylvania, field. President Bush himself did not appear on television again until 8:30 that evening, when he would address the nation from the Oval Office. In the long interval between the first collision (at 8:46:40 a.m.) and President Bush's address to the nation, most Americans had turned to the television news to keep abreast of the still-evolving set of catastrophes occurring across the Northeast that interrupted what had begun as an ordinary day of the week.

Before 9/11, television news had seen steady declines in ratings for years. Though print journalism has its own historical relationship to sensationalism, the television news could not easily compete with it and had been dismissed as style over substance since its debut. By 2001, the glory days of broadcast news, in particular, were long gone. Networks with legacies, like CBS and NBC News, could not keep up with the pace of relative newcomer CNN whose reporting style and repetitiveness changed the news landscape during the Persian Gulf War era. However, even CNN had been flagging in the ratings.[15] Amid the proliferation of cable channels that gave viewers a greater set of viewing options, the television news industry sought to drum up loyalty from the viewers they already had and to attract a new generation of viewers to their product—the news—as well. Network news had a smaller stake in the commercial viability of the media companies that owned them as a result of steady deregulation in the 1980s. By the 1990s, these entities had corporatized, en route to becoming international conglomerates with diverse portfolios. For journalistic television to earn its keep meant that, with foreign correspondents let go and international bureaus closed, news departments had to change tactics and to expand their definition of what was newsworthy. "Awash in the thrilling, marvelous, breathtaking, and trivial," television news programming could more readily overlap with the world of tabloid journalism, which had no duty to the public, than with newspapers.[16] Because print journalism's long-term reporting still could produce the kind of hard-hitting articles that harnessed the full political potential of journalistic practice, a newspaper's obvious belatedness had a considerable upside as far as many news junkies were concerned.[17]

But television viewership spiked on 9/11. The audience for the news tripled that evening from 26 to 79 million viewers.[18] Some 90 percent of news seekers turned to their television to follow what was happening. And the quality of viewing changed too. Because on-air personalities acted as sources of both information and comfort, many became, however briefly, trusted in a way that recalled the relationship between viewers and news anchors in previous generations. Furthermore, network directors and show producers made decisions that limited choice: commercial breaks were suspended; programs ran longer than their allotted times; networks simulcast news coverage on the nonnews channels they owned. Tuning in that day, viewers were most likely to be watching, if not exactly the same story, in terms of interviews, talking heads, or analysis, then at least the same images and same bits of information about what were now being formulated as deliberate attacks instead of, say, an unfortunate accident.

By tuning in, viewers could not just know what had happened: they could also, in the case of the second hijacked plane, get to know something was occurring at the same time as other people on and off air learned it. Because the exact circumstances of the attacks were unforeseen, only a relative few could be considered traditional eyewitnesses of the first collision, that is, watching the event as it unfolded before their eyes somewhere nearby. The media landscape made real-time coverage of the subsequent events possible. Anyone watching television that morning saw the collisions, collapses, escape attempts, and early search-and-rescue events as they were happening, with footage that often reflected the impromptu decision-making involved in capturing events of this kind. The significance of this collective and, for most people, hypermediated experience of 9/11 cannot be underestimated—even some twenty-plus years after the fact. Individuals seemed to bodily register the feeling that the events of the day were historically significant—alongside many other feelings. They also registered the fact that they were navigating this feeling and others *with* others, whether in their immediate vicinity or beyond.

In the weeks afterward, the Bush administration and media personalities would refer to this sense of collectivity to rally support for the War on Terror under the banner of patriotism. As the pressures to perform patriotism mounted and the Bush administration monopolized analysis, interpretation, and response to the attacks, unity shaded into a homogenized unanimity, which could pass for democratic action. With everyone assumed to be in agreement about what had happened and what needed to happen, the linchpins of democratic governance—deliberation, checks and balances, and so on—became superfluous hindrances to realizing the will of the people.

Nevertheless, this swift and rather deft transcoding of the collective witnessing of 9/11 into political capital could not completely resolve the uncertainties and discomfort that the attacks themselves provoked. Many of these uncertainties involve the body as affective and perceptive conduit: What place did the body of those hypermediated witnesses of the attacks have in their experience of it? Why did something so intangible to those witnesses *feel* palpably "real"? How did those bodies end up feeling as if they shared feelings with others, even those they had no intimate relationship with or had never met? How could those witnesses at different levels of geographical proximity relate to one other within the nation? Others take up the political stakes of such connectivity: What political action does the awakening to such connectivity through new *and* older technologies make possible? How do these possibilities interact with the state's priorities—or the priorities of the industries that comprise media? Given the international reach of television media conglomerates and the development of internet technologies, how could those witnesses within the United States relate to those witnesses beyond the nation's confines? Still others would involve the memory of 9/11, both as an event in people's lives or as one enshrined in public monuments. Visiting sites and eventually memorials that had pieces of steel from the Twin Towers or other artifacts helped people connect tangibly with what had they witnessed; the artifacts-made-relics could anchor their uncertainty in the encounter in solid, discrete material.[19]

All of these issues involving technology had existed before the attacks in New York, Virginia, and Pennsylvania or the War on Terror. The experience of the attacks represents further articulation(s) of long-held concerns about the mediatization of private and public life as well as about the media industry's relationship to the health of American democracy rather than the advent of a radically new conundrum. Recall that *The Matrix,* an anime- and cyberpunk-influenced movie wherein human beings live paralyzed and infantilized, plugged into a virtual simulation they believe is real life in order to act as batteries for machines, had premiered not long before this, in 1999.

Mobile phones equipped with cameras, faster computer processing speeds, and more widespread access to the internet would further complicate the media landscape, pushing more traditional media to innovate or to risk obsolescence: newspapers would need to develop websites to stay afloat; new genres, like blogs, would emerge to take advantage of opportunities for networked connectivity. With the media landscape growing in complexity, the body's place in relation to media products, like the news, and to other entities (phones, communication towers, satellites, metals) involved in its manufacture and usage would respond in kind.

Networks prioritized coverage of the aftermath and continued suspending ads, thus foregoing their main source of revenue, for the next several days.[20] In the weeks and months afterward, various members of the television news media advanced the idea that on 9/11 the television news had not just regained its viewership, but it had also bade farewell to the days of "soft news" or market-centered, tabloid-style journalism and embraced its role as the fourth estate in American democracy once more. The trustworthiness, insight, and stability projected by the golden age of the broadcast news—though not the infrastructure responsible for producing these effects—were due for a comeback.[21]

Such claims became near impossible to defend once the Bush administration regained control over the day's events. President Bush's speeches demonstrated a savvy approach to the role of televisual images in what was to come. Referring to the "pictures of planes flying into buildings" and acts of bravery that encapsulated "the best of America," the president's live message from the Oval Office that Tuesday evening offered viewers further reassurance that the US military remained strong and financial institutions unharmed.[22] The commander-in-chief looked into the camera and closed his remarks with statements that would structure foreign policy and foreign policy discourse for decades to come:

> This is a day when all Americans from every walk of life unite in our resolve for justice and peace. America has stood down enemies before, and we will do so this time. None of us will ever forget this day. Yet, we go forward to defend freedom and all that is good and just in our world.

Framing "defense of freedom" as the outgrowth of a desire for both justice and peace, President Bush defined Americans as a nation and then exceeded the boundaries of the nation to include the world over. This framing anticipated the decision, announced in the State of the Union address on September 20, that defending freedom and protecting "all that is good and just" actually meant a war in the form of a "lengthy campaign unlike we have ever seen . . . includ[ing] dramatic strikes, visible on TV, and covert operations, secret even in success." The United States would be waging this war not against the group known as Al-Qaeda, which Bush named as the perpetrators of the hijackings that ended in thousands of casualties, but against the emotion of terror itself. For it was terror that would help America's enemies craft the world according to their evil, radical aims. The war necessary to combat it would proceed just as spectacularly as it had entered American homes, bodies, and lives.

The phrase "covert operations, secret even in success" demanded meticulous scrutiny. Such scrutiny never really came from mainstream journalism. Instead, the TV news functioned more like an additional mouthpiece for the Bush administration. Complaints about the insufficiencies of the coverage of post-9/11 decisions started to bubble over in short order. In an article in the *Washington Post,* "Journalism's Surreal Reality Check," Howard Kurtz recalled that during "the Persian Gulf War a decade ago, news organizations openly chafed at restrictions on their movements imposed by the first Bush administration . . . but now journalists were working closely with the local and federal government with most of the information that they purport to 'leak' really coming from authorities."[23] During the September 26 episode of CNN's *Reliable Sources,* Kurtz grappled with issues ranging from breaches to journalistic objectivity to the constant replays of the same, horrifying images and soundbites during marathons of coverage.[24] In an article in the November 4 issue of *The New York Times,* writer Caryn James lamented, "After a rock-solid performance in the first week after the attacks—news anchors calmly informing the country for days on end, the nation united by television in a way it rarely is anymore—a shakier tone has dominated. Hard news is more suspect than ever and commentary more useless." The weeks leading up to the first phase of the global War on Terror substantiated these concerns about self-censorship, submissiveness, and uniformity.[25] Amid surges of patriotic fervor, calls for national unity brooked little dissent from the war consensus. Famously, when Rep. Barbara Lee (D-CA) alone voted against the Authorization for the Use of Military Force that gave Congressional consent for the War on Terror, she faced death threats, racialized and gendered abuse, and accusations of treason.[26] And when Bill Maher discussed the intimate history of the United States with the regimes that the administration framed as the nation's immoral and cowardly enemies, ABC responded by cancelling his show, *Politically Incorrect*.[27]

On October 7, 2001, the Bush administration announced that military activity had begun in Afghanistan.[28] Networks quickly found various ways to capitalize on the war in Afghanistan in order to sustain viewership. They littered chyrons with segment titles that sounded like action movies. They coupled industry familiars like Wolf Blitzer with military experts and officials to populate new programming. Preexisting shows reveled in the technology of warfare, even in terms of sets designed with interactive maps and tactical-looking stations. Outside of the studio, dedicated embedded reporters gave viewers access to images of the military's weapons, vehicles, and gear as well as the foreign terrain and activities of troops. This style of coverage courted and entertained viewers while not infrequently marginalizing various forms of protest that were occurring both nationally and internationally and were therefore mobilizing a host of sodalities other than the nationalism that fit within the official narrative approved by the Bush administration.[29] The industry's commercial self-interest had overlapped with the administration's goals to curate a public that consumed warfare in its most sterilized and self-congratulatory form.

Synchrony's Classicism and the Body Politic

Like his industry colleagues on rival networks, Dan Rather from CBS and Peter Jennings on ABC, NBC News veteran Tom Brokaw used his platform to support the newly announced War on Terror. Brokaw does not belong to the golden age of television journalism whose early icons include Edward R. Murrow and later ones include Walter S. Cronkite. Still, his own image as an NBC mainstay leans very much on that era: as a white paternal figure whose booming voice and unflappable presence could lend at least the air of *gravitas* to stories on everything from the *Today Show* to *NBC Nightly News*, Brokaw enjoys widespread recognizability and favorability in American media culture. Because of these characteristics, he very often straddles the line between generic celebrity, on-air personality or news presenter, investigative journalist, and even historian. In practice, this flexibility offered the network that employed him a commercial opportunity that we will discuss in due course, but for most Americans, he was simply an establishment figure who could offer a sense of stability in a time of uncertainty, as traditional news anchors are expected to do.

In its broadest strokes, Brokaw's December 2001 contribution to the *San Diego Union-Tribune* compares the circumstances of the attack on Pearl Harbor to those of 9/11, and America's entry into World War II to the decision to wage a global War on Terror. Entitled "Two Days That Will Live On in Infamy," the op-ed employs a Pearl Harbor buzzword to reflect on the media's role in 9/11 and to look forward to a future after the War on Terror. Since the presidency of Franklin Delano Roosevelt, referring to an event's infamy alludes to the moral character of actions that a foe has committed and, just as important, to the retaliation that the American people collectively decide such an action warrants and which they resolve to deliver. Considering the circumstances of the 2001 attacks in light of those at Pearl Harbor, Brokaw joined a familiar post-9/11 chorus. Comparisons between the two events "flooded the media" as the United States dealt with the immediate aftermath of the terror attacks and as the Bush administration hastened toward a military response. Both the lexicon and iconography of the attacks in New York City recalled World War II heroics.[30]

Mild rebukes of American complacency and racism lend the piece an air of criticality, but a quick succession of paragraphs implants 9/11 within infamy's semantically intricate web to "abjure the political."[31] Brokaw mainly uses that criticality to endow his vision of American unity, exceptionalism, and heroism with more depth: clichés about democracy, the corporate media's fulfillment of their duty as the fourth estate, multiculturalism, and, more subtly, gender equality pepper the piece. Using "infamy" to think about the events that took place that day, the months that had intervened, as well as the near future capitalizes on the commemorative context of December 2001, that is, the sixtieth anniversary of Pearl Harbor, to emplot the September 11 attacks within the nation's history.

This commemorative foreclosure of both 9/11 and the War on Terror's historical and affective meaning involves an equally shrewd approach to the experience of time. The telejournalist's most obvious gambit—the comparison between then and now—coexists with several others. Brokaw's look forward to one of the nation's possible futures depends on the similarities he finds between the period of World War II America and America in the run-up to the War on Terror: he relates the cyclical rebirth of the ethos and productivity of the GI generation to the synchronizing force of the television news coverage of the 9/11 attacks.

To synchronize entails making something "operate at the same time, rate, or pace as something else." Synchronization, as Elizabeth Freeman so neatly puts it, "creates the social": it is synchrony to which we owe the functional harmony of the organs that make up our human bodies, and this temporal coordination of different entities produces the functional harmony of families and organizations. And because synchrony is indispensable to how we as human beings sense our belonging to those social groups, Freeman describes it in terms of social reproduction: synchrony can afford a way out of "eugenic thinking . . . [and] be crucial for imagining engroupment and descent among populations that do not biologically reproduce," or, where the power needed to synchronize subjugates others, it can produce the aesthetic effects of harmony and vitality.[32] In that case, being dazzled or comforted by the perception of harmony, energy, and collective cooperation can obscure the fact of domination and thwart resistance to it.

Comparing how Americans learned about each set of attacks, Brokaw writes: "When it became clear that these were deliberate, coldblooded acts of war, the nation bonded electronically—by radio in 1941 and television in 2001. On that long ago Sunday and the more recent Tuesday, Americans were glued to news broadcasts, bringing this vast land to a standstill." The NBC News staple marries his vision of a single national space to that of a polity made to quit their divergent tasks, their different clock-times, and various schedules in favor of simultaneous inactivity. A one-time military technology, television has been dogged by the threat of inactivity and stupefaction—that it would keep housewives from completing their chores, emasculate men by making them passive, that it would wreak similar havoc on children—since it entered American homes in the 1950s.[33] Brokaw's caricature of Americans being "glued" to their TV sets beckons toward that history and the anxieties about embodied difference that it provoked only to reroute them. Avoiding descriptions of the attacks themselves, Brokaw makes those immobilized bodies of American TV viewers available for the rapt uptake of the "bread and butter" of news, stories about traditionally masculine acts of valor. "In 1941 radio listeners heard of young sailors diving into burning waters again and again to rescue their buddies, many of whom had been catapulted off exploding ships. On television in 2001, stories quickly began to emerge of firefighters and police officers who raced into the smoke and darkness of the World Trade Center towers, ignoring personal safety in their heroic efforts to rescue those trapped inside." Stilled before television screens, "we" duly and collectively took in the best of what we were, just as "we" did as we learned about the attack on the naval base.

Imagining Americans "bonded [to each other] electronically" and "glued to news broadcasts," Brokaw details how the news broadcast transforms the United States into a veritable Fordist factory.[34] Disavowing the current media landscape and the larger economy in which it is situated through technological nostalgia *and* deploying infamy's semantic web share a corporeal through-line. American viewers function as that factory's synchronized and "standardized" workers: the ability of television news to arrest individual bodies and to circulate vital energy between those bodies consequently revives the body politic. Brokaw tries to harness the speed, energy, and will of the masses for the benefit of the nation as quasi-imperial totality or, as he will call it, praising the achievements of those who fought in and lived through World War II, the American "colossus."[35]

Jumping back and forth as it does between physical bodies (viewers, victims, and first responders) and metaphorical or symbolic ones (the body politic, America as one contiguous "land"), the piece operationalizes synchrony's ability to effect social reproduction in service of multicultural liberalism's usual bromides, especially in connection to World War II.[36] Its opening paragraphs chide the United States for an overconfident, fortress mentality that made it vulnerable to attack in both cases. The middle paragraphs highlight the missteps made in response to those attacks. Here, the news figure considers the rise in anti-Arab and anti-Muslim hate crimes in the context of the internment of Japanese Americans. Noting this repudiation of discrimination, a reader could conclude that the op-ed does not espouse an unfettered patriotism that will excuse *anything* done in the name of the nation's safety. Still, the op-ed contains a conceptualization of the nation worth examining. For when Brokaw summarizes, "civil libertarians are demanding that Arab-Americans not be deprived of the fundamental rule of law simply because of their ancestry," this framing looks to the problems of ethnicity and assimilation rather than a culture that continues to manufacture race and, yes, legalize racism.[37] Encouraged to look away from "ancestry" and institutional racism through supposedly color-blind spectacles, the reader can more easily imagine those TV viewers recast from the male and white-norming mold of the Greatest Generation.

In 1998's *The Greatest Generation*, Brokaw proposes that the men who belonged to this age cohort were not just the best Americans ever but the best generation produced anywhere and thus worthy of "veneration" as heroes.[38] The book earned mixed reviews. Some praised Brokaw's "panegyric" for crafting heartwarming anecdotes.[39] Others criticized its claims to actually represent a generation rather than the few service*men* it profiled. Reviewers of this stripe highlighted how the book ignored the social forces that created the ethos he identifies as pervasive; Brokaw thus oversimplifies the divergence of attitudes that existed among Americans toward entering World War II. Race, class, gender, and sexuality—some of the forces that contributed to that divergence—receive only the most superficial consideration, if any. Megan Rosenfeld put it matter-of-factly in the *Washington Post:* "Brokaw tells us right away that the women who kept the home fires burning were terrific, but are not part of this group. The African Americans who fought valiantly despite having to live with a segregated military are represented by one Johnny Holmes. . . . But their stories are not really included, either." Rather than presenting a nonfiction account of an actual generation of Americans, *The Greatest Generation* burnished the "mythology . . . that after Pearl Harbor young American men 'step[ped] forward in unison to answer the trumpet's call.' "[40]

Speaking of ancestry in the shadow of this generation, as the op-ed does, reveals one crux of synchrony's cultural significance. The synchronizing powers of television do not only affect the individual bodies of the Americans in the moment of witnessing by bringing them to a halt. The vitality and uniformity produced by a synchronized standstill has a nationalistic, eugenic aspect, to harken back to Freeman's words on the temporality. As a means of reproduction that does not involve biology, synchronization creates Americans no longer weighed down by the baggage of racialized "ancestry" and stirred to behave in line with one vision of the American ethos. By watching television and inculcating its lessons, those formerly troublesome bodies can be assimilated and satisfactorily reproduce the ideal society at last.[41] The Greatest Generation would function as the nation's ancestors in common henceforth.

The op-ed will tip its hat to more economic concerns towards its conclusion. Looking toward wartime and the future that it could make possible, Brokaw observes:

> For the United States, the beginning of World War II signaled the end of the Great Depression. The beginning of the war on terrorism was another blow to what had been a high-flying American economy.
>
> Both [the beginning of World War II and of the War on Terror] changed the domestic lives of Americans, but World War II had a far greater impact. More than 15 million men and women eventually were in uniform, and on the home front families made real sacrifices, rationing meat, sugar, gasoline and other items that contemporary Americans will take for granted during this new war.
>
> The critical comparison between Pearl Harbor and the events of Sept. 11 remains to be made, of course. As devastating as it was at the time, Pearl Harbor was the beginning of modern America. World War II and the post-war years shaped the colossus the United States represents today.
>
> The question confronting the United States today is whether its unparalleled political, economic and military power can be mobilized in a way that produces not just another victory for our values but also another generation of greatness.

Here Brokaw acknowledges that participation in the war effort takes place on the battlefield *and* the home front, and makes sure to honor the women in uniform as well as the men. He thus remedies one of the complaints about his best-selling book *and* attempts to universalize an aspect of the era he admires so much. Alluding once more to the Great Depression, bringing the war home seems to entail sacrifices of mostly the consumptive sort. Focusing on goods approaches—though never fully materializes—an admission that entering the war could cause people to feel regret, worry, or concern that they had taken a step backward into the hardship they had just barely survived. However, instead of this chink in the armor of consensus, Brokaw reminds readers of the postwar manufacturing boom and American prosperity.[42] Whatever fears may have circulated on the eve of war, Americans entered "modernity" through participating in it and enjoyed geopolitical hegemony after it: the author notes that the United States went on to build "the strongest military in the history of mankind" and to wield "unparalleled political, economic and military power." The Greatest Generation turned the United States into a monumental superpower capable of conquering the world astride.

I use the phrase "conquering astride" to connect the connotations "colossus" has within the histories of capitalism and imperialist thinking in America to Brokaw's classicizing of the World War II generation. In the 1883 poem memorialized by a plaque at the Statue of Liberty, "The New Colossus," Emma Lazarus compared the neoclassical statue of a torch-bearing woman to "the brazen giant of Greek fame," that is, the Colossus of Rhodes, an oversized statue of the god Helios and one of the wonders of the ancient world. "The most revered and renowned example of this type" of statue, the Colossus of Rhodes inspired the design for an artwork commissioned by Nero, the infamous last Julio-Claudian *princeps*; the Flavian amphitheatre—the structure known colloquially as the Colosseum in Rome—owes its nickname to the enormous statue of Nero which was eventually moved to the site from another location in the city.[43] The poet contrasts the Statue of Liberty's restrained posture to the Rhodian statue that was once believed to stand astride a waterway as being indicative of a different set of national priorities: rejecting a nationalism that aspires toward classicism's masculinist classism, Lazarus famously imagines Lady Liberty saying, "Keep, ancient lands, your storied pomp! Give me your tired, your poor, your huddled masses yearning to breathe free." Images of Cornelius Vanderbilt and other immensely wealthy industrialists standing, to use Lazarus's phrase, "with conquering limbs astride" circulated in newspapers and spawned parodies of various kinds: these images represented the scale of power wielded by one male figure who towered over or had no rivals. Concepts of scale recur in Brokaw's hopes that America's "unparalleled . . . power" will lead to "another generation of greatness," bringing a measure of security to the American people, rather than a single individual; the rivalry at hand would pit the United States against other nations. However, Brokaw's deployment of the term suppresses the critical thrust of its usage in connection with industrial hegemons to, *contra* Lazarus, create its own "storied pomp" about American capitalism, wealth, and global dominance. In so doing, he echoes arguments about the United States's role in geopolitics that predated 9/11 and that circulated much more frequently after the attacks "spurred more hawking neoconservative intellectuals and pundits to appropriate, even to revel in, both the concept of empire and historical comparison with ancient Rome": as Maria Wyke has discussed, by the time the United States was preparing to invade Iraq in 2003, "political debate about American empire had thoroughly saturated both the national and international press" with figures either cautioning against or championing American empire as a colossus and its president, George W. Bush, as a would-be emperor.[44] In the more immediate aftermath of September 11, Brokaw appropriates the latent classicism that frequently underwrites claims of American exceptionalism, places the classical period for America in the period after World War II, and comes close to expressing a feeling for empire, however benevolent.

Employing "colossus" in a piece of writing so invested in standards and time-travel also reveals a particular approach to modernity. As Dilip Parameshwar Gaonkar clarifies, "the term modern generally designate[d] the consciousness of an age that imagines itself as having made the transition from the old to the new."[45] This kind of modernity entails a particular kind of classicism: "the old representing venerable antiquity haunts and instructs the new. The old, as the custodian of the classical, sets the measures and models of human excellence that each new age must seek to emulate under altered conditions without ever hoping to surpass it." For Brokaw, those who served in World War II function as the standard by which all cohorts should be judged, especially but not exclusively those generations of Americans that have come after it; the greatest hope for this post-9/11 period of uncertainty as a nation and as people endowed with bodies in an economy increasingly disinvested from bodily labor as such is to alter their character in conformance with a now gone national ethic. Notice that Brokaw never makes demands on the state or the societalization of a type of capitalist accumulation itself: the welfare of the American people, their ability to act as fitting vessels for the Greatest Generation's spirit and to maintain, if not continue to build, this colossus, depends wholly on their attitude instead of the socioeconomic conditions that prevailed during and after World War II.[46]

However much nostalgia for the technology and men of yore Brokaw peddles here, it would be a mistake to ignore the article's own commercial context. Brokaw might represent the last glimmer of a previous generation's journalistic culture, yet his relationship to NBC exemplifies the profit-maximizing strategies that large multinational media corporations normalized in the post-Fordist era. Brokaw's *The Greatest Generation* was "one of the fastest selling nonfiction volumes of [its] decade."[47] Historically accurate or not, the book very much connected with American audiences. Its "remarkable publishing success" demonstrated the wisdom behind what the *Wall Street Journal* called a "little-known arrangement" with NBC whereby the media corporation would own almost 25 percent of the book and thus earn royalties from it. Such a financial arrangement incentivized what in early 2000s business-speak was called *synergy:* the exploitation of in-house publicity and marketing linkages created by large corporate mergers and acquisitions.[48] Brokaw enjoyed increased publicity across NBC Universal (including on the networks MSNBC and CNBC, and on popular shows like the *Today Show*) and the development of programming that could further the success of the book and its sequel (*The Greatest Generation Speaks* [1999]).

For these reasons, though the final paragraph of the op-ed may look back wistfully in time, attempting to mitigate the uncertainties of the war in the present with the achievements of the past and to associate coverage of 9/11 with the golden age of radio, Brokaw's comments actually reflect a very contemporary circuit of power and goods. The connectivity Brokaw promises through the synchronizing force of the news might more readily function as corporate synergy than democratic dynamism. In its offer of stability and a prosperous future, the newsman's op-ed reminds readers of the publishing niche that he had recently created for himself and NBC. It was as *consumers* of particular goods and a particular attachment to the past, not as politically active citizens trying to create a future marked by peace, that the media positioned Americans who tuned in to the news in the immediate aftermath of the 9/11 attacks and as the War on Terror proceeded.[49]

From Replays to Delays

If Brokaw yokes the rebirth of the Greatest Generation in all of its high Fordist glory, in part, to the synchronized standstill that fell over the United States as the television news broadcast the 2001 terror attacks, Ben Lerner thinks about media-influenced repetition and simultaneity in far less fecund terms. From the opening images of *Angle of Yaw,* Lerner's second poetry collection, to its most obvious discussion of 9/11 in "Didactic Elegy" and onward, the synchrony and repetition that will characterize the media spectacle desensitize and deaden the body as they "standardize" it: rather than forging bonds that allow docile bodies to revitalize the past, dulling the affective acuity of the body encourages an interpersonal disconnection that veers toward narcissism and erases memories of any images and feelings besides those that have been sanctioned by the state. Attentive to affect and not just to the mass's purported (ir)rationality, Lerner's effort to sense what others felt on 9/11 generates questions that contest the prevailing narrative.

The temporalities of what he labels a negative lyric reject the pretensions of a banally emotional 9/11 poem in favor of one that memorializes the unmet desire for connection and connectivity typical of the period.

Angle of Yaw describes a world where politics amounts to little more than "the appearance of significance" (65): "every politician knows" despair is an "oculogyric crisis" whose "remedy" lies in empty gestures and vainglorious displays rather than actual medical care (96). Television screens, jumbotrons, mirrors, and lenses offer up more things to see, but seeing's significance remains variously troublesome. One prose poem describes plastic lenses in glasses as a "mediate plane between [people with agoraphobia, numerophobia, and social anxiety] and the object of their fear [which] apply a comforting pressure to the bridge of the nose," making them not just a device for ophthalmic correction but a barrier against and substitute for interpersonal interaction as well (54). Positions associated with wisdom and power, like the bird's-eye viewpoint or the sight of the Earth from the International Space Station, cannot deliver either. Speaking of astronauts, the narrator observes, in an etymological pun, that unlike heroes who have experienced sublimity, "astronauts sleep strapped to their beds . . . like the lunatics they are" (53). Even God watches human history through a trimetrogon, an apparatus with three camera lenses inside (72).

The opening section of the collection, "Begetting Stadia," mocks the kinds of belonging and collectivity fostered by the mass media spectacle of sports. Using the plural in Latin and ancient Greek for the word "stadium," "stadia," and the similarly archaic-sounding word "beget," especially familiar to readers of genealogical catalogues in texts like ancient Greek and Roman epic poetry or the Bible, this opening section of *Angle of Yaw* thus primes its readers for the loftiness of old-time and even sacred genealogy, only to evacuate humans and humanity from the process of reproduction. As much as the arena suitable for seating a mass viewing audience very obviously speaks to the presence of a collective, the poem specifies that "demands incompatible with collective living / beget stadia / with indefinite seating" (3). Satisfying the demands of the market, we construct spaces only suitable for entertainment *ad infinitum.* Continuously associating infinite repetition with death or, at least, machinic nonlife, this section sees the shape of the arena's structure echo the coordinated movement of bodies in the arena—the wave—that will eventually consume the individual sports fan in its tow (99) or even bring the reader, whose page turning re-creates the wave, into harm's way. The collection suggests that those who inhabit this environment are constantly lost in and overwhelmed by images made to pass for meaning.

Later in "Begetting Stadia" fans will play at democracy by synchronizing their bodily movements. Comparing the racist gesture made by some fans of the NFL team now known as the Washington Commanders to a boomerang suggests skepticism about what synchrony offers beyond the appearance of belonging and inculcation in racializing and racist tribalism:

> Configured to return to the thrower when hurled
> and configured to return the thrower to the herd,
>
> intended backfires configure warmth
> for the polis and polis fans.
> Context attributed to the skin at birth
>
> picks teams:
> shirts and skins,
> redshirts and redskins
> and tomahawking redskin fans.
>
> "In 1825, the natives of Port Jackson hurled their halos and lay down."
> Support your polis: chop the air.
> (8)

By repeating actions in sync with others, an individual joins the fandom. But things get less straightforward as the poem develops. For example, the feeling of warmth mentioned could be literal—the energy expenditure of performing "the chop" would produce heat—or metaphorical, referring to emotional intimacy. Referring to the polis and polis fans only further encourages confusion of the literal and metaphorical (along with the part and the whole). Because it is unclear whether the "polis" refers to the team and its fandom, nominally attached to the city, or the city(-state) itself, those gathered in the stadium may be either sports fans in the conventional sense or supporters of a political formation. The second sense of the phrase recalls an earlier parody of pee wee football formations through juxtaposed references to the military tactics associated with Quintus Fabius Maximus Verrucosus during the Second Punic War (the Fabian strategy) and Mickey Mouse (6).[50] In this instance, political action becomes as derivative as the militaristic activities and life skills that sports claim to index: "support[ing] your polis" by simply reproducing the racist gesture and synchronizing with other people in the stadium has been made to suffice for an act of citizenship.

Given sport's relationship to bodily technologies and self-making, it isn't surprising to find these concerns about the docile body attached to the stadium. Instead of focusing on the athletes, however, the poem highlights the bodies of those in the audience and the audience as a body politic: the spectators undergo just as much corporeal training and "standardization" as the members of the team they root for. In the last case, fanaticism suits an era when supporting the troops could mean buying camouflage jerseys, chanting "USA" in response to military actions, or rebranding French fries as freedom fries.[51]

In section II, "Angle of Yaw," Lerner makes clear that the problems of media saturation encompass more than the latest electronic device or advances in computing. Books may only function as objects of sight: "The average reader often turns two pages at once, without perceiving a breach in narrative. He picks up a book, quickly flips through its pages, and believes it read" (26). As a result, reading and writing deepen the predicament of corporeal mis- and dis-connection. Contrasting reading advertisements and decrees to reading a book via the positioning of the body, for example, one prose poem laments that reading material of the former sort "[fails] to teach us the humility a common life requires" because it allows us to continue holding our heads up instead of down as we apprehend it with our gaze (39). If publicity is "the willful deadness of surface" (55), as the poem claims, everyday encounters with advertisements affect the individual reader as much as the mass audience to which she belongs so that all of us fail to have habits compatible with a life in common with each other. In the first section, death is analogous to the corporeal desensitization that hollow encounters produce: in the second section, many of these advertisements actually involve personal grooming products (such as toothpaste or shaving cream) and those viewing or consuming them end up decapitated, with chest wounds, or receiving otherwise fatal body blows.

Section III, "Didactic Elegy," focuses on poetry's place within the image's post-9/11 political economy. Noting, as his predecessors the Language poets had for decades, that poets share their medium—language—with figures from politics and commerce who bear some responsibility for societal fraud and that lyric utterances can be easily mistaken for sincere expressions, Lerner suspects that lyric poetry's sentimentality might make readers less sensitive to that fraud in a public-facing way and therefore less likely to rectify it. Affirming the presumed safety of their private homes or their individual heads and preciously singular voices, for example, lyric merely compounds the crisis it seems to resolve.[52]

The poetry world has its own institutional baggage in this vein: this world induces its citizens to conform through repetition and synchronization bearing the names of poetic modes, genres, and techniques. Even as most of the collection's ironic detachment grounds itself in countercultural antagonism, "Didactic Elegy" recognizes irony and other techniques of estrangement and countercultural questioning as commonplaces of a certain kind of poetry as well. The section thus owns its unoriginality and lack of radical spontaneity.[53] It subjects its own approach to close scrutiny, if not exactly swapping certainty and conviction for potentiality and suggestion, then intermingling them: "ignorance that sees itself is elegy" (67). Because of this not quite (un)certainty, naming this section "Didactic Elegy" performs its most knowingly ironic gesture.

Delay attempts to put ironic detachment from national sentimentality and the image-saturated media environment into poetic practice. Exemplifying the fault lines of modernist "difficulty," the negative lyric seeks to make the struggle with the "impossibility" of self-knowledge, subjectivity, and interconnection its subject without falling into confessionalist traps whereby those struggles appear as "mere positivity" (61).[54] In a series of Silliman's New Sentences, Lerner explains that "the lyric is a stellar condition/ like the relation between a star and starlight" (66). "Designed to collapse in advance" and "lag[ging] behind the subjectivity it aspires to express" rather than being self-evidently contemporaneous with it, the negative lyric commits itself to absence in order to communicate to its future audience how much we currently desire presence in the form of images. Whenever the negative lyric does appear, the "image that transmits the impossibility of transmission" will operate more through affect—"the absence of the I is felt as presence"—than visuality. And for that reason, it is hard not to interpret the claim that the negative lyric is "repetitious" as another etymological pun, one that refers both to the poem's future iterability (*repetere* as "repeat": that "image" of intransmissibility will loop) and to the desire it registers (*repetere* as "seek to recover": that connection or even substitute for connection it cannot deliver will continue to be sought after). Inducing pangs for connection, the negative lyric nudges its audience to continue searching elsewhere for its true desideratum, to quit the lyric in favor of other kinds of encounters that can fully sate the need.

The negative lyric's terms arise out of a discussion about a type of poem able to withstand the "reassignations of value" caused by "events extraneous to the work" like the attack on the World Trade Center (62). For Lerner, the 2001 collapse of the Twin Towers as viewed on television dramatically recalibrated the contemporary significance of absence and presence, seeing as the destruction of the building complex imbued its absence with great symbolic meaning and, no less worrisome, value. In an image-saturated media environment such as ours, the symbolic power of the Towers would not go uncommodified for long after their collapse. Lerner's poem voices the concern that poets could peddle imagery of the attacks no less parasitically than the US government or other public figures had done.[55] Tempted to worry about their work's "relevance" and its "loss of capital" in the wake of the "extraneous event," the author/poet/critic might latch onto those images in order to recapture what they lost and go down a rabbit hole of anxiety- and oblivion-inducing binge-watches of the attacks. Doing so, the critical poet runs the risk of dulling their own sense of what happened and of simply reproducing the standard explanations, definitions, and descriptions.

Preoccupied with creating a poem whose value and status "extraneous events" cannot diminish, the narrator envisions a lyric poem that takes on aspects of ancient Greek heroism:

> . . .
> What was once a gesture of negativity has lost its capacity to refer
> to the difficulties inherent in reference.
> Can this process be made the subject of a poem?
>
> No,
> but a poem may prefigure its own irrelevance,
> thereby staying relevant
> despite the transpiration of extraneous events.
>
> This poem will lose its relevance if and when there is a significant resurgence
> of confidence in the function of the artwork.

> If artworks are no longer required to account for their own status,
> this poem's figures will then be fixed and meaningless.
>
> But meaninglessness, when accepted, can be beautiful
> in the way the Greeks were beautiful
> when they accepted death.
> Only in this sense can a poem be heroic.
> . . .
> (62)

Imagining the negative lyric as a hero who accepts his own death, Lerner recalls the ideology of the "beautiful death." The adjective "beautiful" had both moral and aesthetic connotations in ancient Greek. Commemorative speech genres, including heroic epic, elegy, and funeral oration, drew on the concept of the "beautiful death" when they attached immortal glory and admiration to those who died while performing acts of martial valor, or laid unstinting shame upon those who fled battle or otherwise shirked their duties to themselves, their fellow fighters, and the other communities to which they belonged. Ancient Greek epic poetry heaped praise on the body of the hero who dies while at the height of his power as a fighter, man, and human being, and on his character, celebrating his achieving a perpetual youthfulness rather than the inevitable decay of old age.[56] Tyrtaeus, a seventh-century BCE Spartan elegiac poet, will lament the coward who "disgraces his family and so contradicts his splendid form" by retreating to the country away from duty's call, and glorify the young man who "dies amidst that first line of warriors stabbed many times over with a spear through his chest," drawing on Homeric precedent to do so in this and many other extant fragments of his work.[57] Lerner's narrator seems to posit that composing a poem with an indifference to its fate will, paradoxically, guarantee it an afterlife.

However, the narrator quickly realizes that, instead of endowing their poems with the immortal status of the classic, poets may find themselves more readily in a "classical" bind with respect to the relationship between individual bodies and state-sanctioned commemoration. Immediately after introducing the strategy, the narrator reflects:

> After the towers collapsed
> many men and women were described as heroes.

> The first men and women described as heroes were in the towers.
> To call them heroes, however, implies that they were willing to accept their deaths.
> But then why did some men and women
> jump from the towers as the towers collapsed?
> One man, captured on tape, flapped his arms as he fell.
>
> Rescue workers who died attempting to save the men and women trapped in the towers
> are, in fact, heroes,
> but the meaning of their deaths is susceptible to radical revaluation.
> The hero makes a masterpiece of dying
> and even if the hero is a known quantity
> there is an open struggle over the meaning of her death. According to the president,
>
> any American who continues her life as if the towers had not collapsed
> is a hero. This is to conflate the negative with the counterfactual.
> The president's statement is meaningless
> unless to be American means to embrace one's death,
> which is possible.
> (62–63)

Addressing the struggle over those who jumped from the Twin Towers, the meanings of heroism, and the imagery of post-9/11 poetry, Lerner connects the negative lyric to the "gap [that] separate[s] the representation of the one who has *died beautifully* . . . and the ideology of the beautiful death, where the bodies vanish in a highly elaborate process of abstraction."[58] Funeral practices varied across different ancient Greek-speaking communities. Studying Athenian funeral oration in particular, Nicole Loraux demonstrated that the speech genre tended to spend more time exalting the city than the individual, and so pays the individual body, however much on public display, far less attention than the body politic for which the hero perished. The Athenian memorial service for the warriors who died performing military service to the city-state effectively monumentalizes the city-state and thus contributes to a larger cultural program that spans several institutions, social roles, and life stages whereby men learned to play the part of citizen, including what and how to speak, what to do, and how to (talk about) feel(ing). Through various cues in these speeches, the patriotism of those living—in attendance at the public funeral and living in accordance with civic ideals—"matched that of the dead."[59] As a result, it is the city and not the warrior that truly continues flourishing and that continues demanding a particular set of actions from its citizens. Wrestling with the Bush administration's attempt to fix the meaning of heroism, to foreclose interpretation of the jumpers' act, and to scrub their especially troublesome bodies from the collective memory confronts the contemporary ideology of the beautiful death.

Lerner proceeds carefully here. As in the case of *Tumbling Woman*, the section runs the risk of crossing lines of public decorum. To avoid doing so, the lyric persona allows rescue workers to remain uncontestably heroic and selfless, while questioning the meaning assigned to those others caught on camera. Interest in what the individual jumpers must have been experiencing and feeling as they evacuated the Towers produces a yearning to memorialize their last moments as something other than an inevitable, indistinguishable, and easily legible death. Note that the poet never purports to speak on behalf of the victims. Rather, the poet bears responsibility for the poem as speech act: one cannot create in this climate without acknowledging that image-rich poetry of a certain kind can further the government's agenda or contest it, can obfuscate and abstract or come to grips with and explore.

Attuned to these conditions and pitfalls, "Didactic Elegy" tries to make the negative lyric's interest in the visual nature of the attacks work on its audience less normatively. In the case of those who jumped from the Towers, each death is meaningfully singular even as it can be replayed via videotape (or digitally, for that matter). Replaying events and reviewing images of them primed for sensual observation exemplifies critical repetition. Instead of mindless binge-watching or, equally standardized, trauma-induced return to the image, critical repetition endeavors to allow the critical poet to feel for herself and to thereby challenge the prevailing "counterfactual" sentiments about what we should see and feel about what happened. It also entails questioning standardized ideas about the American ethos. Such decisions could very well redound back onto the poet's "investment": they may cost the poem and the poet the status she seemed to desire insofar as this interest in the details of the event dispenses with the pose of "meaningful" irrelevance, one mark of the contemporary, seemingly unracialized experimentalist.[60]

The Countermonumental Quotidian

In her essay "Poetry in a Time of Crisis," poet and scholar Juliana Spahr recounts her experience of 9/11 to explain why she so desired poetry "attentive to collective responsibility." Spahr witnessed the collapse of the first tower on 9/11 while standing on a Brooklyn street corner, briefly accompanied by neighbors before everyone "scattered back" to their individual homes. Rather than " 'mov[ing] us inward,' " as one former poet laureate claimed poetry *ought to do,* this experience stoked a desire for poetic "models of intimacy that are full of acquaintance and publics," for poems that "turn outward" when addressing how "difficult" living amid and being aware of such crises can be.[61] *This Connection of Everyone with Lungs* does just that, turning lyric's intersubjective, frequently romantic interest further outward, into a mechanism for sensing antiwar solidarities: the collection's attentiveness to the body's mediatized experience of the 2001 attacks and the subsequent War on Terror attempts to transform the moment when everyone returned to their homes into a less isolating and politically passive experience.

"Poem Written after September 11, 2001" doubles as the first section of the collection. Spahr spends its first stanza explaining how our integument—the skin—gives this collective entity we call a body its definitive form. The opening deictic, "There are these things," introduces a list of items, and will be echoed by "this is a shape":

> There are these things:
> cells, the movement of cells and the division of cells
> and then the general beating of circulation
> and hands, and body, and feet
> and skin that surrounds hands, body, feet.
> This is a shape,
> a shape of blood beating and cells dividing. (3)

The two phrases on the poem's opening page shift accordingly from plural to singular, with the list of separate constituent parts congealing into an appositive phrase. Enlisting biology to describe the human body building up from individual cells to the skin, the human body's largest organ, Spahr's focus on the circulatory and integumentary systems renders the human organism a collective entity that functions through carefully coordinated activity.

Afterward the poem focuses on that which occupies negative space and, to our eye, lacks shape altogether. Described as "space between" and "space around," air enters bodies from the outside and leaves bodies to return to the outside world. Human connectedness originates, partially, from the fact that we have this air in common: the subprocesses from the introductory stanza—cells dividing and things circulating within the human body—make the air and the things that travel in it actually part of the fabric of our bodies and allow us to continue functioning.

Naming the toxic, postcollapse particulates moving from the air into bodies via lungs instead of referring to those iconographic images of the Twin Towers, "Poem Written after September 11, 2001" addresses the attacks in its final lines:

> The space of everyone that has just been inside of everyone mixing inside of everyone with nitrogen and oxygen and water vapor and argon and carbon dioxide and suspended dust spores and bacteria mixing titanium and nickel and minute silicon particles from pulverized glass and concrete. (9–10)

Lyric, as we have already discussed, is an especially baggy term in modern literary studies. In one articulation of the term's meaning, the lyric poem takes as its subject the intimate relationships between lovers (triangulated by the reader), especially the lover or beloved in absentia. Here particulates flowing through spaces inside, outside, and between bodies recall the dynamics of that social relationship, especially the intercourse of things that creates corporeal intimacy. However, the stanza subtly contorts what might be called a familiarly intimate, enclosed, and even sexualized lyric scene into one with markedly public, industrial, and scientific valences. Deprioritizing sight and sound as the senses through which humans most accurately witness an event taking place similarly contorts the pillars of absence and presence around which that notion of lyric poetry often pivots: the mixing of discrete entities it points to mixes "everyone" up together involuntarily and, as far as those aforementioned senses are concerned, imperceptibly. The second poem in the collection tackles the issue of collective will and political resistance more directly. But this poem's last stanza anchors the movement from discrete entities to organisms as collective entities dependent on the coordinated activity of constituent systems, and beyond, to a world organism, inaugurated by the opening stanza and carefully sustained throughout.

Operationalizing the rhythm of breathing conjoins the emergency to the everyday, temporalities that might seem diametrically opposed. The phrase "as everyone with lungs breathes the space" recurs anaphorically throughout the poem. It will continue to expand from its first appearance in a twenty-two-word stanza at the end of the poem's second page up to ninety-two words before contracting into a two-stanza refrain separated by a page break, "In this everything turning and small being breathed in and out by everyone with lungs during all the moments / Then all of it entering in and out," that begins to close the poem (8–9). Exemplifying poem as performance, the stanza's expansion and contraction mimics the contraction and expansion of the lungs themselves. The absence of commas makes the increasingly long stanzas a challenge to recite aloud and so nudges the oral reader to become especially diligent about managing her breathing. Briefer, less taxing refrains toward the end of the poem make the prior work of reading even more apparent. Therefore, just after a reiteration of the ninety-two-word stanza and another, much shorter refrain, "How connected we are with everyone" (9), the stanza that refers to the bits of disintegrated building matter circulating in the air through our individual corporeal systems and throughout the world system after 9/11 entwines whatever exceptional vulnerability had been attributed to the event of the attack and to those especially proximate to it—at the World Trade Center, in New York City, and within a certain geographic radius—with every single body's necessary, normal, quotidian, and unremarkable interpenetrability.[62] All of this living with each other, amid and by grace of the air, takes work on everyone's part. It taxes as much as it sustains. The fact that we constantly experience that penetrability in both life-affirming and life-endangering ways emphasizes the refrain that ends the poem: "How lovely and how doomed this connection of everyone with lungs" (10).[63]

In "Poems Written from November 30, 2002, to March 27, 2003," the collection's second section, paying incessant attention to the news reveals the conjuncture of emergencies with the everyday. The steady rhythm of breathing still matters ("Beloveds, what do we do but keep breathing as best we can this minute atmosphere?" [26]). But the poems that make up this second section more persistently confront the technologically mediated experience of the War on Terror and similar disasters worldwide. Or, as one poem states, "We watch it all happen on television" (69). Spahr explains, in an italicized note that prefaces the second section, that she had begun watching news "more seriously" after her premonition that the United States would not invade Afghanistan as a response to 9/11 proved false: awareness of this self-styled naïveté, coupled with exposure to the political (in)efficacy of difference in Hawai'i, the island state where she, as a nonnative transplant, resides, prompted her to rejig her conception of intimacy, "the afar," and lyric's possibilities. The section's first poem begins on the day she "realizes that it was most likely that the United States would invade Iraq again," and the journal-like formatting of the individual poems in this section attests to that quotidian struggle to "understand how this would happen" (13). Watching, reading, discussing, pondering, and reacting to all the moments when she does not directly engage the news shapes the way she conducts her day-to-day life, the activity's recurrence noticeable even in its intervallic absence.

Spahr thus renders the two-pronged nature of habit especially clear in this section.[64] Habitually taking in the news impacts how Spahr inhabits her family home and the relationships tethered to it. Moreover, because stanza lengths, line breaks, scope, and poetic referents allow these poems to mimic the expanding and collapsing frame we observed in "Poem Written after September 11, 2001," inhabitation also includes a global nexus of "lovely and . . . doomed" relationships. Still subject to the forces of global capitalism, living in Hawai'i and therefore outside the continental United States did not make her any less complicit in war or exploitation. Instead, as Piotr Gwiazda observes, several moments literalize what it means for her poetic persona to be embedded within the military-industrial complex ("In bed, when I stroke the down on yours cheeks, I stroke also the carrier battle group ships, the guided missile cruisers, and the guided missile destroyers" [74]).[65]

Attuning oneself to these various connections on a daily basis prompts a meaningful realization about "the stuff of the everyday in this world" (57). Repeatedly confronting the doom that befalls those whom she feels connected to, the term "emergency" loses its status as exceptional, surprising, and therefore deserving of media attention, according to some rubrics of newsworthiness: everyday recurrence normalizes disasters and injustices as mundane for some, at home within the spaces, frameworks, and times of our lives rather than truly interrupting any of them.[66] Reframing "emergency" thus casts doubt on exceptionalist narratives of national innocence and greatness that legitimize retaliation, e.g., for attacks, as morally necessary. It also reintroduces interpretive uncertainty into discussion about responses to those attacks since it lines up different analogues for the attacks themselves. Yet, everyday recurrence undergirds the effectiveness of referring to these distantly intimate relationships and connections with the multitude through the nonstandard pronoun "yous" and the markedly tender "beloveds": each time they are read or spoken aloud, the awkwardness of the grammar calls attention to the naturalization of various ideologies, including nationalism and heteronormativity, that the standardized pronouns index or, as Spahr says while analyzing the work of Bernadette Mayer, "the linguistic system's categorical violence."[67] Repeated habitually throughout this section, these words function in time as *usefully* mundane corrections to the sociopolitical status quo.

Like Lerner, but inclining toward emotional complexity instead of ironic detachment, Spahr acknowledges failure and impossibility throughout the book's individual poems. In *This Connection of Everyone with Lungs*, each effort to protest and each observation of other protests with which she feels some solidarity contends with the "inability to control what goes on in the world in our name" (71). The moments Spahr spends directly engaged in protests does not put an end to the suffering and injustices being encountered by her beloveds every day and eventually relayed to her by daily news reports: such is the downside of experiencing a "call to act despite the lack of answers" (58). Enumerating the series of setbacks alongside the sudden victories signals how each act of protest must continue to balance a determined hope with a legitimate sadness. Sudden enlightenment never comes. Instead, Spahr states in the prefatory note that she "gained no sophisticated understanding as [she] wrote these poems" (13).

"Poems Written from . . ." attests to the struggle against the conformist arrest of the information deluge, against being lulled into that Brokawian standstill so amenable to further cooptation on the nation's behalf. In it, Spahr renders bodies everyday countermonuments by treating them as both the sensate interfaces that apprehend the news, that hear the birds singing of war (69), or that press up against their beloveds *and* as the sensible interfaces that remind others of the interpretability of entities, of actual and potential solidarities, and even of what stands to be harmed or destroyed. This countermonumentality resists the reinstallation of bodies into an idealized past with its heteronormative and monogamist domestic scaffold, as in Brokaw's op-ed: it moves toward an array of heres and nows and *others* that everyday activities—including the everydayness of warfare—constellate instead.[68]

Allusions dot this constellation, placing the reader in the company of poetry similarly attuned to warfare's quotidian nature. Reading *This Connection,* one hears unmissable echoes of Spahr's poetic predecessors, such as June Jordan in "The Bombing of Baghdad" (especially "The bombing of Baghdad / did not obliterate the distance or the time / between my body and the breath / of my beloved"), Muriel Rukeyser (especially "The War Comes into My Room" and "Endless"), and Adrienne Rich.[69] "January 20, 2003" in particular adapts Sappho 16, a fragment of a monody that probes the ties binding erotic desire and erotic attachments to warfare and societal upheaval in the ancient Greek cultural imagination. Contemplating desire's "emphatically public" "ricochet," Spahr's poem continues turning lyric's quintessentially intimate, if not romantic, yearning into an on-ramp to other, larger social relationships.[70]

"January 20, 2003" follows the structure of Sappho 16 rather closely. The ancient fragment's priamel (1–4) sets the narrator at odds with prevailing opinions about what constitutes the most beautiful thing on the Earth. Initially, social groups differ in their opinions about which of the armed forces surpasses the others in beauty. The narrator's preference for something categorically different rearranges the terms of comparison, and a mythological exemplum tries to bring that difference back into the culturally legible fold:

Οἰ μὲν ἰππήων στρότον, οἰ δὲ πέσδων,
οἰ δὲ νάων φαῖσ' ἐπὶ γᾶν μέλαιναν
ἔμμεναι κάλλιστον, ἔγω δὲ κῆν' ὄτ-
    -τω τις ἔραται
πάγχυ δ' εὔμαρες σύνετον πόησαι
πάντι τοῦτ', ἀ γὰρ πόλυ περσκέθοισα
κάλλος ἀνθρώπων Ἐλένα τὸν ἄνδρα
    τὸν [. . .]άριστον
καλλίποισ' ἔβα 'ς Τροίαν πλέοισα
κωὐδὲ παῖδος οὐδὲ φίλων τοκήων
πάμπαν ἐμνάσθη, ἀλλὰ παράγαγ' αὔταν
    . . . σαν
. . . αμπτον γὰρ . . .
. . . κούφως τ . . .
με νῦν Ἀνακτορίας ὀνέμναι-
    σ' οὐ παρεοίσας
τᾶς κε βολλοίμαν ἔρατόν τε βᾶμα

κἀμάρυχμα λάμπρον ἴδην προσώπω
ἢ τὰ Λύδων ἄρματα κἀν ὄπλοισι
    πεσδομάχεντας.[71]

Some declare an army of horsemen, others an army of infantrymen,
still others [declare] a naval fleet the most beautiful thing
on this dismal earth, but I say it is
    whatever someone loves.
It is quite easy to make this understandable
to everyone. For Helen who far exceeded
mortal beauty left an
    excellent husband behind
and went sailing off to Troy
and paid neither her child or her beloved parents
any mind at all, but [the goddess of Love?] seduced her
    [unwilling?].
For . . .
nimbly
brought to mind Anactoria
    who is not here
Whose lovely footstep and face's radiant gleam
I would rather see
than Lydian chariots and infantrymen
    amidst their weapons of war.

The first page of "January 20, 2003" initially cycles through fairly direct translations of the priamel. Synonyms replace one another across lines. Or individuals stand in for a military group via synecdoche (fleet/rowers). In one instance, the verb of speaking changes. Spahr alters the ratio of "some" to "others" sometimes or shifts where the substantives appear from stanza to stanza. Most notably, though, Spahr extends the poem by repeating the priamel, and she inserts markedly contemporary words into it ("Abrams tanks," "Bradley fighting vehicles," "155mm Howitzers"). Fragment 16 ends with the narrator prioritizing the sight of Anactoria's "lovely footstep and radiant face" over that of Lydian chariots and armed footsoldiers. Spahr's cataloguing of modern weapons and equipment in these opening stanzas bombards the reader with the array of items produced by the modern military-industrial complex while jumping forward to that part of the ancient text.

The priamel's predicate—that social groups frequently declare the bevy of things associated with warfare to be superlatively beautiful (or noble)—appears at the end of the first page; experiments with the priamel continue on the following one. As in the case of war's collectives, weapons and personnel, Spahr cycles through various ways to render the predicate, deploying synonyms (fairest/most beautiful), repeating the phrase on the same line, or placing it in different parts of the line. After a stanza summarizes the normative opinion, a stanza pivots to the countervailing one: "But I say it's whatever you love best." Line after line, "I say" repeats the counterclaim and alters it from "whatever you love" to "the persons you love." Eventually, "I say it again and again" withers to "again and again." Choosing to translate a line that begins a second portion of the poem or that begins another fragment, μεν οὐ δύνατον γένεσθαι ("not possible to happen"), as "I try to keep saying it to keep making it happen," Spahr's lyric voice accentuates the struggle of trying to overcome the barrage that contributes to our normative conditioning.[72] Closing with "I say it again, the sight of the ones you love, those you've met and those you haven't," Spahr's adaptation pluralizes the object of the narrator's love and the efforts to announce that preference.

In the ancient Greek text, the speaking voice asserts "it is easy to make everyone understand this [claim about whatever one loves best]," transitioning from the priamel with its personal declaration to mythological exemplum. The story of Helen abandoning her parents and child in Sparta out of love for Paris most obviously bridges the matters of erotic desire and warfare, since these actions provide the pretext for the decade-long siege of Troy. This well-known exemplum sets the matter of personal desire—and, to some extent, depending on words missing from the fragment, will—in problematic relation to preexisting social conventions and institutions (Helen's marriage to Menelaus and the power it was meant to secure). The pivot to shared memory as a means of understanding-in-common doesn't last long, at least in the text we have, because the exemplum then jumpstarts yearning for Anactoria who, like Helen, has left her company for elsewhere. The poem then returns to the speaker's idiosyncratic preference and experience over the male-centered culture of warriors and, by extension, the kind of poetry that celebrates it. "January 20, 2003" translates neither the transitional sentence nor the exemplum that follows it.

Because they aim to establish information in common and configure social and geopolitical relationships, news broadcasts play a cultural role similar to that exemplum, though. In addition to the prefatory note's admission that obsessively watching the news produced no special insight, the narrator of "January 13, 2003" equates the news with distraction. That same poem sets the news apart from more immediate relationships—idle chat or reconnecting physically with beloveds who have recently returned home does not include conversation about what she learned from news reports. However, that information bleeds into the very next poem, "January 20": cataloguing military groups and armament, the narrator relates items from the news and discusses with the external reader the things they didn't manage to discuss with their nearby beloveds in the previous poem. The rest of the collection will explore solidarities that oppose the war consensus, the multitudes gathered to actively protest large-scale injustices, and the labor turning them into communities and of communicating with them. But in this poem, the narrator is attempting to incorporate that information into their approach to the world. Whereas the ancient transitional statement boasts how easy it is for the narrator to explain one different, seemingly incommensurate perspective to the audience, "January 20, 2003" belabors how challenging it has been for the narrator to learn to value others as beloveds and to follow through with that conviction on a day-to-day basis in a particular milieu.

Emphasizing the difficulty of the contemporary milieu also translates the ancient poem's exploitation of archaic lyric's "public, cultural work."[73] Sappho's poem repeatedly goes beyond juxtaposing ideas and feelings experienced in common and those experienced privately or individually. Haunted by the chorus, it cleverly exploits the circuits of desire in which the relationship to Anactoria exists and that frame the turmoil of her absence.

Though fragment 16 is most likely a monody—that is, intended for a solo performer—and we do not know on what occasion it was meant to be performed, "Sappho's (probable) monodies routinely position themselves in meaningful relation to *choreia,* integrating . . . the language, imagery, tropes, and postures of choral performance and occasion, and, by extension, their broader cultural contexts and connotations."[74] The chorus is an institution that enculturates individuals by having them train their bodies and voices to perform in public as part of a group. Moving, playing, and/or singing in sync, its members exemplified the perfect fusion of many disparate elements and that allowed the audience to collectively feel wonder when watching them perform. This same synchronous harmony could reflect (on) the ideals of community and, by provoking an illusion of audience participation, further enhance a sense of intersubjective connectivity.[75] In the fifth stanza of fragment 16, when the narrator prefers the sight of Anactoria's face and footstep to the sight of the people and things that make up the Lydian military, an obvious lexical echo binds the yearning to see Anactoria's step (βᾶμα) to the departure of Helen for Troy (ἔβα). Less obviously, that step's descriptor (ἔρατόν) resonates with both the unsanctioned erotic desire that motivated Helen to undermine her first marriage and the kind of societally sanctioned arousal and routing of desire that choral performance is imagined to achieve: paying attention to Anactoria's step recalls her past participation in a chorus of young women, with the spotlight on Anactoria's radiance possibly identifying her as the (once) nubile chorus leader, and, consequently, speculating about where marriage has taken her.[76]

As a parachoral instance, or moment when a poem alludes to a physically absent chorus and the spacetime of choral performance, the fifth stanza also points to a correspondence between the group that Anactoria once belonged to and the military units that Sappho does not love most.[77] Whether the poem's first collective noun (στρότον) is assigned to the cavalry, the infantry, or the navy, the group created from a mass of fighters has been taught to abide by a corporeal schema whose value is both tactical, useful for accomplishing their tasks, and cultural, useful for stoking esprit de corps and connection to the larger society. This correspondence between the military and chorus as groups with corporeal schemata whose synchrony contributes to the status quo helps the poem cohere from beginning to end. It also tempers what might appear as unmitigated radical difference in Sappho's preference. For the very institution that affords a relationship between Sappho and her beloveds, the chorus she either trains or participates in by composing for it occasionally (if not on the occasion of this poem's performance), trains these young women as individuals to lead normative lives, that is, to marry, to leave the chorus if not the city, and to reproduce the social order. The solo performer's allusion to the dancing body and, by extension, the chorus gestures toward a crack in the normative power of synchrony— toward the individual mind's deviation from a shared time and space and the norms that prescribe them. In sum, the absently present bodies of the chorus and the military both act as reminders of how society can harness bodily capacity to move through space and time in order to engender and to reflect societal harmony (to various ends), and, at the same time, how bodies can elude the total cooptation of those capacities and function as countermonuments to unsanctioned emotions, sensations, relationships, and memories.

Depicting the struggle of writing in response to and against the synchronizing force of the news broadcasts that try to set information in common, to catch viewers up to what has been happening over the same timespan across the world, and to create an affective collective, Spahr's yoking of the news to the erotic captures the tension of parachorality in fragment 16. Moreover, when "March 27 and 30, 2003" describes the lyric self stroking a lover's cheek and simultaneously stroking a weapon of mass destruction, that is, lying in bed with the military-industrial complex, we might think back to the various objects, individuals, and groups set in relation in Sappho 16 as well. The caress befits this lyric scene because it is a stereotypical gesture of intimacy and care, one we learn to imitatively re-perform. The scene prompts the reader to imagine the virtual interaction of several bodies and things. That interaction outs the virtuality through which the lyric voice has sought to render the self and its relationship to others as individuals, as groups, and as whole multitudes, and the effort of making "our bed . . . part of everyone else's bed" rather than "just our bed" vivid since *This Connection*'s first page. It reminds us of the feelings, the spaces, the movements, the sensations, and the institutions that constitute the normatively corporealized self. It can also remind us of the actions, desires, gestures, sensations, and connections that undermine those norms and attempt, sometimes with great difficulty, to fashion alternatively embodied (inter)subjectivities. Being embedded in those normative social systems and in those schemata—as opposed to being wholly detached from them—makes tapping into the body's manifold capacities necessary as an agent for change, both on an incremental and on a large scale, during times marked as everyday and as exceptional. Those capacities reveal how truly lovely and how truly doomed we always are.

Rhythm

Revisiting the work of Lerner and Spahr as counterpoints to Brokaw's op-ed clarifies how post-Language poets wielded insights born from complaints about lyric poetry and lyric subjectivity as tools against the monumentalization of 9/11. Techniques meant to address lyric's shortfalls linger on the mental, emotional, and corporeal effects of witnessing the attacks. Lingering on and leaning into these effects allows them to make time for dissenting opinions from the war consensus, for critiques of the industries that profited from that consensus, and for the uncertainties involved in the attacks that their monumentalization pretends to resolve. While Lerner continues and, as we have seen, mocks the sideswipe at political engagement that experimental poets of a certain stripe take when keen on demonstrating their poetic bona fides, in *This Connection of Everyone with Lungs,* especially in the second section, Spahr models how poetry contributes to and can participate in traditional forms of political activism but not suffice for it.[78] Considered in tandem and in light of poets like Claudia Rankine—whose experimentation would once have been overlooked in favor of stiflingly identitarian readings—enjoying mainstream critical and commercial success in this era, these collections represent a shift, however small, in what the white poetic and literary establishment recognizes as worthwhile and yet still politically engaged.

I conclude this chapter by revisiting two poems written by Adrienne Rich in *Tonight No Poetry Will Serve,* the last original collection she produced before her death in 2012. Capping the chapter with the work of Rich might come as a surprise, although she had been a major figure in American poetry over her accolade-rich career. Known—and once, in some quarters, dismissed—as a political or feminist poet, Rich gave attention to writing as a social practice that meant making her poetry part and parcel of a life spent in active solidarity with others engaged in antiwar, anti-imperialist, antihomophobic, antisexist, and antiracist struggles, whether they were in the United States or abroad, in the world of poetry or outside of it.[79] The stakes of Rich's unabashedly political writing have never meshed well with those of the Language poets, even though some of their practices emerged from the sociopolitical disenchantment of the Vietnam War era.[80] We have already devoted so much of this chapter to Language-y poets. Considering Rich's work offers a glimpse into a different segment of the poetry world and its approach to the nuances of what some critics of recent fiction have labeled the "affective dominant."[81]

Scholars have attached the term "countermonumentalism" to Rich's poetry before. The Gulf War and the War on Terror share significant geopolitical and televisual through-lines, although significant technological advancements and changes in the media industry mark the period between President George H. W. Bush's attempt to check the power of Saddam Hussein with Operations Desert Storm and Desert Shield, and President George

W. Bush's attempt with the Iraq War. Scholars have argued that the poem "Atlas of the Difficult World" responds to the rhetoric and visual culture of the Gulf War with a corrective catalogue linking it to a long prehistory of violence, erasure, conquest, and misleading nationalism. Constructing an "atlas" of these conflicts and their long-term consequences elevates struggles that unite people across the nation and, no less important, elsewhere.[82] Despite the beginning of the poem's fifth section also enjoining the reader to "Catch if you can your country's moment, begin / where any calendar's ripped-off," most critics focus less on time and its affective dimensions and more on space and the poem's relationship to physical monuments and geographic locations in their usage of the term.[83]

Tonight No Poetry Will Serve follows *The School among the Ruins* (2004) and *Telephone Ringing in the Labyrinth* (2007) in their attempts to examine violence, nationhood, and intersubjective connectivity during the post-9/11 period. Reading all three, one could claim that the later work topicalizes the attacks, the subsequent wars, and American imperialism less directly than its predecessors; that it doesn't, as happens in the others, mention veterans missing limbs or children sheltering in their school as bombs rain down upon them. The collection's differences in this regard register what it means to be writing just a few years later into a war that would continue for at least two decades. The shift in its poetic strategies could be symptomatic of shifts in the perspectives and the tactics that such a long span of warfare—and of fighting against warfare—requires.

In particular, *Tonight No Poetry Will Serve* allows the defiant optimism and resolve that come from a life spent fighting injustice to sit alongside fatigue, uncertainty, and the sense that "no poetry can service to mitigate [torture and violence]."[84] These feelings might keep time with resignation, but they do not exactly amount to it. On par with the powerful final poem of the collection, "Powers of Recuperation," the definition of "to serve" that appears before the table of contents substantiates this claim. The title of the collection boldly announces what it will *not* do, however, as the reader of the definitions learns, such defiance must cope with the fact that "to serve" can equally denote obedience or satisfaction; of the six definitions offered in the collection's paratext, half belong to that former meaning and the other half to the latter. Rather than despair, the rest of the collection suggests that poetry cannot function, or serve, in either way perfectly. Poems, poets, and the concept of poetry, materialized in institutions and practices—none of them functions, or serves, in isolation. This realization prompts reconsideration of what writing and reading poetry works *with* in order to bring about a world more conducive to life across the globe. After all, as Rich observes, a poet is just one of the many "everybodies" in this world.[85]

Forming a diptych that hinges upon reading the *Iliad,* Rich enlists two poems to ask what purposes Homer's aesthetic valorization of warfare and death serves at the current moment. According to the dates that accompany them, Rich composed both "Reading the *Iliad* (As If) for the First Time" and "Don't Flinch" in 2009. "Reading the *Iliad* (As If) . . . " appears in the first section of the collection, and "Don't Flinch" appears in the fourth and penultimate section. As the parenthetical phrase in its title suggests, the earlier poem attaches its attempt to actually feel the shock of the violence Homeric epic so vividly portrays to a counterfactual temporality: imagining the first encounter with the archaic Greek poem allows its subject to imagine reconfiguring their relationship to death, warfare, and its memorializations. "Don't Flinch" pushes the potentiality of the counterfactual encounter with the epic further while employing a different set of temporal coordinates. Constructing a scene around repeated attempts for the poem's lines to "pulse into sense," the poem involves affect as well as interpretation in its exploration of how best to live while mindful of the dead.

Encountering a battle scene in "Reading the *Iliad* (As If) . . .," the poem's subject tries to lend more immediacy to the repetitively forceful actions of warfare. Detailing the action as if reading the poem proceeded like watching a movie, the subject describes "blood . . . / in the spear thruster's arm as in / the gunman's neck / the offhand moment—Now!—before he / takes the bastards out"(15). Following the capitalized word "Now" with an exclamation point, Rich enhances the ekphrastic thrust of the sentence: the punctuation and adverb pairing recalls the callouts of graphic novels and comics; planted within a sentence the phrase interrupts narrative progress much as callouts do in those other contexts. When, in the second stanza, "Beauty!" appears similarly punctuated, the interruption pauses the action. In Iliadic battle scenes, narrative momentum makes constant demand on the reader's attention so that, even as names, personal details, and moments of glory accumulate, readers may not notice the gruesomeness of the tally of the injured, dying, and deceased strewn across the epic's hexameters. Catalogues, on the other hand, impede narrative progress while items, like the tally of the dead, are enumerated, taxing the performer's memory and the audience's ability to focus on any one single act of violence. Here, a catalogue-like series of things spied on the shore at Troy after Greek ships arrive replicates that dynamic. Parataxis objectifies body parts seamlessly until the callout halts movement through the sentence. So halted, readers can take note of the decay beneath the sheen of militaristic splendor, a grotesque juxtaposition: "flesh before gangrene."

When another pairing of this kind occurs, though, punctuation emphasizes the extent to which Rich makes her own poem serve as a countermonument to the epic's aestheticization of warfare. Rich includes in the collection's notes Simone Weil's observation about the ancient poem's ability to reflect human affairs: "For those dreamers who considered that force, thanks to progress, would soon be a thing of the past, the *Iliad* could appear as an historical document; for others, whose powers of recognition are more acute and who perceive force, today as yesterday, at the very center of human history, the *Iliad* is the purest and the loveliest of mirrors."[86] Comparing a poem to a mirror appeals to the privileged relationship with truth that sight has enjoyed—a sensorium that equates seeing with believing ignores the uncanny aspects of mirrors and instead associates them with security, certainty, and/or revelation. As "pure" mirror, that is, presumably, one that doesn't distort, the poem would reveal us and our history for what we and it actually are.

Though the graphic-like callouts accomplish that task to some degree, the end of the poem troubles sight. As it approaches the topic of grief and commemoration, it associates those revelatory interruptions more with indecision. The final stanza reads:

> Ugly glory: open-eyed wounds
> feed enormous flies
> Hoofs slicken on bloodglaze
>
> Horses turn away their heads
> weeping equine tears
>   Beauty?
> a wall with names of the fallen
> from both sides passionate objectivity (16)

The stanza's first five lines survey the carnage of the battlefield before alluding to *Iliad* 17, where Achilles' immortal horses weep upon learning that

Hector has killed Patroclus. Homer's description of the horses soiling their "luxuriant manes" as they hang their head in grief reflects on the aesthetics of the fallen warrior, given that, at this point in the narrative, the integrity of Patroclus's corpse is at stake, as well as the aesthetics of mourning, where soiling oneself is a commonplace. The Homeric narrator's focus on the horses' appearance also anticipates Zeus's perspective on the scene unfolding before him: for upon seeing the pair weeping, pity for them having to "share in the pains that wretched mortals suffer" moves him just enough to endow them with energy to protect their rider as they go through the melee toward the Greek ships but not enough to stop the fighters from killing one another (17.441–54). As the stanza shifts its focus from detailing the battlefield to mourning the dead and memorializing war, Rich adapts the limited efficacy of the beauteous sight in the Homeric scene to suit a different (set of) commemorative context(s), allowing the bloodshed to make the stakes of this scene "more real." Applying the compound adjective "open-eyed" to a wound that exposes decomposing flesh to scavenging flies creates a contrast between the reality of battle and the fantastic scene that tries to recuperate it. Here, fixating on the horses' beauty would have us turn away from such grotesquery much as the horses turn away from the spectacle of carnage staring them in their faces.[87] The phrase, "Beauty?", interrupts this scene's unfolding, as the exclamations did in previous stanzas, and reroutes the poem's direction. Punctuated differently from those prior phrases and dramatically indented on the page, the question implicates the aesthetics of the gory scenes from the battlefield, the politics of burial, and the reprieve that the horses' grief and Zeus's pity at the sight of them means to offer.

In place of that reprieve, the image conjured by the words that follow "Beauty?" could also posit a different kind of memorial, an object that takes into account the suffering that warring groups heap upon each other (and thereby punned upon with "passionate objectivity"). This memorial to the ubiquity of suffering does not quite exist, at least in a nationalist context, unless one pairs Maya Lin's Vietnam Veterans Memorial and its countermonument, Chris Burden's *The Other Vietnam Memorial*: the nearly 15-foot, Rolodex-like artwork lists names to represent the three million Vietnamese people the artist estimated died as a result of "US involvement in Vietnam" over two decades.[88] Such an object is just as counterfactual as the desire to see with fresh eyes violence of the kind the ancient poem relishes. And even if it were to exist, the beauty of the object so mired in death would remain just as questionable.

Questions animate "Don't Flinch," but they pertain more to sensory perception than to aesthetic judgment (beauty). In it, rhythmic engagement with other sensate and sensible items facilitates the emergence of the human subject. Awakening readers to the fact that the human being is stuff amid stuff, that is, not yet food for "worms doing their normal work" of decomposition, the poem manages to create a sense of intimacy between narrator, reader, and figure despite conveying little—if any—customarily personal(izing) information as such. The figure finds itself surrounded by a sense of liveliness, the potential for life, if not life itself.

The poem begins with an unnamed "you" getting distracted by and away from the light "pulsat[ing]" on a nearby rooftile. Repudiating death, the figure tosses a newspaper in favor, *again,* of trying to get the lines of Homer's *Iliad* to "pulse into sense," and then questions whether a smell is smoke or a sound, music. The news about "(who tramples whom) is antique," and the threat of the individual dead who mattered to this subject or another person just like them begins to take hold.[89] At this juncture, a question interrupts the not yet ekphrastic scene about flesh-eating worms to ask, "How could this still shock or sicken you?" (69).

We have seen these tactics before. In "Reading the *Iliad* (As If) . . .," the narrator pinpoints a pulse ("blood making everything more real pounds") on the way to thinking about the insufficiency of contemporary built monuments and ancient Greek heroic epic's own limitations as commemorative genre. The poem uses interruptive phrases, moving from exclamation to interrogation, to evoke the struggle to remain "open-eyed" to carnage. Such questions gesture toward rendering more real and less routine the brutal carnage people suffer everywhere. Here, the possibility of desensitized indifference loomed large after "you" exasperatedly switched media, from newspaper to epic. Should it have taken hold, the poem would sketch the figure's reading practice concretizing them into something even less attuned than the worms are imagined to be. Instead, the lament finds a pulse insofar as leaning into the affectivity undergirding being shocked and sickened reveals vitalizing attachments to friends who have died. As the poem unfolds, moving through affective states accompanies the movement of the figure's gaze, hands, and attentive energy so that interacting with environmental stimuli continuously brings a different kind of "you" into being.

Put into more theoretical terms, sensing the persistence of the attachment to those deceased friends jump-starts the figure's entrainment to the pulses that still abound, that is, to the other relationships and interactions that this assemblage affords and that remain to be actualized.[90] Such potentials suggest reevaluation of the sensibilities of the verminous "chewers chewing" and of death as radical rupture. The poem's unfolding in fact depends on rhythm as both pattern-imposing temporal regularity (the cycle of life and death, the cyclical retreat to the epic poem) and the contingent, unpredictable, and potential-laden relationality of time itself so that the human figure's observation of cycles indexes a more expansive and life-affirming affective capacity.[91]

Taken this way, the human subject resembles those visible and auditory phenomena it asks about in the poem's concluding lines. For like them, it has not yet been definitively formed or perceived. The body, spurred by other beings and inanimate objects to feel by remembering the dead they loved and who have been forgotten or erased by traditional media ("Friends go missing, mute/nameless"), becomes a countermonument capable of actively honoring relationships of various kinds. Instead of nurturing an attachment to the past amenable to political passivity and a refusal to imagine different futures, this body's countermonumentality invests us in the potential and the possibilities of interactive coexistence.

Lerner, Spahr, and Rich count themselves among those who felt they had experienced 9/11 through their televisions or at a remove from the space dubbed Ground Zero and yet disagreed with the consensus that war was the right response to that feeling. Made to witness horror after horror as the War on Terror continued, they rejected the affective resolution offered by the Bush administration via the television news and other media industries. The critique Rich offers in *Tonight No Poetry Will Serve*'s Iliadic diptych differs stylistically from the critique we find in her earlier collections. And the quarrels about lyric that suffuse both Lerner and Spahr's work don't loom over these poems. Nevertheless, "Don't Flinch" and "Reading the *Iliad* (As If) for the First Time" lean into the curious position of the body at this historical juncture of warfare and media technology, and so engage in an important facet of the post-9/11 affective landscape. The administration sought to foreclose 9/11 as historical, thereby asserting control over what people should think, feel, and do to honor those who died in the attacks. These poets enlist time to wield the uneasy power that comes from feeling countermonumental, alone and with others.

CHAPTER 2

Out of Sync

IN JESMYN WARD'S NOVEL *SALVAGE THE BONES*, CLAUDE BATISTE attempts to synchronize with his daughter's pregnancy the day after Hurricane Katrina barreled down on his family's Mississippi homestead. The members of the Batiste family have been out of sync with each other since Rose, Claude's wife and the children's mother, left for the hospital after a complicated home birth and never returned. In the seven years since, whether as coping mechanisms, genuine passions, or some combination of both, each member of the family has pursued interests that have kept them on different, often conflicting schedules. This asynchrony reaches a critical point when the storm's floodwaters overtake their house and the Batistes must coordinate with each other to escape via the roof and to find refuge. Before Claude's son Skeetah can explain his sister Esch's hesitation to jump into the watery vortex below them, Claude pushes her into it, where she struggles to maneuver her pregnant body and to swim as she used to. If he had just waited, if he had been paying better attention before the storm, if they could all effectively communicate with each other, Claude would not have inadvertently jeopardized his daughter's (and grandchild's) life, and Skeetah would not have had to give up one of the most important people in his life to rescue her, in turn. Recognizing the seriousness of his error the day after the storm, Claude apologizes, then inquires about her pregnancy timeline and, after Esch admits to being unsure, he slips into the first-person plural to discuss preparations: "When we can, we need to find out . . . so nothing goes wrong" (247).

Winner of the 2011 National Book Award, *Salvage the Bones* is often summarized as a novel about Katrina, the 2005 hurricane that still holds the record as the costliest storm in American history.[1] But, in narrating the period from August 19 through August 30, 2005, with each chapter covering one day, Ward's second novel dedicates only one chapter to the storm and just one other to the day after it: the harrowing scene that culminates on the roof, that quintessential Katrina-era image, occurs in its penultimate chapter. Esch is a deeply observant narrator, steeped in family and local histories. Recounting these histories during the ten days before the storm, Esch explains how the Batistes developed a synchronous bond with each other on their homestead, known as the Pit, and with other families in Bois Sauvage, the rural Black enclave where they live. Emphasizing the extent to which this synchrony has helped them survive racialized poverty also reveals why losing it—that is, becoming asynchronous with each other *and* with national(ist) culture—matters so much. The novel portrays Katrina's outcomes as epiphenomenal to a weakened citizenship that has made families like the Batistes particularly vulnerable to the destabilizing forces of emergencies for centuries.

Depicting how the temporal dynamics of the Batiste family relate to a performance of citizenship, *Salvage the Bones* dramatizes the sociopolitics of (a)synchrony. Recall that synchronization—making one thing "operate at the same time, rate, or pace as something else"—"creates the social." Synchrony helps any group to cultivate functional harmony as well as a sense of belonging. Its opposite, asynchrony, either destroys that harmony and sense of belonging or arises out of their absence. Perhaps less obviously, it can also hamper real and perceived access to the rights (such as the right to redress), responsibilities (such as the duty of care), and protections that affiliation provides. Crucially, as Elizabeth Freeman has written about extensively, asynchrony with one group may actually be synchrony with another: social groups with alternative habits, morals, and so forth can emerge and reproduce themselves by developing, living, and sharing an approach to time that intentionally differs from a group that does not serve their needs or goals.[2]

The first wave of news about Katrina very often framed the racialized poor in the areas affected by the storm as deviants from a post-9/11 culture of preparedness whose refusal to evacuate before the storm outed their asynchrony with the nation. According to this logic, because they were too lazy and irrational to prepare themselves for the future, they had earned their due, albeit regrettable, recompense. Poor in terms of disposable income, the inhabitants of places like Bois Sauvage have historically not been able to count on the support of outsiders to meet the challenges of everyday life, let alone large-scale disaster. They have thrived by relying on each other—pooling their resources and skills, keeping traditions alive, and sharing the knowledge that they have inherited. For this reason, evacuation comes with obvious risks: being displaced means losing access to tried-and-true lifelines while relying on those that are new, alienating, or have perpetrated harm before. Braving a disaster such as Katrina in the place where they have a safety net and have outlasted other struggles that could rightly be considered emergencies offers the hope of survival in cultural and spiritual terms, if not in strictly material ones. Unfortunately, national coverage did not initially endow the Deep South's racialized poor with the ability to make such rational decisions based on their life experiences.

The synchrony of 9/11 with turbocapitalism had proven amenable to news-friendly stories, the manufacture of sympathy, and the discourse of national unity in 2001. In 2005, conventional media outlets did not find it as lucrative, appealing, or easy to wade through the quagmires of residential segregation, Swamp Acts, slashed budgets for public services, historically low wages, and bottom-of-the-barrel rankings for quality of life in a segment about Katrina between commercials. Instead, readily digestible narratives about Black criminality and a lack of preparedness dominated coverage of the storm, marking some of its hardest-hit victims as outsiders who, when cordoned off, could not threaten the social order or the rhetoric of American exceptionalism.

Aided in no small part by technological developments like photo-sharing platforms that allowed community members to circulate their own photos and responses to formal news outlets, counternarratives eventually emerged that couched the experiences of many of Katrina's racialized poor victims in terms of what scholar Rob Nixon has called slow violence instead of irrationality, laziness, and defective Americanness.[3] Out of sync with the notion of the event, electoral cycles, quarterly reports, insurance policies, and the (turbo)capitalist *tempus quo,* acts of slow violence are neither sensational, spectacular, nor immediate. They often occur at a rate not conducive to historical recordkeeping and, if noticed, are easily forgotten. Allowed to fester over time, they have dispersive, accretive, and exponential effects.[4] Wealthy individuals and nations tend to lay exclusive claim to environmental consciousness. Having to fight for recognition as environmentalists or as legitimate sufferers, the socioeconomically disenfranchised who exist on the front lines of phenomena like climate change—by virtue of gender, residential segregation, colonialism, forced displacement, and so on—face momentous if not insurmountable hurdles rectifying the situation themselves or convincing those more empowered to act on their behalf.[5]

Salvage the Bones exemplifies the thrust of these critical narratives in numerous ways. National and even international coverage tended to focus on New Orleans. Ward herself experienced the storm at home in Mississippi. Concerned that "people weren't really paying attention to what had happened along the Mississippi Gulf Coast," she wanted *Salvage the Bones* to "serve as a counterpoint" to the national conversation.[6] In addition to matters of voice (who gets to tell their story) and place (what locations get to represent the event), Ward's novel addresses that conversation's chronopolitical oversights: by enabling Esch to survey her recent experiences alongside the long-term history of her family and community, Ward creates a narrator whose acknowledgment of the past contextualizes her family's refusal to evacuate the Pit and thus challenges the discourse that damned the racialized poor for their predicament post-storm.

Medea, the princess who hails from the Black Sea in ancient Greek and Roman myth, may not be the first figure that comes to mind when one considers intervening in debates about Hurricane Katrina, racialized rural poverty, and the politics of asynchrony. Name-checked early on in Ward's book, Medea more clearly serves as a sentimental resource for Esch in the absence of her mother, her grandmother, and any female companions. In the novel's first chapter, Esch shares that she must read Edith Hamilton's 1942 anthology, *Mythology,* over the summer. After completing a section about erotic encounters with mostly unhappy outcomes, she strongly identifies with Medea: "Here is someone that I recognize. When Medea falls in love with Jason, it grabs me by my throat. I can see her" (38). The father of her child, Manny, who is also a friend of her teenage brothers, prioritizes his relationship with a relatively wealthier and more stylish girl from their school. Now that she more obviously needs him for support in addition to sex, the informality of their relationship weighs on her heavily. Fearing that she will disrupt their friend group and end up even further isolated than Manny's rejection and her family's dysfunction makes her feel already, Esch keeps news of pregnancy to herself for most of the novel. She wades through her feelings about Manny and the possibilities of motherhood by calling on Medea repeatedly as the novel progresses.

Scholars and reviewers who address the reception of Medea in *Salvage the Bones* tend to be preoccupied with Euripides's tragedy, which famously dramatized Medea committing filicide on purpose, and the epic by Apollonius of Rhodes, *Argonautica*, which chronicles Medea's initial encounter with Jason, because Hamilton's anthology includes them.[7] As a result, they tend to focus on Medea's romance with the hero and to construe allusions to Medea as harbingers of maternal violence or emotional excess. Esch considers terminating her pregnancy only briefly, however, and, as I have already mentioned, Esch's narrative is as much about the threats her family turmoil poses in light of the sociopolitics of the Deep South as it is about her crush on Manny. Taking Hamilton's anthology at face value, studies of Medea's influence on *Salvage the Bones* tend to not reckon with the ramifications of Claude's relationship with his children, the fact that Skeetah's legal name is Jason, and other nonromantic allusions to Medean myths, including to Medea's "mutilated brother," as an extension of the novel's politics.

Arin Keeble has argued that Katrina-era literature responds to the way sentimentality depoliticized domestic fiction after the 2001 terrorist attacks. During the post-9/11 surge of nationalism, domestic fiction's stereotypical figures, conflicts, and traumas merely allegorized state neglect, providing cover for neoliberalism, the security state, and the transnational military-industrial complex.[8] Defining Claude by his alcoholism and his lack of interest in parenting, Keeble especially spotlights the relationship between Esch and Skeetah as a substitute for their father's caregiving, a claim to which we will return. She also notes how Ward grounds emotional outbursts, sentimental speeches, and trauma in the realities of slow violence, thereby blending the sentimentality and allegorizing of post-9/11 domestic fiction with a hard-nosed realism. Accordingly, Keeble considers the novel and other texts involving Hurricane Katrina as doing for domestic fiction what the hurricane itself did for the nation: watching the inept, inhumane, and often extralegal responses to the calamities facing their fellow citizens in 2005, Americans could face the flaws of the American social and temporal order without fearing reprisal for their lack of patriotism as in 2001.[9]

In *Salvage the Bones*, Ward capitalizes on the fact that the stakes of love, family, exile, and motherhood in stories about Medea were never simply personal. Aspects of the ancient stories about Medea adapted to changing laws, ideologies, predicaments, and customs in ancient Greek and Roman cultures. Ward likewise adjusts plot points, political conditions, and temporal details from these stories. The novel's subsequent dramatization of the politics of (a)synchrony invites readers to reckon the risks that accompany strengthening and weakening familial bonds; that accrue when gender, race, ethnicity, class, and other hierarchized differences are accounted for; and that imperial aspirations, anxieties, or achievements heighten. Situating the novel amid the circumstances of Hurricane Katrina demonstrates how preparedness in post-9/11 America and slow violence configured love, family, and community. Just as importantly, *Salvage the Bones* gets to the heart of longstanding American myths about security.

Medea, Temporal Technologist

Ward joins a list of authors who link Medea and temporal manipulation. Notably, in Euripides's tragedy about Medea's experience while displaced in Corinth, overcoming the time limit imposed upon her complements a portrayal of her as a deviant woman whose impiety, manipulative speech, and daringly masculine spirit pollute the places she occupies. But Roman versions that emphasize how Medea (and Jason) murder her brother in order to slow down her father and to escape Colchis portray her weaponizing time in a particularly shrewd manner. In those stories, Medea's ability to leverage asynchrony to her own ends reflects anxieties about belonging, empire, and justice.

Multiple Medea myths coexisted throughout Greco-Roman literary history, although relatively few have survived. Medea's name appears in some of the oldest extant texts in ancient Greek. However, none of those texts tells a single, authoritative story about her entire life.[10] In many versions, Medea—a princess from an area near the Black Sea, Colchis; granddaughter of Helios (the sun god) via her father Aeëtes; priestess of Hecate and/or practitioner of "magic"—plays helper-maiden to a hero from Greece (Jason) who is trying to regain his ancestral throne from his uncle (Pelias). These versions narrate some of the consequences of helping Jason on his quest, consequences that include betraying her own father, abandoning Colchis aboard Jason's famous ship, the *Argo,* and causing the subsequent destruction of other families, some intentionally and others less so. Versions vary as to whether she herself killed or simply watched her brother get killed, but in either case, his death serves a practical and temporal purpose rather than a purely vengeful one: Jason and Medea get the time they need to escape their pursuers.

Euripides's *Medea* portrays the Colchian as a vindictively intentional murderer of her children. In some versions of her myth, Medea is an unwelcomed ruler in Corinth, rather than a trailing spouse. Her children die from failed attempts to safeguard them, not from a murderous desire for vengeance; the Corinthians impiously kill them before an altar to Hera, or Medea, knowing about threats to their safety, fails to make them immortal and they die anyway.[11] Despite this rich history, for many contemporary audiences, familiarity with Euripides's play means that filicide, if not also erotic revenge, makes Medea "Medea."[12] Euripides's tragedy sees Jason attempt to marry the Corinthian king's daughter in his continued quest to seize power for himself. To do so, he must rid himself of the partner who once sacrificed her familial connections and homeland in order to help him. In the drama's first speech, the nurse mentions how Medea tricked the daughters of Pelias into chopping up their father, a ploy that capitalizes on their filial desire to restore him to youth and good health (*Med.* 9). Later, Medea will lament that she killed her brother, Absyrtus, and Jason will specify that she did so near the family hearth, thereby emphasizing her disregard for familial piety and her contamination of the *Argo* (167, 1334).[13] These allusions complement Euripides's characterization of Medea as *both* a foreign, rhetorically savvy woman of action who defies Athenian (if not "Greek") gender norms *and* one stereotypically prone to feminine irrationality and erotic madness (see 1339–40). They also emphasize the danger she poses first to Creon, persuaded by her performance of suppliant motherhood to give in to his sense of social tact (αἰδώς) to allow her a single day to find asylum for herself and her children (340–56), and then to Aegeus, a king from Athens, who offers her asylum in exchange for helping him father offspring (708–55).

Euripides operationalizes Aristotle's ideal timespan for tragic plots, one day.[14] Medea knows the challenge that being unmoored from her family and her city presents; she begs the chorus of Corinthian women to keep silent if she contrives a way to punish those who have betrayed her (255–62). Immediately after Creon accedes to her request of a day's stay, Medea tells them that it will suffice (371–75). In the next twenty-four hours, she secures a place of refuge, assassinates Creon and his daughter (Jason's new wife) with bridal gifts, kills her children, and, finally, escapes to Athens in her grandfather's chariot.

Temporal strategizing plays a role in other ancient Greek texts, too. We know through small, attested fragments that Pherecydes of Athens described how Medea and Jason killed her brother (a baby), brought his corpse aboard the *Argo*, and then scattered his remains in the water to escape the Colchians' pursuit of them. Apollonius Rhodius's Hellenistic epic, *Argonautica*, narrates Jason's mission to regain his ancestral throne, including his first encounter with Medea, her help with the trials set by her fear-inspiring father, and the couple's subsequent flight from Colchis.[15] Deputized by their father, Absyrtus leads the Colchians' pursuit of the Argonauts and secures a considerable advantage by arriving in the Adriatic first, effectively trapping them (4.328). Once it is agreed that the Fleece could be taken away if Medea were returned to await judgment about her rightful place, Medea reminds Jason of his oath to her and the costs of leaving her behind. In response to both Jason's reassurance and his need for a full-on battle to be delayed (ἀλλά τιν' ἀμβολίην διζήμεθα δηιοτῆτος, 396), Medea plans to entrap Absyrtus so that Jason can murder him and she can evade any impediment to her remaining with the Argonauts (415-18). Her plan succeeds. Though Medea watches the murder from behind a veil, her brother stains her garments with his blood, an act that directs attention more to her culpability than her distance from the grisly scene (471-74).[16] Absyrtus's death provides an aetiology for the Absyrtian people, since Jason buried his corpse where the ambush occurred. As for the delay, while the Argonauts reason that the Colchians, bereft of their slain leader, will waste time deciding what to do next, it is actually the goddess Hera who hinders them and thereby assures the escape of the *Argo* (499–510).

Ovid's tragedy, *Medea,* has not survived. Still, the Colchian commands a substantial portion of *Metamorphoses* Book 7, "writes" one of the letters that constitute the *Heroides* (12), is featured in the letter her romantic predecessor "writes" to Jason after he abandons her (and her children) for Colchis (*Her.* 6), and appears across his exilic works.[17] Roman literary culture began translating and adapting ancient Greek texts in its earliest stages, so it is common for Roman authors to draw from the Greek well and Medea figures early on into this process as well; they had access to these myths and to others no longer extant.[18] Working with Greek texts widened the range of responses that the Roman texts could produce, in no small part because Medea herself is not Greek, yet she is intimately bound up in the history of ancient Greek-speaking communities and the colonial projects in which they were involved. The Medea figure could negotiate complex cultural concerns, affording Roman audiences aspects to identify with and to disidentify from simultaneously.

In *Tristia* 3.9, Ovid describes Medea committing rather than simply conceiving of fratricide. Medea's decisively quick (*protinus*) weaponization of asynchrony in this version especially hinges on familial piety—Medea's continued abandonment of it while in the thrall of erotic love and her more sympathetically drawn father's being compelled by it:

Dum trepidant Minyae, . . .
dum sequitur celeres ancora tracta manus,
conscia percussit meritorum pectora Colchis
ausa atque ausura multa nefanda manu;
. . .
Ergo ubi prospexit venientia vela "tenemur,
et pater est aliqua fraude morandus" ait.
Dum quid agat quaerit, dum versat in omnia vultus,
ad fratrem casu lumina flexa tulit.
. . ., "vicimus" inquit:
"hic mihi morte sua causa salutis erit."
Protinus ignari nec quicquam tale timentis
innocuum rigido perforat ense latus,
atque ita divellit divulsaque membra per agros
dissipat in multis invenienda locis.
Neu pater ignoret, scopulo proponit in alto
pallentesque manus sanguineumque caput,
ut genitor luctuque novo tardetur et, artus
dum legit extinctos, triste moretur iter.
Inde Tomis dictus locus hic, quia fertur in illo
membra soror fratris consecuisse sui.
(*Tristia* 3.9.13–34)[19]

While the Minyans scramble, . . .
while the anchor follows swift hands as it's hauled out of the water,
the Colchian, fully aware of her offenses, struck her breast
with a hand that had dared and was about to dare many unspeakable things;
. . .
When she spied approaching sails she said, "We are caught,
my father must be detained by some trick."
While devising a course of action and turning to look at everything around
her,

she by chance caught sight of her brother.
. . . She said, "We have won:
his death will save me."
Right away with a hard sword she pierces the
innocent side of her brother, who neither suspected nor feared such an
attack.
Then she tears apart the limbs wrenched from his body and strews them
throughout the fields, so they'd have to be found in multiple places.
To make sure her father would know what had happened, she exposes
[her brother's] increasingly pale hands and bloody head on a high cliff,
so that her father might be held up by fresh grief and,
while gathering lifeless limbs, slow his mournful journey down.
Since then, this place has been called Tomis, because here
a sister is said to have torn the limbs of her brother to pieces.

The poem takes up one of the *Tristia*'s prevailing concerns, the toll of forced displacement. Linking Absyrtus's death and mutilation to aspects of his new home through etymology, as other authors did, Ovid suggests that exile presages his own violent, even emasculating disintegration (*rigido perforat ense*). Points of similarity between Ovid's situation and that of multiple characters lends the poet plausible deniability in case anything he writes should hamper the slim possibility of being recalled to Rome from the Black Sea: is he a malign wrongdoer in exile (*Medea fugiens*, 9), a pitiable victim of random violence (Absyrtus), or even another figure?[20] Moreover, the asynchrony created by Medea's stratagem configures the poet's exilic alterity in terms of a frustratingly absent presence (and vice versa). Living on the edge of empire creates the same spatiotemporal disconnect for the poet as Medea's murderous betrayal of her family and departure from her homeland: the more Ovid grows accustomed to life in his new "barbaric" home, the more he is estranged from his former life. This reality suspends the poet in a disturbing half-life since resisting acculturation only exacerbates his debilitating isolation: he doesn't even find joy in celebrating his birthday (*Tr.* 3.13).[21] Euripides features hands prominently in his description of oaths, supplication, and gender-defying violence (e.g., Eur. *Med.* 1239). In addition to that intertext, Ovid's emphasis on Medea scattering Absyrtus's limbs throughout nearby fields and exhibiting his hands and head on a rock also recalls the death of Cicero, another Roman sent into exile.[22] The fact that his experience has Roman (and not just "uncivilized" foreign) precedent rejigs the terms hierarchizing imperial center and periphery.[23] If Roman *imperium* can enact such "barbarism," what truly distinguishes Rome from other places?

Seneca's *Medea* deals in different fashion with the promise and peril of imperialist expansion. A philosopher, statesman, and author, Seneca is probably best known as a Stoic who tutored the *princeps* Nero in his life, and for his eventual death by suicide. It is uncertain whether Seneca wrote *Medea* throughout his life, while he was in Nero's good graces, or once Nero banished him to exile. Consequently, the drama may not necessarily critique Nero's character or leadership as much as it furthers how other Roman authors had "encrusted [stories about the *Argo*] with the semiotics of a negative critique of the development of civilization" in keeping with the "grammar of imperial Rome."[24] The problems with and possibilities of empire (civilizing mission, contact with strangers, overreach and governance, effect on national identity, imminence of collapse) existed long before Nero's reign and would continue so long as the empire kept on extending its dominion.

Seneca's dramaturgy highlights Medea's asynchronous relationship with the chorus. Euripides's Medea courts the pity and the compassion of the Corinthian women of the chorus. Prefiguring her interactions with Creon and Aegeus, Euripidean Medea performs "pitiful helpless woman" to reap some benefit from spatiotemporal proximity. In their first appearance onstage, they reassure her, via her nurse, of their friendship and advise her (Eur. *Med.* 179–81). Specifying the shared conditions of womanhood, Medea counts on the Corinthian women sympathizing with her plight of being discarded as unimportant, yet being necessary for the reproduction and maintenance of society. Whether as an innovation or as a holdover from a lost earlier tragedy, Medea and the chorus never share the stage in Seneca's drama.[25] Asynchronous staging creates the effect of "choric presence and absence," and emphasizes Medea's social isolation.[26] Instead of sympathizing with her, the Senecan chorus condemns Medea as a dangerous, even nonhuman (Sen. *Med.* 862–65) foreigner whose tenuous claims to marriage (106) hinder the legitimate process their city is counting on to produce rightful heirs. Medea thus fits the bill of dangerous women from the East in the Roman imagination (think of Dido and Cleopatra), capable of thwarting a political destiny vested in the success of a man and patriarchal inheritance.

Even without the chorus's support and without Aegeus (or someone similar) offering her refuge, the Colchian on the Senecan stage has all the time she needs at her disposal. Just as in Euripides's play, Seneca's Creon grants Medea a daylong allowance after she plays the role of bereft suppliant (*supplex . . . precor,* 282; *precor brevem largire fugienti moram,* 288). Medea suggests that a brief timespan should inspire no fear in him (*Quae fraus timeri tempore exiguo potest,* 291), but Creon suspects that any meager amount of time is too much in the hands of someone so dangerous (*malorum machinatrix facinorum,* 266; *nullum nocendum tempus angustum est malis,* 292), with his adjective *angustum* taking up the spatial semantics of Medea's chosen descriptor, *exiguum.*[27] Later after Medea reasons that killing one son would be insufficient recompense for her grief—too meager a sum (*nimium est dolori numerus angustus meo,* 1011)—Jason asks her not to delay committing the second murder so as not to prolong his pain (*Iam perage coeptum facinus . . . moram dona,* 1014–15), echoing Medea's request for a daylong delay from the king of Corinth (*moram largire,* 288).[28] Although that request continues to render this Jason a more compassionate and caring father than the Euripidean one, Seneca's Medea exhibits more daring. Speaking to her grief rather than to her one-time partner and reminding herself of the contract she forged with Creon (*accepto tempore,* 1017) highlights her autonomy. Leaving the confines of the house, she heads for the roof where she imagines, metatheatrically, that people will applaud her next act—murdering her second son in broad daylight for the first time in the myth's known performance history. Refusing Jason's request, she exhorts her pain to go slowly and to enjoy the murder's effect on him (*Perfruere lento scelere, ne properas, dolor,* 1016). This exhortation to delay inverts Medea's dismissive imperative in Euripides's drama (μένε καὶ γῆρας, 1396): telling Jason to "wait for old age" looks to a time when he will mourn not having the children to care for him, a time she once feared for herself (1033–34).[29] The intertext highlights how little at this same point in her arc this version of Medea fears aged precarity, and thus complements her transformation of sociopolitical isolation into moral and temporal independence. Because her day need not equal any other person's day (*meus dies est,* 1017), she can take as much or as little time as she wants.

Victoria Rimell has explained how Seneca's Medea embodies aspects of the Roman imperial machine. When Medea says that if she were pregnant, using a word (*pignus*) that semantically links a child to financial and legalistic surety, she would probe her insides and drag it out of her body too (*in matre si quod pignus etiamnunc latet / scrutabor ense viscera et ferro extraham,* 1012–13), she treats her own body as empires treat female bodies and territory.[30] Constantly opening up things for exploration and scrutiny, she directly recalls the play's description of the *Argo*'s journey, its cleaving open the sea and through it, the world, for the spread of Roman imperial power fated to have neither limits nor boundaries (*imperium sine fine*). Moreover, the Colchian's ever-growing rage (*furor crescetque semper,* 406–407), opening her breast to the Furies (*pectus en Furiis patet,* 966) of the brother she dismembered, and bringing the gore of filicide closer to her internal and external audience also mimics empire's consequences. Seneca's chorus envisions the fears from Virgil's *Eclogues* (1.59–63), written a generation before, when it describes the people at the ends of the world drinking from rivers much closer to Rome than their homelands (Sen. *Med.* 301–79). Initiating contact with people and places that had seemed remote also enabled those faraway people to initiate contact with Romans and their territory, threatening the safety, purity, and cultural integrity of the Roman people (such as it is).

Rimell pays particular attention to space, figuring Medea's embodiment of Roman imperialist anxieties in terms of uterine contraction and dilation. Subject to Roman law in Seneca's tragedy, Medea would lose legal claims to her children in exile: she asks for an extra day in Corinth to say goodbye to them rather than to find them refuge (*dum extrema natis mater infigo oscula,* 289). By moving the slaughter of her son outside, Rimell argues, Medea reverses childbirth and reappropriates the matricide that Jason and the king of Corinth's decisions had imposed on her in practice. Killing her brother, sailing the seas, and indulging her anger speaks to the kind of expansion endemic to imperialist conquest, whereas the death of Pelias, the collapsed world postconquest, and Seneca's description of the poison folded within the bridal gift all refer to the constricted spaces that haunt empire. In the case of Rome, that haunted space includes its self-declared origins, "the monstrous womb of the Trojan horse, wreaking its creative destruction."[31]

In terms of time, Rimell argues that Medea performs "the temporal equivalent of spatial conquest" when she assumes the role she knows has been assigned to her.[32] Focusing on constriction and dilation includes the historical present and the future. The adverb *nunc* ("now") announces the violation of the sea as feminized space (364–67), which corresponds to the Roman misgivings about their conquest, and recurs when Medea declares that she has come into her character (910), voicing the Roman anxiety about being subjected to the same power they exert on others. Since imperial control aims to render the future a known entity, as the present is assumed to be, Medea seems in sync with Rome's imperialist *tempus quo.*

Even so, Medea's autonomy dissociates her from the feminized imperial subject, weakened when not producing more subjects to be governed. Her tumescent fury apes political authority before finally deposing of its figureheads (for instance, the king of Corinth). Medea more closely resembles a masculine military leader, escaping in the chariot gifted to her by her grandfather, the sun god, as the city of Corinth burns, or even a celestial body than the docile reproductive tool empire desires.

Indeed, Medea—and others like her—would pose far less of a threat if they were neither needed nor wanted to reproduce the social order, but they are. Narratives may try to offload cultural anxieties onto that foreigner/desired object. But they can also emphasize that vulnerabilities or crises about the sociopolitical order predate their arrival and that, should that object fail to resolve the preexisting crisis, they do not completely shoulder the blame for that either. Euripides's tragedy ends with Jason bereft of his children and of his new alliance, while Medea escapes. But leaving Corinth doesn't resolve any of the issues dredged up by the play. The foreign woman with the boldness and rhetorical savvy of a man, able to create as much as she destroys, escapes the consequences of her actions by going to Athens, to another man (Aegeus) who needs her help to reproduce himself. If the structural circumstances (displacement, isolation, and gendered precarity) were to recur, she could resort to the same tactics to save herself. In turn, since each murder pollutes the person who committed it and the place where it occurred, Medea's relocation to Athens threatens to contaminate that city too (846–55). In the case of Roman empire and Seneca's version, Rimell points to the dissolution of familial bonds involved in the Trojan Horse, Aeneas's loss of his first wife, and his final marriage's disruption of a previous marriage pledge as cultural origins Rome would rather avoid confronting. Given that Rome's *other* origin story also involves fratricide, the Romans can't simply offload Medea as a foreign source of contamination. Their history has too much in common.

Expanding our understanding of the myth's chronopolitics reveals further dangers to Roman *imperium* and its self-image. Even as Medea appears to fit within her story cycle and cultural paradigms about, say, gendered behavior, she unshackles herself from the feelings meant to control her, like shame, and thereby grows less predictable. Synchrony, the performance of conformity to the *tempus quo* (*accepto tempore utimur*), allows Medea to arrogate the rights and protections that come from belonging when needed. Asynchrony abrogates the attendant responsibilities or limitations. Out of sync, Medea counts on these norms, stereotypes, and myths of empire to predict the future and thereby secures a tactical advantage against her enemies. Fitting within the "grammar of imperial Rome" as the menacing outsider or "witch" presages one set of issues; demonstrating one's disregard for it introduces a disquiet about that grammar's blind spots. Put another way, choosing to desynchronize from the *tempus quo,* one can autonomously disidentify from an imperial subjectivity along with its constructs of gender. Asynchrony, as the outcome of that choice, can therefore impose a limit on imperial governmentality and, when it comes to characterize whole groups and not just individuals, can even signal imperial collapse.[33]

Seneca's concluding dialogue mires the audience in the problem of injustice that trails Medea's (a)synchrony. Immediately after killing their son publicly, Medea asks: "Do you recognize your wife? This is my usual escape. Heaven's highway has opened up" (*coniugem agnoscis tuam? sic fugere soleo. Patuit in caelum via,* 1021–22). Her language refers to the flight that concludes Euripides's previous tragedy, yes. It also indexes the spatial dilation initiated by the *Argo* and pursued by the Romans, punishing Jason, punishment for Absyrtus's death, and the dilation of the day she was given to evacuate Corinth in this play (*pateat,* 377; *patuit,* 550; *patet,* 966; *patebit,* 423). Furthermore, Medea riffs on Jason's complaints about suspense (*moram . . . dona,* 1016) by bidding him to physically recognize her completion of the customary plot points of her myth. Doing so removes him from the tenterhooks he had been on waiting for the murder of his second son while exposing his folly. For when Jason tells her to bear witness that her escape route is devoid of the gods (*per alta vade spatia sublimi aetheris/ testare nullos esse, qua veheris, deos,* 1026–27), recalling their history of fugitivity reinstalls Medea in the epic narrative with which he is familiar and ignores the fact that Medea in her ancestral chariot successfully assumes divinity.[34] Left in a burning city with his ambitions annihilated, Jason reasons that if the gods did exist, Medea would be made to pay for her crimes. But Jason has misunderstood because he and the Corinthians have paid the price for attempting to disregard Medea and because she is always (accompanied by) divine power.

Having reconciled the present and the past deployed by Jason to chasten her, Medea does not operate according to the same systems of justice as he does.[35]

Seneca's tragedy thus extends the outcome of temporal disaffiliation that had featured in preceding Medean myths. Ovid's *Tristia* deploys Medea's manipulation of time to consider the tension between exile and belonging. But to some extent, Ovid's self-castigation and personal attachment to his former home temper whatever critique of *Romanitas* or empire Medean myth implies: asynchrony merely punishes. Seneca's Medea adopts a self-serving timeframe and a no less dangerously self-serving morality. By the end of the drama, she has refused to be constrained by isolation, self-criticism, or, even trauma, with its recurrent, disempowering return to the past.[36] She acts with full awareness of the role she is expected to play in the drama and in the society producing that drama, forcing internal and external audiences to confront things about themselves that they would rather ascribe to others. Referring to Absyrtus's murder, exhibiting filicide, and playing with staging, Seneca links asynchrony to a reassessment of the cultural codes that govern behavior and belonging.

Preparedness, Slow Violence, and Belonging in the American South

Reflecting on the devastation caused by Hurricane Katrina (and Hurricane Rita), in a speech before a special session of the state legislature on September 27, 2005, Governor Haley Barbour tried to unite all Mississippians under a conspicuously color-blind tentpole. Barbour began with heroes that spectacle-dependent political rhetoric in America typically spotlights, namely, conservation officers, police officers, and members of the Coast Guard. The Mississippi native then pivoted to a heroization of preparedness via "local officials who ordered mandatory evacuations . . . and the 'inland families' who took in friends and family members <u>before</u> Katrina struck." Barbour placed his optimism for Mississippi's renaissance "in the fact that rich or poor, black or white, worker or businessman or the person who had nothing before the storm hit—all of them are focused on the future."[37] In the archived text of the speech, the word "before"is underlined. Barbour's emphasis on the adverb favorably aligns those Mississippians who apparently prepared for misfortune with conventional heroes and thus suggests that the synchronous community he envisions follows the lead of a particular segment of the population.

Barbour never chastises anyone outright in his speech: his remarks praise the can-do attitude of Mississippians as a galvanizing force statewide. Surveying the damage across his state convinces him that "Katrina didn't discriminate," a claim that, in turn, supports his visions of a synchronized multiracial state propelled by plucky self-determination. The governor tethers that attitude to a historical narrative about Mississippian self-reliance that stretches back to the Civil War: Mississippians not "whining or moping around . . . into victimhood" when they realized "there was no one to help" them after that "man-made" disaster resemble those Mississippians he and his wife had just met, people intent on rebuilding the state themselves.

To better understand the subtext of these remarks, recall that preparedness had been used to chastise how *other* segments of the population approached the future. Much of Barbour's rhetoric is redolent of Lost Cause arguments about the Civil War and, consequently, states' rights. It might therefore be dismissed as typical of a governor with Republican establishment bona fides. By designating Katrina's outcome as a "natural" disaster, praising those who acted before the storm hit, decrying "victimhood," and deploying color-blind rhetoric multiple times, Barbour also attempts to deflect charges made by native Mississippians, southerners, Americans elsewhere, and members of international communities who, in the weeks preceding this speech, witnessed how local, state, and federal officials responded to the storm and found the response insufficient. These critics argued that the storm had a disproportionate effect on the racialized poor and feared that any plan to rebuild Mississippi that did not address the man-made history of racialized inequities in the state, before and after the Civil War, would simply establish them anew.[38] Governor Barbour was right when he said Katrina didn't discriminate. Critics pointed out that the history he used to epitomize a unified, color-blind Mississippi also demonstrates that people—in their capacities as government officials, as members of zoning boards or the chamber of commerce, as home inspectors, as realtors, loan officers, and fellow citizens—did discriminate. Poor Mississippians weren't whining victims without gumption, they had not suffered because they did not want to prepare, and they weren't asking for more than their share of consideration or funding. The precarity and vulnerability that impeded their preparedness and informed their skepticism of plans being advanced by public officials cannot be simply excised from the state.

Barbour's heroization of preparedness also responds to well-known concerns about the safety and self-image of the United States post-9/11. "A shadow discourse about technologies of prediction and preparedness" haunted the Katrina era because the hurricane occurred less than four years after the 2001 terror attacks, in the early years of the War on Terror.[39] Touching down on August 29 and September 18, 2005, respectively, Katrina and Rita actually bookended an anniversary of 9/11. The 2001 attacks had demonstrated the need for efficient and coordinated disaster response across state lines and between the various levels of government. Increasing levels of preparedness, assessing risk with precision, and developing efficient emergency management systems all aimed at keeping the homeland safe. If, as many claimed, America had been caught unawares by an attack that happened "out of the blue" in that instance, the nation could not be caught unawares again. Achieving preparedness, or at least constantly working toward that level of readiness, would provide the state the illusion of control amid great uncertainty. Katrina had called the bluff on these aspects of preparedness. Though Pennsylvania senator Rick Santorum charged that the National Weather Service had not *sufficiently* forecast the hurricane's path, state-of-the-art technology predicted the storm days before it arrived in the Gulf of Mexico, and in the preceding years various cities had run through scenarios that were eerily reminiscent of what actually happened.[40] This failure of the government to protect its citizens from a disaster it knew would strike casts doubt on its ability to prepare for the disasters that, to echo former secretary of state Donald Rumsfeld, remained unknown, and to deliver on its promise to protect the rest of the world, in turn.[41]

In addition to signaling government bureaucracy, technology, and armed forces, preparedness focused on maximizing individual readiness enlists regular Americans and transformed the body and the home into sites of nationalist discipline. In its 2004 report, the 9/11 Commission declared that "individual civilians need to take responsibility for maximizing the probability that they will survive, should disaster strike." Americans could do their part to keep themselves safe from the catastrophic effects of the next "emergency" or even from the insecurity of crime on a routine basis. The routines of readiness matter: because it is unclear when one has reached an ideal level of preparedness, emergency readiness and the production of security involve constant labor and a hypervigilant form of self-governmentality. Post-9/11 preparedness could therefore also be considered as a performative discourse related to citizenship, one that informs how American civilians do their part to produce security and thereby behave patriotically.

In theory, every American can prepare for the future and thus adopt the American ethos. In practice, the state authorized performances of preparedness that often entailed a consumerism out of reach of those affected by poverty. In 2004, the same year as the 9/11 Commission published its report, the Federal Emergency Management Agency (FEMA) named September "Preparedness Month." Studying the materials FEMA prepared as part of its public awareness campaign, Marita Sturken has observed how posters appealed to a consumerist, multiracial, *Leave It to Beaver* notion of domesticity with each member of a nuclear family having at hand various items and instructions for evacuating.[42] Imagining a nuclear family unit in the relative isolation of a single-family house with any other houses that might be nearby cropped out of frame, the family can safely ride off together in a minivan to the safe unknown because they have bought all the right stuff. That early campaign seems to have been buried on the agency's website. However, handouts available on the website ready.gov in 2021 still emphasized the need for Americans to start a "rainy day fund" and to purchase hazard insurance in case an emergency should arise. While this advice might appear eminently sensible, checklist items or hazard insurance won't protect everyone. Most Americans, even those who work at least one full-time job, if not two, and have paid for their education or have family members with any medical needs, cannot afford to save vast sums of money on a regular basis. This was true during Katrina, especially since end-of-the-month paychecks and first-of-the-month income subsidies could not be dispensed nor received: a "rainy day fund" would hardly have financed their evacuation or relocation for prolonged periods of time, and recovering from the hurricane took *years*. It proved even more true during the COVID-19 pandemic as tourism and hospitality jobs disappeared while costs for everyday goods either remained the same or increased. And as climate change affects weather patterns and subjects people to unprecedented flooding, wind storms, and cold, insurance agencies are finding ways to exclude these hazards from their coverage, further limiting the practicality of the government agency's advice. Preferring to focus on surviving "the event" favored by our national imaginary, such advice fails to acknowledge the slow violence that led to the long dying of the poor or the infrastructure that could lead to their thriving—a robust, easily accessible, and equitable healthcare system, high-quality equitable public education, a livable minimum wage, sustainable town planning, and other aspects of the public safety net.

Within this context, suggesting that poor Mississippians most affected by the storm had not prepared for it not only casts doubt on their approach to the future, it questions their performance of citizenship and undermines their rights, privileges, and protections. In 2001, acts of terrorism brought the destruction and instability that Americans had associated with foreign countries and "developing" nations to their shores. Hurricane Katrina had a similar effect in 2005: the insecure conditions that many Americans imagined as far away had grown "incredibly close." On September 2, Louisiana senator John Breaux famously described New Orleans as "Baghdad under water"; the mayor of Biloxi, Mississippi, declared Katrina as "our tsunami," referring to the catastrophe that had unfolded in Indonesia and Sri Lanka less than a year before; and Governor Barbour famously compared Mississippi to a place the US leveled with an atomic bomb: "I can only imagine that this is what Hiroshima looked like 60 years ago."[43] In similar fashion, those who suffered the most in the storm had brought back into view aspects of American life that had been pushed offshore, rendered invisible, or forgotten about. Some coverage of the storm's aftermath labeled those mostly racialized poor who had not evacuated before landfall as *refugees* rather than as Americans.[44] Echoing some of the Roman imperial anxieties we have already discussed, this language allowed them to be marked as needy outsiders and sources of contamination that made expurgating them necessary for the nation's safety and for the preservation of valuable resources. It thus helps to explain the biases underlying Louisiana representative Richard H. Baker's infamous comment about the storm ("We finally cleaned up public housing in New Orleans. We couldn't do it, but God did.") or why, when the National Guard arrived in New Orleans, residents noticed that they seemed tasked with the duty of containment and restoration of law and order rather than with organizing or distributing aid.[45]

This part of the Deep South had already weathered criticism that its people and their cultures did not comport with the nation. Studying this history, Anna Hartnell has described how New Orleans' Instagram-friendly French Quarter especially "gestures back to . . . an unacknowledged aspect of U.S. history wherein [the nation] picked up the imperial mantle from its French predecessor." For a time, the United States reaped the intended benefits of the Louisiana Purchase of 1803: New Orleans was an important commercial hub for nineteenth-century industry. Nevertheless, the port city's inhabitants and their various cultures challenged homogenizing conceptions of the nation. Francophone Creoles especially complicated racial binaries demarcating Blackness from whiteness, as the landmark Supreme Court case *Plessy v. Ferguson* exemplified.[46] The twentieth century only deepened the area's connection to French and American imperialisms: for example, Vietnamese refugees established "Little Saigons" in both New Orleans and East Biloxi, where the humid climate and fishing industry proved amenable to rebuilding their lives after the Vietnam War.[47]

Sometimes, racial and cultural difference could be commodified. Most visitors to New Orleans confront the politics of the city's transnational past only indirectly.[48] The city and its residents has been cast as culturally and temporally exogenous salves for the laborious demands of contemporary American life.[49] Tourism endorses experimentation with gambling, alcohol, and sex; facilitates costumed antebellum play in the case of heritage tours and plantation weddings; and titillates visitors with exoticized versions of syncretized Catholicism and Black diasporic spiritual practices. Plane travel allows tourists to leave transgressive behavior behind as quickly as they took it up: having let the good times roll in "N'awlins," a substantial portion of Americans can recommit to the buttoned-up, antipleasure, Protestant work ethic that normatively governs their lives come Monday.

Instead of capitalizing on this alterity, Katrina conspicuously saddled New Orleans with all of alterity's ideological baggage. Poststorm catastrophes reminded Americans that the city was a place open to the dangerous forces of the outside world, yet, no less dangerously, within America's national borders. A share of the general public began to grasp that their good times there had come at the expense of the majority of the city's inhabitants. For others, though, watching spectacular news segments and wondering how such cataclysms could happen in the United States without a truly external antagonist led to more staid conclusions: choosing to live in New Orleans meant giving too much license to leisure and illicit pleasure, and too little care to the hard work and responsibility that preparedness demands. New Orleanians might be Americans in name, but they had embodied an exotic attitude toward labor. No longer characterized by its past of genteel plantation owners who embodied white wealth and created docile slaves mired in frivolity, New Orleans was a stereotypically racialized ghetto where Black lawlessness and laziness had run the city riot, as Michael Bibler has argued that recurrent "narratives about the inevitable tragic downfall of New Orleans" had long imagined.[50]

Bois Sauvage, the setting of *Salvage the Bones,* is not New Orleans. The novel takes place in a markedly rural town on the Mississippi Gulf Coast. Sensationalized (inter)national coverage of the situation in New Orleans rendered Mississippi's racialized poor especially invisible. Because slow violence festers in the dark, visions for a future in Mississippi that disavowed the poor, however subtly, as in Barbour's speech, or overtly, as with comments made by other public officials, would exacerbate the conditions that had brought them into precarity and turn "rebuilding [into] a kind of destruction itself."[51] The novel emphasizes how classed and racialized slow violence in the United States intersects with Katrina's landfall, the Gulf Coast's complicated relationship to the national self-image, and preparedness as a discourse of citizenship. By sketching the Batistes' relationships with one another and their neighbors in Bois Sauvage, the author thereby attempts to short-circuit the representational problems of slow violence post-9/11 without ignoring synchrony's inability to completely resolve the long-term injustices that structure American life.

(A)synchrony's Kin

A few hours before a torrential downpour engulfs the Pit, a TV beams an image of domestic heteronormativity and consumerist hope into the Batistes' living room. Frustrated with each other, family members have spread out over the house: Skeetah has locked himself in his room with his dog, China; Claude writhes in pain after he loses most of the fingers on his right hand in an accident in his bedroom; Esch, Randall, and Junior sit on improvised mattresses made of wood pallets, sheets, and limp pillows, eating boiled eggs with noodles before the television. Depicting "a newlywed couple convert[ing] a room in their house from an office into a mint-green nursery," the program sells the young Batistes a vision of home improvement that their present and historical circumstances have shown to be unattainable, namely, that with a few easy tweaks you can make your home perfectly secure and comfortable (216).[52]

Generally, home improvement programming indulges the joy of consumerism and deemphasizes the expense and labor involved in remodeling.

By focusing on the transformation of a home office into a nursery, the show the Batiste children watch that night further attempts to insulate the home from the reality of labor traditionally understood as "productive." The nursery invites viewers to luxuriate in sentimentality. Yet, the room's new paint color (mint green) merely softens the one-time home office's relationship to money. Moreover, Rose Batiste died after childbirth; Esch is currently pregnant; Claude could not afford to pay for repairs to his house, and an accident has made it impossible for him complete the DIY storm-proofing he planned. If the Batistes' experiences don't reveal the realities of domestic life that home improvement channels obfuscate, the fact that the children watch the program on a small TV sitting atop a broken one, while the flood waters soak their makeshift mattresses, surely does.

Throughout the novel Ward reminds readers that poverty increases the difficulty of Esch's everyday life. Putting Katrina aside—as the postponement of the storm until day eleven does—Esch's experience alone barely fits within the narrative's twelve-day duration. In the ten days that precede the storm, our narrator negotiates the fading memories of her mother; her father Claude's grief, which he often expresses in anger, by indifference to his children, or through his alcoholism; her sexual relationship with, and unreciprocated love for, Skeetah's friend Manny; the suspicion, then confirmation and reveal of her pregnancy; helping care for her youngest brother, Junior; helping Skeetah care for China; and helping Randall care for their father. Rose's gardening skills once provided her children with fresh vegetables on a regular basis, and on one family vacation she even caught a fresh shark for her family to enjoy. Now, Esch struggles to find nutritious food of any kind to eat. Confirming the pregnancy requires that Esch secure a ride to a store, since there doesn't seem to be any public transportation, *and* that she steal a pregnancy test. Thoughts about terminating her pregnancy include the grim realization that, as a poor young woman, the cost of any safe options prohibits her from accessing them. Without a confidante to turn to and without money, she has had to "snatch" possible solutions to the predicament of pregnancy from the conversations she has overheard at school: even these dangerous ideas—drinking bleach, running into a car, or overdosing on birth control pills—must be stolen from elsewhere else (102). We know, from the memories about life before Rose's death and from the twelve days Esch narrates to us, that Katrina counts as only one of the many metaphorical storms through which she has had to persevere while feeling confused, hungry, sick, silenced, and mostly powerless, sometimes all at the same time.

Connecting Esch's personal experience to familial and local histories uncovers environmental and structural neglect. Esch's mother and grandmother had shared their life stories with her and so transmitted valuable information about the Pit, Bois Sauvage, life in the civil rights era, and so forth on to the next set of Batistes. Some memories historicize her mother's death: her mother dying shortly after childbirth looks back to the death of seven of her siblings in childhood, feeds into Esch's anxieties about motherhood, and anticipates the family's trip to the hospital when Claude injures his hand preparing his truck for post-hurricane work. As is still the case in the United States for Black mothers, mortality rates run high in this family, in no small part because of their limited access to healthcare. The long ride to the hospital and Esch's sense of unfamiliarity and shame in the space reflect the family's continued estrangement from the medical infrastructure. Likewise, when Esch goes to the school gym to watch Randall play basketball, Esch puts the school within the context of desegregation and 1969's Hurricane Camille: "the elementary school used to actually be the black school for the district before the schools were desegregated in 1969, after the last big hurricane, when people were too tired finding their relatives' uprooted bodies, reburying them, sleeping on platforms that used to be the foundations of their houses . . . walking miles for freshwater, for food, to still fight the law outlawing segregation" (140). The anecdote takes what could be interpreted as progress toward racial equality and Barbour-esque Mississippian unanimity and describes it as an outgrowth of a particularly racialized neglect.

In fact, this combination of natural cycles, state neglect, and racialized injustice recurs when Esch describes the park that tries to "impose civility" on Bois Sauvage and its residents. Because the park is only given maintenance once a year, the nearby woods and the grass have overrun the baseball field, the play structure is falling apart, and the basketball hoops have no nets. So, while in the scene "convicts in green-and-white jumpsuits" . . . halfheartedly" tend to the grass, forced to do hard labor for cents per hour, their indifference reflects on the policies of containment, disinvestment, and wage theft uniting the predominantly Black enclave to the carceral system and the security state writ large. Esch figures her neighborhood as an incomplete civilization project: "The wild things of Bois Sauvage ignore them; we are left to seed another year" (117). Scenes like this anticipate the robocall that happens the night before Katrina's landfall. Just like the radio that had "told [them] nothing practical" during a previous category 3 storm, the call contains little information beyond the fact the state will bear no responsibility for their failure to evacuate. Frightened, Esch only recalls the "iron throat's" unspoken pronouncement: "You can die" (217).

This community's disposability cannot be untethered from a transnational, multiethnic heritage that America rarely acknowledges. Ward models the fictional enclave Bois Sauvage after DeLisle, Mississippi, her hometown, located in Harrison County and close to the Bay of St. Louis. DeLisle's nearest big cities are Biloxi and Gulfport: even if they do not count as "Black cities," the French Catholic colonial past of these places nevertheless troubles American notions of white Protestant homogeneity. Bois Sauvage means "wild wood" in French. Esch's maternal grandmother, Lizbeth Temple, dies while praying the rosary. In addition to recalling the various ways that water has shaped their lived experience, Esch's paternal last name, Ba(p)tiste, reflects this same past. Details about Esch's appearance remind readers of the problematic inclusion of this area, once governed by the French with their particular racial hierarchies, into the United States: Esch specifies that her body lacks stereotypical signs of Black womanhood in the white-norming racial imaginary of America, and reveals a lineage of race-mixing or what her mother, Rose, called "a throwback trait" (7). China's relationship with Skeetah has similar dimensions: the conspicuously white-colored dog named after a country in the so-called "Far East" belongs to a racialized breed (pit bull). The Batistes and China thus bring up the discomfort that the region created for the nation at large by revealing the constructedness of racial difference: admitting that multiple modes of construing race could co-exist at any one time, on the same continent and within the same nation, erodes the concept's presumed self-evident immutability and intrinsic meaning.

Likewise, the Pit offers testimony about a troublesome past that could otherwise be forgotten. Esch was under the impression that men build houses for their wives because Papa Joseph built a house when he married Lizbeth. When Claude Batiste married Papa Joseph's daughter, Papa Joseph helped Claude build the new branch of the family a house on his land, too. Lovelorn Esch focuses on the gesture's sentiment, that a house symbolizes love and commitment. But this one story touches on the racialized history of informal resource exchange, land settlement, homeownership, infant mortality, and environmental debility all at once:

> My mama's mother, Mother Lizbeth, and her daddy, Papa Joseph, originally owned all this land: around fifteen acres in all. It was Papa Joseph nicknamed it all the Pit, Papa Joseph who let the white men he works with dig for clay that they used to lay the foundation for houses, let them excavate the side of a hill in a clearing near the back of the property where he used to plant corn for feed. Papa Joseph let them take all the dirt they wanted until their digging had created a cliff over a dry lake in the backyard, and the small stream that had run around and down the hill had diverted and pooled into the dry lake, making it into a pond, and then Papa Joseph thought the earth would give under the water, that the pond would spread and gobble up the property and make it a swamp, so he stopped selling earth for money. He died soon after from mouth cancer, or at least that's what Mother Lizbeth used to tell us when we were little. (14)

"An impossible site but an ideal situation," New Orleans offered colonialist explorers prosperity and wealth if they could "master" the watery hazards that threatened it on all sides.[53] They founded the city on these principles of containment, resistance, and extraction, gambling on its long-term viability. Aggressive logics of extraction also shape the Pit, increasing its vulnerability to the forces of erosion and diverted waterways.

Once Joseph realizes the hazards of his enterprise, he refuses to gamble his family's long-term future while propping up the houses of white men any longer. For the Pit to be turned back into swamp would bring his family steps closer to the privations of slavery and the period immediately following Emancipation when maroon communities, first, and then communities of legally emancipated individuals inhabited the spaces white Americans did not want, like swamp and marshland. A homeowner raising a small amount of livestock, Joseph forewent the additional income in favor of preserving what little agricultural land was still viable, and keeping the rest of the plot safe for his only surviving child, Rose. By ensuring that his daughter would have a place to live, Joseph used his wealth in land to provide his daughter a measure of security that could never be taken for granted in American history.

Though we never learn the extent of what Papa Joseph taught Claude, the novel portrays Claude preparing for the storm to the best of his abilities. It is tempting to define Claude by his addiction, grief, and neglect of his parental duties. However, from his first appearance in the novel Claude obsesses about the hurricanes that keep developing over the Atlantic Ocean. He watches the news on the small, yet still functional television and parrots the reports coming through the radio. While he still has full use of his hands, the Batiste patriarch recruits his children's help in his efforts to board up the house with the scraps of wood they have available, to fill up the bathtub and empty jugs with water they will need when the processing plant is out of commission, to stock up on shelf-stable food, and to fix up the dump truck on the lawn so he can act as a makeshift waste disposal service for those within driving distance while normal services remain suspended. In fact, he wakes up Esch and her brothers on the first day of the novel by telling them they all have a lot of work to do. Once he loses the fingers on his right hand, his repair work comes to a halt and his plan to earn more money grows increasingly untenable. We learn late in the novel that Claude has already managed to save a few hundred dollars for his family since he knows life after a storm can be unpredictable. At the very end of the novel this detail will factor into our reappraisal of Claude's ability to care for his children's emotional needs. Here, even as the injury pushes him deeper into the grip of depression, Claude continues to plan as far ahead as a medicated haze of physical and emotional pain will allow.

The narrative thus demonstrates the numerous ways that the Temple-Batistes have exhibited a spirit of preparedness long before the post-9/11 articulation of it. Both men creatively navigate inequalities of the formal labor market: in addition to working the land and having a job, Joseph tries to support his family in any way he can. He also stewards his land responsibly. His farsightedness also involves the nonhuman creatures and entities that contribute to the ecosystem of the homestead and so anticipates and perhaps influences, for example, Rose's interest in gardening and farming and Skeetah's nurturance of China. Esch expresses embarrassment about the state of the Pit, especially the items she considers (and others also could consider) trash. Yet her parents' and grandparents' habit of salvaging parts and fixing things rather than throwing them away reflects a more sustainable approach to objects than simple consumerism. Indeed, Rose "tried to keep the house up, but needing a bed for [Esch] and Skeet to sleep in, or needing a pot when hers turned black, was more important than keeping the house a shrine": the land, the house, and the accoutrements that Rose inherited from her parents repeatedly keep the Batistes back from the brink of total financial ruin (58).

Suggesting that the common conceptualization of preparedness and security depends on invisibilized, often intergenerational wealth, the novel emphasizes that, although the Batistes exhibit the spirit of preparedness, they fall short of performing preparedness in sanctioned ways. They lack the disposable income necessary to purchase checklist items, and they don't currently own a functional car. In fact, when Esch sees people stocking up on hurricane supplies while she is trying to steal a pregnancy test, she imagines that they are wondering why she is not doing the same and experiences a shame that recalls when white-columned homes made her feel "small, dirty, and poorer than ever" (29–30, 252–53). Most obviously, when their wealthier neighbors evacuate, the Batistes remain at the Pit.

Their temporal differences play out more subtly. The Batistes constantly confound the distinctions between labor and leisure that American culture imagines as a safeguard against insecurity, recalling the way the branding of New Orleans or Biloxi's label as the playground of the South feeds into the myth of the doomed southern city. At no time does the Batiste household seem to obey the rhythms of the standard workweek. *Salvage the Bones* is set in the summer, and since the Batiste children are minors, they spend mostly unscheduled time on the margins of social institutions. In the case of Claude, we never find out where he used to be formally employed. Instead, Esch tells us that shortly after her mother's death, her father started receiving disability checks because he was in a car accident. To supplement that income, he "picks up odd jobs working on oyster boats or towing scrap metal" (61). A generation before, Papa Joseph was *also* trying to earn additional income in the informal economy when excavation began to harm the Pit.

Ward assigns each of Esch's older brothers interests that have racialized baggage and that similarly blur the distinction between leisure activity and "productive" labor. Esch describes Randall's athletic nimbleness with painterly precision and animalizing language: handling a basketball, he is "all quick grace and long haunches"; dodging defenders, he recalls "a bayou crane alighting so he doesn't even sink into the black marsh before taking off in flight" (2, 143). As a sport with low barriers to entry, it isn't surprising for a Black teenager from a nonwealthy background to have hoop dreams. Nor is it uncommon for those dreams to come up against the hard reality of stiff competition: advancing to the professional levels does take connections, monetary investment, parental support, *and* talent. Injuries to Randall's knee and hands jeopardize the already slim possibility that he will ever make a living through basketball. During the novel, he seems confident that he will be able to earn a scholarship to a basketball camp where he can meet scouts, only for the scholarship to go to someone else. While Randall's chances at the riches and glory of the NBA offered a respected (however racialized) route out of generational poverty, Skeetah nurtures a passion for dogs that will likely brand him a criminal. Skeetah does earn money performing a more traditional task—mowing and weeding the lawn of the Catholic cemetery nearby. But he does this just so he can afford to buy China the most expensive dog food on the market. Longer term, he plans to earn money fighting and breeding pit bulls.[54] As he struggles to learn the ins and outs of husbandry and frets over the health of the puppies in China's litter, Skeetah doubles for Rico, the owner of the litter's sire. Rico, we are told, "makes so much money fighting him he only has a part-time job as a mechanic at an oil change shop, and he spends the rest of his time driving his dog in his pickup truck to illegal dogfights set back in the woods" (13). Esch thus describes Rico inverting the balance between formal work (part-time) and side-hustle (full-time) or leisure activity. In sync with Rico, Skeetah would also be asynchronous with the timing that most comports with normative productivity, patriarchy, and the domestic sphere where these ideologies converge.

Other character arcs play out similarly. Losing both his job and his wife in short order transforms Claude from a householder who dressed for work in a normatively masculine uniform of steel-toed work boots and jeans into a man who leaves home only reluctantly and will soon lose the ability to work with his hands. Rose's death has adultified Esch.[55] Randall shares caregiving duties with her. Even though Claude's off-loading of Junior's care rushes Esch's development into a traditional gender performance, it is striking that part of her concern about the visible symptoms of pregnancy revolves around clothing: the square body that she found insufficient when compared to Manny's acknowledged girlfriend, Shaliyah, had fit so well in the jeans, cotton shorts, and tee shirts that she shares with her older brothers and father. So, while the clothes resist Esch's sexual differentiation, the mothering imposed upon her at an early age complements the sexual experimentation she began at age twelve with Skeetah's friend Marquise. The fact that she has had multiple sex partners and that she especially enjoys sex with Manny characterizes her as "fast" developmentally. But reclaiming sexual pleasure leads to her pregnancy and makes her into the ultimate example of illicit Black female productivity. Skeetah's relationship with China frequently crosses the human-animal line in ways that disturb the hypermasculine criminalization of Black men who organize dog-fighting *and* queer but consumerist approaches to pet ownership. Esch casts him as China's "lover [and] father," while the pit bull fits the bill of "doting daughter" (98). However, the mutuality of their bond means that China, this fierce fighting dog, also mothers Skeetah. While mothering pushes Esch to one end of the spectrum of racialized femininity, Esch thinks it inhibits Skeetah's normative performance of masculinity and heterosexual development. She worries that girls won't find him attractive because he smells like a dog.

In the past, the Batistes' synchrony would have made their home a refuge of sorts or, as Arin Keeble frames it, "a place of routine and familiarity that . . . structure[s] their lives and provides some protections" from poverty that contributes to precarity.[56] Keeble construes the tasks and circuits in which Esch spends time as a reflection of the fifteen-year-old's unresolved feelings about her mother's death: her daily cycle of activities mimics the "insistent return of the [trauma-inducing] event." While some part of Esch's day belongs to a routine—waking up late, occasionally reading, eating—much of it doesn't follow a schedule and changes when an opportunity or need presents itself, whether that is for the pregnancy test, or because friends show up, or when Randall has a game, and so on. Esch is not the only one traumatized, though: all the family members are buckling under the weight of Rose Batiste's death and have been using a variety of interests to cope. Indulging these interests makes idiosyncratic demands on each family member's time. Those demands do not necessarily square with the schedules of another family member.

In addition to the irregularity of the events she narrates, Esch mentions her family's asynchrony numerous times. On the third day of the novel, when she wakes that morning, she surmises that "maybe they've scattered: Junior under the house, Randall to play ball, Skeet in the shed with China and her puppies" (38). The next day, she admits: "Before China had these puppies, I'd go days without seeing [Skeetah]. Days before I'd be walking through the woods looking for eggs or trying to see if I could find Randall and Manny, or walking to the Pit to swim, and I'd stumble on Skeetah, training China to attack and bite and lock on with an old bike tire or a rope" (60). Other details, like Esch reminiscing about the way Mudda Ma'am used to, but no longer watches Junior, suggest that the family is falling out of sync with Bois Sauvage as well. Skeetah recalls that Rose, just before she left for the hospital, enjoined her children to take care of each other. Having fallen out of sync with one another as well as with other families in Bois Sauvage, they now risk losing their entire safety net.

Chrono- and choreographed allusions to the dynamic between Medea, Jason, Absyrtus, and their father, Aeëtes, reflect the family's disconnection, how they misunderstand and miss each other. On day four, when Esch tells us a bit more about Claude's work history, we realize that her tired, slightly frail father walking up the steps is a mere glimmer of who he used to be. Though Claude still manages to inspire fear in his children, Esch wonders if Medea also spotted the frailty in her father and if that influenced Medea's abandonment of him in exchange for a future with Jason:

> His T-shirt is dark at the pits and neck and down the middle of his back. His boots hit so hard on the floor that he sounds like he's going to go through the rotted wood. He's not that much bigger than us. Is this what Medea saw, when she decided to follow Jason, to flee her father with her brother? Did she see through her father's rich robes to the small-shouldered man beneath? (61)

Just afterward, Claude orders Skeetah to help him prepare the house for the storm. The exchange between the two is fraught, with each one not completely willing or conversant enough to help the other. Eventually, Claude tries to physically intimidate Skeetah into doing what he asks, only for both father and son to realize that physicality alone won't work anymore. Her father's fingers just miss Skeetah's arm because of the teenager's slithering stride, and his eyes catch Esch's glance at the very same instant. As Skeetah eventually backs down, Esch acknowledges her father's frailty and confusion, and Claude reasserts his will over them all, the encounter demonstrates, quite literally, how tenuous a grasp they have on each other. Claude's attempt recalls Aeëtes's parental desperation to collect the hands and limbs of Absyrtus. But it also smacks of an imperiousness reminiscent of Apollonius's Aeëtes and Medea's experience with male authority figures in other stories. Claude prevails. Not only does he win the argument, and so they do what he says, but in getting up to the attic, he more importantly prepares them for the coming storm, fulfilling his parental duty.

Similarly, when Randall disapproves of Skeetah's plan to break into their white neighbors' barn to get supplies for China, he grabs Skeetah's arms. Skeetah had folded his arms across his chest, turning "his muscles [into] rope[s]," but frustrated at Randall's attempts to control him, he "unlashes his arms and they come whipping out from his sides" (73). No longer restraining himself, Skeetah reminds Randall that, while he might be the oldest sibling, he is not a parent. Besides this "bitter" rebuke, Skeetah explains, in response to Randall's concerns about danger, that he has taken all necessary precautions to minimize the possibility of them getting hurt or even killed during the raid *and* that he had planned to use the money he could earn from breeding China to pay for what their dad could not, Randall's basketball camp. Like Esch and Claude, who believe that Skeetah's passion for dogs has separated him from the needs of his human kin, Randall did not imagine that Skeetah had been planning to share with him whatever income he earned from the puppies. The scene turns from aggressive grabbing and defiantly crossed arms to gestures of endearment and heads nodding in unison:

> Randall's arms cradle [Junior] by the chest. Randall looks down at Junior's head . . . "You'd do that for me?" Randall speaks to Junior's head, so at first I don't know who he's talking to, and then I remember Skeet, who is nodding next to me now. With each dip of Skeetah's head, sweat drips unimpeded from his crown . . . to fall from his chin like a weak summer sprinkle.
>
> "Yes," Skeetah says, still nodding. (74)

Looking down onto Junior's head, Randall's posture mirrors that of his brother Skeetah, who is moving his head up and down. The two don't seem to make eye contact. Still, the moment plays out as an inverse of the interaction on the staircase, with Esch once again emphasizing the stakes of what has happened.

This won't be the last time Randall misinterprets Skeetah, but the conversation opens up a path for mutual understanding that had previously eluded them. Skeetah has noticed that he and his brother both suffer from Claude's seeming unwillingness and inability to pay for the things they want. Randall will eventually take risks on his brother's behalf as well. When Randall grows frustrated that Skeetah has only brought enough dog food back from the store and not enough human food, he enlists Esch to go on the same mission he had tried to prohibit Skeetah from making. Hurting his hand and his knee in the hopes of providing his family with food, Randall exhibits the self-sacrificing caregiving Skeetah will show on numerous occasions, simultaneously fulfilling his mother's wishes for his human and nonhuman kin, and defying blinkered stereotypes about Black masculinity.

In fact, it is Skeetah who leads the way to their life-saving synchronization on the night of the storm. As the house tilts and the water finally reaches the attic, Skeetah refuses to die in the tiny space above the rafters. He summons the determination we have seen him exhibit throughout the novel and begins banging on the roof with his foot to find a way out. Randall cranks up a chainsaw to create a wider way outside. Within minutes, he climbs "into the hungry maw of the storm" with his youngest brother, Junior, clinging to his back (230). The rest of the family follows.

Before the storm, the Batistes coexist under the same roof but do not often spend time together in the same room intentionally engaged in the same activities. On the roof in the middle of the storm, Claude "tried to gather [all his children] to him," to keep them safe (231). Realizing they must go elsewhere, Skeetah has another idea: he shows Esch that Papa Joseph's house sits on the high ground and that they can cross into its attic via a nearby tree. They all agree. While Claude is injured and can only attempt to cross by himself, Esch, Randall, and Skeetah each carry another member of their family with them. Skeetah wears his pit bull, China, the way parents wear an infant. Randall continues to carry a terrified Junior. Esch notices "both of them [are] holding their bundles closely" (232). She herself brings China's puppies and the child in her soon-to-be-noticed protruding belly. Carrying another loved one increases the difficulty of managing the wind, the rain, the rising floodwaters, the height, and the distance all at the same time. Still, as one person readies for the next stage of the journey, there is at least one person watching their back and another who has prepared the way.

Nevertheless, years of asynchrony threaten to reproduce an ordeal that they all desperately want to avoid. Claude impetuously forces Esch into the water one beat before processing what Skeetah said, that she is pregnant. When Esch struggles to navigate against the current, it's not only that Claude has endangered his child's and grandchild's lives, but that, blinded by grief, Claude has failed to notice how all of his children have grown up. When she was a little girl, Claude threw her into the water and so "taught" her how to swim. But Esch is no longer a baby, and she has needed other kinds of instruction in the meantime.

Luckily, Skeetah notices Esch struggling. In response, he whispers into his beloved dog's ear, lets China fall into the water with one hand—counting on her continued strength and swimming skills—and with the other pulls Esch out of it before she drowns. Sacrificing one of his kin to the watery vortex, he retrieves another from the water's Charybdis-like "fanged pink open mouth" (234). Skeetah's determination and sacrifice recovers Esch from the swirling waters as she struggles to swim. She describes "Randall almost break[ing] her wrist with his grip as he haul[ed her] up" into the other attic (236).

During this scene, Skeetah's strength, Claude's frailty, and Esch's pregnancy all resurface, but in spoken ways rather than the previously unspoken ways. This time, it is Esch who just misses her proper landing in the water and flails, beginning to drown. It is Claude yelling to Skeetah, "this ain't the time," ignorant of Esch's pregnancy and mistakenly believing that Skeetah suggesting Esch follow in his immediate wake as he makes a path to the attic reflects a greater investment in China's puppies than in his sister (234). While Skeetah slips from his father's grip on the stairs, that night Claude clings onto a branch with his "bad hand" and reaches out in vain from the tree for Esch with the other. But there are two other sets of hands available: Skeetah's determination and sacrifice recovers Esch from the swirling waters as she struggles to swim, and Randall's grip and strength will yank her from it up into the attic. Instead of breaking limbs and scattering them into the sea to rupture familial bonds as with Medea, Jason, and Absyrtus, the Batistes all work together to overcome their individual debilities and to survive the flood waters on their homestead.

Esch emphasizes the shared nature of the family's condition in the aftermath of their escape. After they make it to the attic of Papa Joseph's house, Esch clings to Skeetah's body, feeling his cheek against her forehead, to counteract the distress he feels as he looks for China in the receding waters below. Day twelve, just before he jumps from the window to break the intimacy of their enclosure, our narrator realizes the family members are "*all* bleeding, all gashed" (239). When their father leans over in reaction to Skeetah's desire to leave them behind, she realizes he struggles "to find purchase to stand up" because of his previous injuries, before noting, in the same sentence, that "none of us could [stand up] with the bones of the ceiling folding so low" (240).

After Skeetah goes in search of China, Esch, Randall, Junior, and Claude walk to Big Henry's house. As Claude's strength fails, Big Henry falls back to help him, placing a comforting hand on his back, and Esch confesses to herself (and consequently to readers) all of the things she wishes she had said to their friend yet can't muster expressing. For Randall, slightly separated from the rest, things play out differently. He establishes that his former best friend has fathered Esch's child and has chosen to wash his hands of any connection to her. Esch, in turn, takes ownership of her part in the relationship by admitting she pursued sex with him. In addition to sorting out details of the pregnancy, the siblings' conversation makes clear that while Randall will always be the eldest, Esch has grown up. She awakens him to her development much as Skeetah had to do for him in the scene about their neighbor's house.

Ward once again choreo- and chrono-graphs tellingly:

> A girl separated herself from the crowd, sat down next to Manny on the truck, laid her head on his shoulder. Shaliyah. Manny sat there stiffly beside her, still looking at me, at Randall, waiting for a wave, a nod, anything. I slid my fingers into the crook of Randall's elbow, and Junior's leg rubbed the back of my hand. His skin, and Randall's skin, was warm; I walked so that Randall was my shield, my warm cover, my brother.
>
> . . .
>
> Randall . . . didn't let Junior go, and he squeezed his forearm to his waist, folding my arm into his, pulling me with him. We walked to Big Henry's front door together. (244)

Rather than slipping out of each other's hands and squirming away from each other, according to mythological and familial precedent, these three Batistes draw themselves tightly against one other, offering each other protection and comfort. As they step in unison, they disconnect from Manny and his betrayal. He may be seated next to Shaliyah, but his gesture attempts to bridge the distance between him and his former friends. Rather than wave back, they move forward.

Though Randall and Esch reject Manny, the family synchronizes with others. At Big Henry's house, his mother, Ms. Bernadine, nurses Claude's wound with hands "quick and light as hummingbirds" (244). His Aunt Sally brought a backup generator that powers a fan to use overnight while the grid is still down. His uncle brought a tarp to serve as a temporary fix for the damaged roof. Other neighbors have executed the plan Claude had in mind, using personal vehicles to clear trees and other debris from the streets.

Before the storm, misunderstandings damaged Claude's relationships with his children. As they are rightfully still struggling with Rose's absence, their youth and grief mistakes Claude's behavior as negligent apathy. For example, while Randall helps Claude recuperate from his maiming, Esch narrates how Claude only ever came to one of Randall's games and left before halftime. But the very next day, as they discuss the provisions they have available, Esch overhears him call Randall "son," a token of affection she said he had used on only a few previous occasions (195). The small word speaks volumes, not only because it shows Claude's softer side but also because that conversation puts some of Claude's practical decisions into fuller context. The money that Randall and Skeetah lamented not having for basketball camp was being stored up for the family' safety, not hoarded out of indifference. While his injury stymied his plans to make more money with the dump truck, Claude zealously guards the savings just in case the worst happens, and he impresses upon Randall the need for them to figure out a way to make those savings last. Leaving Junior with the neighborhood granny, Mudda Ma'am, or with his older children, was not (only) about shunting responsibility for the baby involved in his wife's death—it gave him time to seek out odd jobs that would bring in income to supplement his disability checks when Junior was still too young for Head Start. Needing to combine enough of these informal and occasional employment opportunities could also explain his absence from Randall's games. For these reasons, when Randall hurts his hand trying to steal provisions, he not only resembles Skeetah who attempted this same maneuver on behalf of all the people he loves, he also resembles his father attempting to prepare for the storm.

After the storm, Claude attempts to correct the misunderstandings that have taxed his relationship with Esch. He admits regret for pushing her into the water. Switching from the first-person singular to the plural and inquiring about her due date, Claude demonstrates that he cares very much about his daughter and his grandchild. Esch still remains too overcome with emotion to voice *all* of her feelings. Between her short answers and her gestures in their conversations, she nevertheless manages to engage in a meaningful, if curtailed dialogue with her father. While the pair talk, Claude holds a photo of Rose, a reminder of what the family stands to lose and of the care they owe each other (247). Claude anticipates Big Henry's reassurance to Esch that, despite Manny's disavowal of her pregnancy and his parental duties, her baby, which Esch has decided to name Rose Temple Batiste if it is a girl, will have "plenty of daddies" (255) in the men who constitute her extended family.

Ward balances the overt sentimentality of these scenes with others that spotlight the hurdles facing the Gulf Coast after the storm. On a drive to St. Catherine, a more racially diverse community even closer to the coast, the young people survey the damage Katrina has wreaked there. Randall describes the neighboring town in terms that recall comments officials made after the storm ("Look like somebody dropped a bomb. Like war" [257]), and, after doing what the national media would have called "looting," Esch reflects on the current state of places that used to marginalize her ("[the] small dim bookstores and the kinds of antiques stores that I would never dream of walking into for fear of breaking something have been savaged" [252]). They also witness "people stand[ing] in clusters at what used to be intersections, the street signs vanished, all they own in a plastic bag at their feet, waiting for someone to pick them up." But they themselves know better: "no one is coming" (250).

After describing the busyness of her neighborhood, Esch's characterization of St. Catherine as waiting recalls Governor Barbour's subtle condemnation of those dependent on the state for the help, both before and after the storm. However, the history Esch has provided helps us construe the scene more judiciously. It isn't that the residents of St. Catherine are lazy, lack resilience, or forfeit compassion because their circumstances are so dire. Rather, their waiting only underscores how the Batistes and their neighbors in Bois Sauvage have been conditioned by generations of neglect to expect little to nothing from outsiders. They can tell that jets passing overhead are going elsewhere. They begin to recover, in the way they have always had to do, the way that everyone who has been treated as disposable and unimportant knows how to do.

Mythologies

Later, the kids go in search of Skeetah and find him sitting alone by a fire, hardened by grief, guilt, and worry, waiting for his beloved canine companion, China, to return. They suggest he leave with them to sleep and to eat, promising to help look for the dog later. Skeetah refuses, in case she comes back to the Pit to find him. He stares into the flames as if "he could pull who he is off and become something else . . . [l]ike he could shed his human shape" (257). Esch has favorably compared humans to nonhuman animals numerous times before and, because Skeetah and China share such a deep bond, it is not surprising that she imagines him metamorphosing at this moment. However, when she claims that her brother also resembles "sand seared to rock" as he looks away from the fire and into her eyes again, Esch reactivates a set of resonances between the Batistes and the families involved in ancient Greek and Roman Medea myths (258).

In keeping with his confounding of various norms constraining Black male gender performance, Skeetah has played multiple roles from that myth over the progress of the novel. Skeetah most easily maps onto the character of Absyrtus as his father tries to grab hold of his arm in that tense scene on the steps. It isn't just that, like Aeëtes, Claude wants to take hold of his son's limbs. Claude's behavior and its misinterpretation reflects the articulations and ambiguities of Aeëtes's characterization, sometimes mysterious, sometimes tyrannical, and in other variations, pious: he badgers and imposes upon his son out of the same parental duty and care that Medea counts on to assure her escape from Aeëtes's pursuit, even if Esch's and Skeetah's resentment does not allow them to recognize it as such.[57] The night of the storm, however, Claude and Skeetah switch roles. When Claude pushes Esch off the branch into the water, his disconnection from his children renders him the Medea (or Jason) to Esch's Absyrtus dashed into the waves. When Skeetah sacrifices China by dropping her in the water in order to rescue Esch, the boy whose legal name is Jason plays the role of both Aeëtes, rescuing his kin from the watery depths, and of Medea, from another version of the myth, trying yet failing to protect her children from harm.

These identifications only grow in complexity given the multiple instances in which China has also played various Medeas. In the novel's earliest scenes, China gives birth to her first litter. The Batiste children might be new to animal husbandry, but they are not strangers to birth trauma. So, when China bites her own puppy as it tries to nurse, Esch's description of her as "bloody-mouthed and bright-eyed as Medea" likens her to the Medea who is intentionally dangerous out of a disregard for duties of care and further associates motherhood with excessive violence (130). As they come to understand that the newborn had a disease that would, if not isolated, prove fatal to its littermates as well, the Batiste children grasp that China's actions originate in care and a desire to protect the other puppies from harm.

Doting on the litter constantly and attempting to care for China, even if it means stealing medicine and food, Skeetah takes up the roles of Medea *mater* and Medea *pharmakis* as well as Jason the healer.[58] Taking on the role of Medea as helper, Skeetah can either soothe and protect China from violence or incite the pit bull to it. Goading her on to fight the sire of her litter in the backwoods, "their own dangerous Aegean," Skeetah implores China to "make them know" her ferocity (160, 175). Despite being more dialogic than Medea's metatheatrical pep talk, Skeetah's order still echoes that moment toward the end of Seneca's tragedy: as she comes into character-defining rage, Medea states, "I will make them know how lightweight and run of the mill the crimes I committed for others were" (*faxo sciant / quam levia fuerint quamque vulgaris notae / quae commodavi scelera* [902–9]).

During the dogfight in the woods, Esch sees Manny on Rico's side as Jason betraying Medea for the king of Corinth's favor and imagines herself as Medea, strong enough to ignore Manny's tacit appeals. The dogfight originates in tensions that erupt right after Esch and Manny have sex in the gym bathroom—Esch suggests that Skeetah suspects the pair have a relationship, despite Manny's dating Shaliyah—and the dogs (and other participants) function as partisan extensions of their male owners' bravado. Skeetah's allusion to Medea's dangerous refusal to continue accommodating Jason emphasizes how this particular fight arises as much from his confidence in China as from a desire to protect his sister. The fight between China and Kilo, the sire of her litter, ends with both animals retreating to their humans for safety and comfort, as if to their parents, and so violence, erotic love, and familial love coincide variously. Moreover, Esch's focus on the love and lavish care that Skeetah provides his dog during the fight recalls the tragic scene's metatheatricality insofar as it lets the external audience know who Skeetah really is and emphasizes how much his loving nature is shortchanged by stereotypes about Black boys.

Still, Esch's description of Skeetah seated by the fire awaiting China and looking like "sand seared to rock" reveals her fears that his caring and self-sacrificing love for others could "go wrong" as it did for Medea. At the beginning of Euripides's drama, the nurse describes Medea in Corinth—not looking at, hearing, or speaking to her friends who offer her advice—as a rock (Eur. *Med.* 28–30). Skeetah is not unfeeling, though. He worries that China may, as other family members did before the storm, mistake his actions in the flood waters as rejection and neglect, that she could not be mistaken about his love for her. Esch realizes that the stories she planned to share with Skeetah about the day they spent apart will no longer suffice. To keep him soft and tender, she and the rest of the group should stay by his side. They decide to remain at the Pit, each one watching over another one of them. Even if Junior falls asleep or if they are in pain, the group's common purpose will coordinate the time spent at the fireside vigil. Esch tries to foster a sense of belonging between the group, Skeetah, and China in absentia by synchronizing everyone.

This synchrony overlaps with Esch's forecasting of the future.[59] Just before finding Skeetah, Esch communicates what she will tell her child about the storm. Figuring Katrina as a mother in the mold of Medea, Esch reflects on what her family has survived:

> I will tie the glass and stone with string, hang the shards above my bed, so that they will flash in the dark and tell the story of Katrina, the mother that swept into the Gulf and slaughtered. Her chariot was a storm so great and black the Greeks would say it was harnessed to dragons. She was the murderous mother who cut us to the bone but left us alive, left us naked and bewildered as wrinkled newborn babies . . . as sun-starved newly hatched baby snakes. She left us a dark Gulf and salt-burned land. She left us to learn to crawl. She left us to salvage. Katrina is the mother we will remember until the next mother with large, merciless hands, committed to blood, comes. (255)

Mentioning the "merciless hands" of the next catastrophe, Esch here repeats Edith Hamilton's translation of line 1239 of Euripides's tragedy.[60] However, by pitting the relatively merciful storm against a future merciless one, Esch's language acknowledges a version of Medea more committed to protecting her loved ones than intentionally destroying them. It is unclear whether the "next mother . . . committed to blood" anticipates another hurricane, her impending delivery, or both. In any event, Esch braces herself for hardship by strengthening the bonds of the community where and with whose members she has always found a way to survive.

In light of this, at the end of the novel, when Esch looks up into "the star-suffocated sky [where] there is a great waiting silence," it is hard not to hear a critical echo of Jason from Seneca's tragedy (258). Seated beside Skeetah, Esch glances upward before pronouncing her determination to wait for China, her "canine sister," to return and to embrace motherhood with her when she does ("She will know I am a mother"). The sky's silence refers, in the immediate context of Skeetah's devastation, to the absence of barking, the missing proof that China has also survived the storm. In the context of the Medea myths woven throughout the novel, the comment reflects Esch's resolve. Euripides's Jason's appeals to Zeus as the giver of justice at the drama's end may be futile, since the god who governs oaths and *xenia* could find Jason guilty of the very crimes Medea punishes him for committing. Seneca's Jason ends the tragedy assuming that the heavens must be devoid of gods for him to suffer the way he has, a misunderstanding that helps us calibrate the extent of Medea's disidentification with her former role in his life and of his misidentification of her. For her part, Esch's comments do not so much replay Jason's powerlessness or confusion or even index Medea's survival through relocation as reveal how she has successfully disidentified with the stereotypes and anxieties about motherhood that have plagued her from the novel's earliest pages: synchrony with family and the community in Bois Sauvage allows her to imagine herself doing what Medea so often failed to do, even in those archaic versions where she is not a simple femme fatale, namely, using love to make help go right.

Of course, love has limits, within the text and in the real world to which it refers. None of this lets outside forces off the hook for the slow violence families like the Batistes must continue to combat. A project of Hip Hop Caucus, Think 100% annually commemorates Katrina in New Orleans as part of a larger program of climate activism, racial justice, and political action.[61] Education, Economics, Environmental, Climate and Health Organization (EECHO), based in Gulfport, Mississippi, formed in the wake of Katrina; EECHO educates and advocates for communities simultaneously impacted by environmental disaster, environmental injustice, and systemic racism. Taproot Earth "emerged from communities from the Gulf South to Appalachia, which are organizing for equitable jobs, infrastructure, and an ecosystem" in the wake of Katrina, the BP disaster, and 2021's Hurricane Ida. They represent just a few of the community organizations—some independently, others with the backing of even larger organizations, and others, like Gulf South for a Green New Deal, unite a network of groups—dedicated to remediating conditions that increase the environmental precarity of certain communities and thereby preparing them for future disaster.[62] Such activism has been described as fighting the Jim Crow of climate change, the next phase of a struggle against racializing policies.[63]

The persistence of racialized injustice and of struggles against them should frame our understanding of *Salvage the Bones*'s relationship to both Medean myths and the mythological anthology that Esch reads. The passage that introduces Hamilton's anthology emphasizes that our narrator does not read Euripides's *Medea* or Apollonius's *Argonautica*. Hamilton's popular, school-friendly collection has been continuously reprinted since its initial publication in 1942 and so has been assigned to many students over the last eighty years. Hamilton makes a point in her introduction to favor versions of Greek myths from classical Athens, when she claims humanistic rationality guaranteed the ancient Greeks a freedom from the terror that characterized life in "primeval slime": "The world of Greek mythology was not a place of terror for the human spirit" because this humanism of the "early Greek mythologists transformed a world full of fear into a world full of beauty." Framing the ancient Greeks as humanists par excellence who had shrugged off the fear that comes with primitivity's intellectual and psychic darkness, Hamilton portrays them as thoroughly modern. Hamilton will later admit to excluding versions of myths that do not fit this view: she tolerates Virgil because, of the Romans, he comes close to the fifth-century Athenian tragedians, but excludes Ovid because he did not *believe* in the myths he adapted.[64]

Thinking about *Mythology*'s success and longevity, Sheila Murnaghan has explained that Hamilton's comments respond to the anthropological interest in "primitive cultures" that was in fashion when this work was published. Anthologies always challenge their authors to develop criteria for selection. But as Murnaghan aptly summarizes, comparing Hamilton's work to another from the same period with a rather different ideological bent: "This wish [to honor the chronological variety of their sources] is, in each case, overridden by an even stronger impulse to deal with the question of Greek identity by identifying and privileging one historical era in which the Greeks were most themselves. The stories generated in that era then take on an authority that shapes and colors, in each case, the entire presentation of mythology." Murnaghan cites Hamilton's exclusion of Ovid as evidence of the importance of belief in Hamilton's spiritual life. For Hamilton the Greeks of the classical period become the forerunners to a "specific [Protestant] spiritual state" where pragmatic humanism sloughs off primitivity and "corresponds to the best of modern experience." Additional evidence comes from Hamilton's earlier book, *The Greek Way* (1930).[65]

However, when Hamilton describes Greeks "freed" from "paralyzing fear of an Omnipotent unknown" and ridding the human spirit of the "terrors" that await in the "primeval forest" in *Mythology,* she also voices some of the prevailing sociopolitical concerns of the 1940s. These portrayals of the Greeks position them in terms reminiscent of the discourse of security and progress that responded to the destabilizing horrors of America's Great Depression (1929–33) and the world wars that bracketed it. In the preface to *The Greek Way,* Hamilton famously gestures toward the insecurity of the Great War and the Great Depression when she appeals to the Greeks for spiritual sustenance: "When the world is storm-driven and the bad that happens and the worse that threatens are so urgent as to shut out everything else from view, then we need to know all the strong fortresses of the spirit which men have built through the ages." Later, reflecting on the few physical remains of these "great" civilizations, she reassures her readers that material privations do not affect one's spiritual riches, an idea that the Depression will ground in more tangible concerns than theological metaphysics alone: "Little is left of all this wealth of great art: the sculptures, defaced and broken into bits, have crumbled away; the buildings are fallen; the paintings gone forever; of the writings, all lost but a very few. We have only the ruin of what was; the world has had no more than that for well on to two thousand years; yet these few remains of the mighty structure have been a challenge and an incitement to men ever since and they are among our possessions to-day which we value as most precious." Later, as she begins the book's historical narrative, she seems to motion toward some great upheaval, once more: "what the Greeks discovered, or rather how they made their discoveries and how they brought a new world to birth out of the dark confusions of an old world that had crumbled away, is full of meaning for us today who have seen an old world swept away in the space of a decade or two. It is worth our while in the confusions and bewilderments of the present to consider the way by which the Greeks arrived at the clarity of their thought and the affirmation of their art." Just after she condemns the anthropological fervor that mixed the Greeks in with other primitive cultures, as Murnaghan mentions, Hamilton bemoans the Egyptians who embodied an "Oriental state" with all of its subjugation and despotism. The Romans were equally removed from "the Greek spirit."[66] Claiming that a certain disposition had persisted with little change in the so-called East, she laments that some cultures refuse to conform to the demands of modernity. This modernity, which America shares with the Greeks, doesn't court the terror and misery of the populace; it demands that people think for themselves, enjoy liberty, and, crucially, possess a measure of security.

On January 6, 1941, less than a year before Hamilton's *Mythology* was published, President Franklin D. Roosevelt delivered an address now known as "The Four Freedoms." The speech began by defining the contemporary period as "unprecedented" because at "no previous time has American security been as seriously threatened from without as it is today," before specifying that the nation's future lies in its rejection of isolationism.[67] Subtly expressing sympathy with a reluctance to intervene in what would go on to become World War II, the president reflected on the fact that the Great War had taught Americans that a threat to democracy anywhere could undermine their own: America's "domestic problems [were] now a part of the great emergency." Even as FDR urged Congress and the nation at large to look outward to the "tyranny" imposed by dictators armed with bombs, he emphasized that security, democracy, and cultural freedom (freedom of speech, freedom of worship) in the wider world meant ensuring the economic well-being of people at home.[68] Amid efforts to revitalize the American economy after the Great Depression through the New Deal, Roosevelt had declared that if the South, "the nation's no. 1 economic problem," did not modernize economically, the nation could not make forward progress.[69] In "The Four Freedoms" speech, isolationist policies threaten the nation with Orientalist backwardness: Roosevelt claims the United States had never been "locked behind an ancient Chinese wall while the procession of civilization went past."

After 9/11, the United States once again sought global leadership by promising to spread democracy and to free the world from fear. Defending the claim that Iraq possessed weapons of mass destruction, the United States sought public and diplomatic support for the War on Terror: no one was safe with such weapons in the hands of a tyrant from the "Middle East."

But, less than four years later, Katrina revealed how many Americans had known no other life except one characterized by insecurity. Disparities in economic and physical well-being that racialized and gendered the freedom from want were still widespread. And as long as millions of Americans remained subjugated to the tyranny of impoverishment, they could never enjoy the security FDR had envisioned or that US foreign policy claimed to offer others.

Esch's experiences of Katrina and the familial history she passes on in *Salvage the Bones* encourage us to ask when people in communities like Bois Sauvage will share in modernity's benefits, when they will get to enjoy American security, when things will change for them. Working in the 1930s and 1940s, Edith Hamilton thought the old fears and power imbalances no longer had purchase on American life. She lamented that the East had never changed enough to embrace the modernity that she believed the Greeks, the imagined founders of Western civilization, helped birth.[70] Hamilton saw no point in courting a skeptical take on the Colchian's story. In dialogue with *those* takes on Medea and the politics that animate them, Ward writes back to Edith Hamilton's exclusionary view of modernity.

CHAPTER 3

Home, Land, Futurity

BY THE TIME THE FIGURE CALLED ODDSEE ARRIVES ON STAGE, the audience of Suzan-Lori Parks's play *Father Comes Home from the Wars* (Parts 1, 2 & 3) (hereafter, *Wars*) will already have witnessed familiar scenes of subjection: several slavery narrative tropes will have been dramatized or narrated, including the auction block, whippings, the hunt for fugitives, lynchings, and bodily mutilation.[1] The play follows the relationships between Black adults enslaved together on a Texas plantation as the Civil War encroaches upon their lives. Part 1 begins with a group speculating about the decision Hero, the person Boss-Master prefers, will announce at dawn.[2] Each person selects a prized possession as collateral to bet whether Hero will accompany Boss-Master to battle while he serves as a Confederate officer or turn down the offer and stay with his beloved, Penny, and surrogate father, Old Man. By taking up his enslaver's proposal, Hero likewise wagers that Boss-Master will fulfill his promise to free him in exchange for his labor on the front.

In Part 3, Hero comes back to the plantation eager to start the patriarchal life of his dreams. Experiences chronicled in Part 2 prompt him to examine the insidiousness of white supremacy and to speculate about how he will approach the gulf that will separate even a Union victory from true racial equality. Though Hero will disclose that Boss-Master refused to free him with his dying breath, the one-time favorite remains tethered to the model his enslaver provided for managing a family and property as a householder. And so, returning with the new name Ulysses, he sets about reinstalling Boss-Master's style of dominion over a plot of land, only with himself as Boss over the rest of the community. Penny, in contrast, decides to join a self-emancipated group pooling their material and intellectual resources to journey northward to "Freedomville." Instead of being subjugated to the man she once considered a spouse, she chooses Homer, the figure who has been a devoted suitor and Ulysses's alter-ego, to be her partner going forward.

At the play's Los Angeles premiere in 2016, the audience in the Mark Taper Forum gasped audibly as Hero fell off a tree stump under the weight of his enslaver's blow in Part 2. In Part 3, a member of the chorus from Part 1 reappeared wearing a shaggy jacket to perform the role of Hero's canine companion, named Odyssey Dog but only ever called Oddsee in performance.[3] As the hybrid dog-human ran in circles, licking Penny's face and wiggling his rump in response to her loving scratches, the audience laughed. Soon afterward, when Oddsee began eloquently musing on the dynamics of power, breaking the fourth wall in the process, the audience's laughter receded. The silence, the rapt attention expected at theatrical performances returned. The show went on.

Though it did not last long, that eruption of laughter stayed with me. It wasn't simply that the levity felt incongruous with the drama's knowing self-seriousness up until this point. True, Oddsee's campy excess offered a reprieve from the customary means of realizing the horrors of the peculiar institution—and, for this very reason, it channeled the history of representing those horrors to win sympathy for those Black beings subject to them from a mostly white audience.[4] Knowing that some of Parks's prior works have been criticized for similarly incorporating humor or sexual playfulness into stories whose seriousness seemed a necessary prerequisite for both respectability and redress had prepared me for the likelihood of a comedic moment.[5] It would take weeks for me to begin to sense that Oddsee's late arrival in the progress of the plot was related to the momentary tonal shift his behavior allowed. What we in the audience witnessed that evening was not solely an expert performance of a dog, or a human ideal about dogs. Nor was it merely an extension of Blackface minstrelsy overlaid with the concerns about animality that have underwritten many forms of anti-Blackness.[6] That eruption of laugher marked the extent to which Oddsee changes the drama's affective status quo in anticipation of Hero's return to the plantation as a free(d) person: Oddsee's bodily excess and hyper-loquacity seemed to scream, *Something new is happening!* as the moment forecast by the play's title was most imminent. But given that Oddsee is a dog who sees differently because his eyes go "this way and that" and who left the plantation of his own will before the play began, his late arrival could never be as straightforward as all that (36). Rather, as I now recognize, Oddsee's apparent role as herald contributes to the drama's more nuanced study of what it means to anticipate freedom and the subjectivities that this imminence creates.

The matter of freedom looms large over *Wars* (Parts 1, 2 & 3). The trilogy ends with the formation of two divergent communities. Ulysses had intended to free his enslaved peers by reading the Emancipation Proclamation aloud, thereby using his ability to read to reclaim his sense of superiority over them. But since the group planned to self-emancipate long before Lincoln issued his most famous speech act, Ulysses's late arrival hinders more than it permits. As the curtains close, the hero stares at the Big House where he once served as valet, accompanied by his dog and the treasures he collected on his homeward journey. Now, going their separate ways, these groups—Ulysses and Oddsee, on one side; Penny, Homer, and the rest of the self-emancipated group, on the other—endorse incompatible views about the meaning of Freedom and what community demands under Freedom's conditions. The play ends with the Emancipation Proclamation still unannounced.

Envisioning *Wars* as a triple triptych, Parks will extend the play's temporal reach beyond the Civil War era. Parts 1, 2, and 3 are regularly performed as a unit and have been published as such. As of this writing, only Parts 4, 7, 8, and 9 have been infrequently staged and neither of the latter two triptychs has yet been published. Her plan for this saga sees Ulysses building a family with Alberta—the woman he mentions in Part 3 as Penny's replacement—and his rival, Homer, marrying his former partner, Penny. The descendants of the two families, both named Smith, will encounter one another.[7] As a result of this transgenerational arc, the play will move from the nineteenth century into the contemporary period. Observing all of *Wars*' nine constituent sections will reveal whether Ulysses (or his extended family) ever got to enjoy what we saw him sacrifice so much for in Part 3.

Wars has often been marketed as an American adaptation of the *Odyssey*. Figures named Homer, Odyssey Dog, Penny, and Ulysses—if not also Hero—invite the comparison. The playwright's use of dawn as a temporal marker; scenes of hospitality; a culture-defining war; the interconnection of trickery, disguise, and recognition; rival suitors; and the matter of fidelity reward that comparison. Though a few critics have argued that *Wars* fails to do justice to Homer's verses, most reviewers draw on these intertextual resonances when they attach the heft of the word "epic" to this play: the nine-part, multigenerational scale, its discussion of America's original sin, and mythologizing allusions all make *Wars* an epic example of American drama. And, lest we forget, such seriousness, when combined with Parks's various high-profile awards, including a Tony and a MacArthur grant, helps sell tickets. For those who might otherwise shrink from thinking about American slavery as an insurmountable institution that structures the present, comparisons to ancient Greek literature and the classics render more palatable the play's less than subtle condemnation of whiteness and American history, mitigating the opprobrium of a young nation with the glint of antiquity.

Counter to these front-of-house choices across the country, Parks herself has rejected the mantle of adaptation. In an interview ahead of that Los Angeles premiere in 2016, Marcos Nájera asked Parks about her father. The playwright responded by citing as the inspiration for the play her father's journey to find professional respect and wages commensurate with his qualifications, instead of Homer's *Odyssey:*

> My dad, Donald Parks, was a career Army officer. He joined the Army ROTC in college—it was one of the few places in this country where an African-American person could join, get a job, and have some kind of guarantee of fair treatment. To become a colonel in the army from where he grew up [in Chicago] was a big deal. He's buried in Arlington National Cemetery and the Bronze Star was the big medal that he got.
>
> *Father Comes Home from the Wars* is inspired by my dad. It was not inspired by *The Odyssey. The Odyssey* is in our drinking water. So you get bits and pieces and shards and shrapnel of a lot of things. *The Odyssey* is a big thing you get. It's a big thing that people latch onto and think I'm doing a retelling of *The Odyssey.* No, I'm not. That's not where I'm coming from. It's *Star Wars!* It's Ulysses S. Grant.
>
> . . .
>
> [This play] was inspired by my dad coming home from war a lot—he did a tour in Korea and two tours in Vietnam—or coming home from having practiced being at war.[8]

Parks's comments here are consistent with those she has made in other interviews. The playwright has also, for example, dismissed correspondences between "Penny" and "Penelope" or "Homer" and "Homer," the *Odyssey*'s author, as merely coincidental.[9] This response to the misinterpretation of the play's background is curious since, in her critical writing, Parks often mentions ancient Greek authors as one of the many influences on her work, both thematically and structurally.[10] But the interviewer does not press her on this correcting of the play's genealogy, and Parks, famously tongue-in-cheek and anti-academic about her writing, speaks with an easygoing manner that obscures the subtleties of this story.[11]

The anecdote Parks shares with Nájera actually redeploys the finely wrought discourse of metals that runs throughout *Wars*, drawing our attention to that discourse's relationship to the temporalities involved in Black liberation. I do not construe Parks's comments as wholesale dismissal of ancient Greek drama or criticism that derives from her commitment to thinking about the full range of Black American experiences. I believe Parks has crafted *Wars* as a rejoinder to Homer's *Odyssey* instead of as a retelling. Correcting the *Odyssey*'s idealizing conservatism about heteropatriarchal descent, *Wars* sparks interest in the various futures available to Black Americans at a time when economic policies, nationalism, and postracialist complacency threaten(ed) to extend the inequities of the present indefinitely into the future and still cry progress. *Wars* mimics that text's optimism in the futurity of patrilineal inheritance and its safeguarding of the social order only to then dramatize the limits of that commitment in the context of American racial capitalism.

As incorporating the "Hands Up, Don't Shoot" gesture into the script of *Wars* connects the violence of antebellum "patrolmen" to the state-sanctioned murder of Black citizens by police officers in the present, so too with Parks's directorial note about Ulysses's gaze off-stage at the end of Part 3.[12] His glance at the unrepresented Big House catches sight of the 2008 subprime mortgage crisis and the racialization of homeownership, as well as the continued circumscription of American citizenship. Even without the completion of the triple triptych, Parks's writing nudges the audience of this drama set during the Civil War to decouple chronology from notions of radical change, equality, and optimism. In coming to grips with how the playwright's approach to Black futurity in *Wars* revises the logic of Homer's epic, we uncover the significance of comparing the *Odyssey* to shrapnel as part of this discussion of Lieutenant Colonel Donald Parks's Bronze Star.

Repeating the Lincoln Myth, Revising Homeland Nostalgia

Parks refers to her signature dramaturgic technique as "rep and rev," that is, repetition and revision. Influenced by the aesthetics of jazz, this form of signifying constantly restages ideas, characters, scenarios, and themes within a play.[13] As a consequence of this prominent repetition, actors can "physicalize words," and audiences can see them "literally incorporated into a life."[14] In addition, "rep and rev" is a generative technique, for Parks is constantly writing new texts in various genres and different media, challenging herself to make "form and content" cohere in new contexts. Her highly allusive style involves multiple texts by other authors, while the recurrence of words, gestures, names, and scenarios in her ever-expanding corpus also creates discursive breadth within it. Because Parks sets her works in different historical periods, intertextual "rep and rev" always implicates the audience's perception of time.

Wars typifies the intertextual network this technique creates. First, the play takes up the scenario of its namesake work, "Father Comes Home from the Wars," one of the experimental mini-plays collected in Parks's *365 Days/365 Plays* (2006), to repeatedly stage the moment when an army officer returns to his family after playing at war all day to increasingly absurd ends. Second, *Wars* refuses to contribute to Lincoln's hagiography. *Wars* conceptually resembles both the Pulitzer Prize–winning *Topdog/Underdog* (2001) and an even earlier drama, *The America Play* (1994). In both these plays, Black men in the modern era work impersonating Abraham Lincoln, allowing paying customers to go so far as to "assassinate" them for a nominal fee. Their moneymaking ventures eventually break up their households even as they promise "to convert the trauma of abandonment into a genuine form of possession" through entrepreneurial ingenuity.[15] Finally, *Wars* reprises aspects of the critically lauded five-part play, *Imperceptible Mutabilities in the Third Kingdom* (1989) (hereafter, *Mutabilities*), which shuttles between America in the antebellum past, several domestic spaces in the contemporary world, a contemporary military base on a spatiotemporally distant island, and a deliberately undefined space-time related to the transatlantic slave trade.[16] In its final vignette, "Greeks (Or The Slugs)," a military service member named Smith returns to his family with a medal that fails both to realize his ambitions and to mean what he had convinced himself and his immediate family members it would mean. Mr. Sergeant Smith had hoped, much as Frederick Douglass had envisioned during the Civil War, that military achievements signified by medals would upgrade his life in one fell swoop.[17] Narrating how he achieved his long-awaited promotion—he caught a man falling from the sky and, in the process, stepped on a landmine that permanently injured his legs—he realizes the routines and scripts that promised to move him up the socioeconomic ladder have done him numerous kinds of harm instead. The person he caught resembles Icarus or Phaethon, figures from ancient Greek myth who learn the limits of their existence by plummeting from the sky to the ground. His espousal of respectability politics—especially with regard to the maintenance of his body and the bodies of his family members—similarly sets him up for a disintegrating fall. *Wars* owes much to *Mutabilities,* not least its confrontation with the racialized distinctions between humans and animals via ancient Greek mythology and, in light of the relationship of "Greeks (Or The Slugs)," to the first vignette, named "Snails," its refusal to conflate moving forward in a drama with making progress toward societal justice.

While Parks's planned intergenerational arc broadcasts one aspect of the interest in futurity expressed in *Wars*, the dates Parks chose to bookend the first trilogy's action highlight the futurity implicated in American housing policies during the nineteenth century. Taking place entirely in the Confederate South, Parts 1, 2, and 3 represent approximately fifteen calendar months between spring 1862 and fall 1863. Abraham Lincoln issued the Homestead Act in May 1862, a preliminary Emancipation Proclamation that September, and the final decree on January 1, 1863, when the Homestead Act took effect. Though it exists in the shadow of the Proclamation, the Homestead Act of 1862 impacts significantly the history of homeownership in the United States: the law facilitated the nation's expansion westward via dispossession of Native American territory and explicitly linked citizenship to homeownership. According to the act's provisions, men and women who were at least twenty-one years old could pay a fee to claim a parcel of land so long as they were already or intended to become American citizens and could be considered "heads of households." After five years of development, homesteaders could apply to "prove up" and to legally own their plot, thereby transforming large tracts of public land into personal property.

When Hero returns from war as Ulysses, intent on owning property, he dangles before the group a sheet of paper with the text of the Proclamation written on it, unaware that a few others could also read the words if given the chance. With this action and Parks's directorial note about him "savor[ing] his power . . . and their expectant looks," the audience gets to see physicalized the futurity these dates import to the entirety of the first triptych. Parks's choice of temporal setting in *Wars* goads the audience, knowing the myth about Lincoln and the Proclamation if not the history of its uneven implementation and limited scope, to regard the sheet of paper with equally expectant looks. However inevitable uttering the Proclamation might have seemed to Ulysses, and treating the Proclamation as the moment to which the action trends might seem to the audience, the ending of Part 3 avoids fulfilling any of the expectations about Emancipation, homeownership, and belonging the playwright set up.

There is historical precedent here: the radically improved future the myth of Lincoln seems to guarantee within the first installment of Parks's epic fails to come to fruition, just as it failed to do in the aftermath of the Civil War. The fact that no one has alerted those enslaved on this Texas plantation about the Emancipation before Ulysses's arrival reflects the historical circumstances behind Juneteenth.[18] Moreover, the Homestead Act did not apply to the millions of Black people who were either enslaved or had been emancipated until the Civil Rights Act of 1866 and the 14th Amendment, ratified in 1868, granted them legal citizenship. Though the final Emancipation Proclamation declared that those Black people enslaved in rebellious states would be "free," able to "labor faithfully for reasonable wages," the order's exemptions meant that more than two-thirds of those enslaved at the beginning of the war would remain "unfree at [its] end."[19] The Southern Homestead Act of 1866 would also try to "create a southern economy based on a yeomanry of Black and White small farmers to replace the regime controlled by plantation owners," but it failed to catapult Black landowning due to the cost of relocation, the added expense of farming land, and entrenched racism.[20] In the case of the Proclamation, replacing enslavement with wage labor would eventually overturn the southern economy, which had been dependent on unremunerated Black labor to generate wealth for white male landowners and their heirs. But overturning one economy does not necessarily produce an equitable replacement, and extortionary labor contracts continued to undermine Black labor power with all of its correlate outcomes.

Analyzing debates from Reconstruction over currency standards, Michael O'Malley observed the persistence of essentializing logics binding metal to racial difference in American thinking after the Civil War. Those in favor of hard money, or a currency backed by the value of an actual item such as gold, "wanted an intrinsic or 'essential' value to regulate speculation and growth, and imagined gold or silver's 'natural' value as a check on all values, something above human tampering which would anchor economic cycles and make social hierarchies 'real' as well. The 'soft money' camp treated value as purely social, purely 'conventional,' and looked for ways to stimulate growth and engineer social equality by increasing or decreasing the amount of money available." The thinking that undergirded "soft" or fiat money underscored how other types of value were also grounded in humans repeatedly making a choice to grant value instead of God and Nature having already determined it. Consequently, racial and civic inequality, which originated in discriminating and differentiating convention rather than in natural, nonnegotiable hierarchies, could be remedied by instituting different conventions and even eradicating hierarchies altogether. For these reasons, adopting fiat money as the currency of this reunified nation threatened to further undermine the meaning derived from white male monopolization of the marketplace as a "self-making" instrument and as a mechanism for realizing the potential white skin (or blood) already symbolized.[21]

In some ways, these cultural anxieties about money and race were nothing new. The financial transactions of chattel slavery had long since revealed discomforting ideas about money and the marketplace before these attempts to standardize the nation's currency: enslaved people "had a generative, speculative potential to make wealth, like money loaned on credit, like paper bills circulating on faith, but also a fixed character that could never be negotiated away or altered, like the value embodied in gold bars." For this reason, they "literally embodied the contradictory desires at the heart of capitalism; they were like money, and like money they were founded in irrationality and paradox."[22] Since these issues are inherent to American racial capitalism, Reconstruction-era debates merely emphasized how logics of value continuously engineer white supremacy.

The persistence of racialized disparities in wealth, healthcare, and other indices of well-being and in the rights of citizenship ushers Parks's critique of the idealized past of Emancipation even further into the present. Produced in 2015, *Wars* revises aspects of its Parksian intertexts in response to the contemporary dynamics of anti-Black racism in American society, especially as it pertains to homeownership as an exercise of citizenship. So, for example, while moneymaking enterprises break up a community, as they did in *The America Play* and *Topdog/Underdog,* in *Wars* the nuances of these ventures recall the financialized economy's effect on American homeownership. And whereas Parks gestured toward ancient Greek mythology to explore Blackness, animality, and respectability politics in *Mutabilities, Wars* revises that exploration through its attentiveness to hybridity and national belonging, and not just docile bodies and the human-animal distinction. On one level, such attentiveness responds to what Anita Hill identified as a particular "crisis of home" facing everyday Americans, as well as Barack Obama's first term in the office of president.[23] Scholar Tavia Nyong'o has explained how the Obama campaign had attempted to capitalize on interraciality to promise the nation racial transcendence and redemption. After the election, the Obama administration had to manage the outcomes of incentivized anti-Black discrimination in the mortgage industry during the financial crisis and confront racist essentializing discourses in monetary theory. Obama's presidency led to a "surge of interest in gold among right-wing activists," many of whom conceptualized gold as more real and reliable than this counterfeit leader and his economy. Correlations between the election of the nation's first African American president and the far right's marketization of gold could suggest, as O'Malley has argued, that "the gold standard offer[ed] not just stable prices but the moral purity of the founding fathers and a fantasy of 'natural' hierarchies."[24] Anticipating the reactionary election of Donald Trump and the virulent white supremacism underlying his populist brand of politics, the popularity of this fantasy about gold undermined multiracialist theories of racial progress that assumed Black Americans could simply "prove up" to equality through respectability or that the bad feelings of racial injustice would simply phase out through race-mixing instead of responding in kind.[25] Hybrid futurity was never going to save the United States from itself.

Details about Black American experiences with the real estate and banking industries leading up to the 2008 crisis once again revealed the paradoxes of capitalism. Racial covenants and redlining once excluded Black Americans from homeownership and the long-term security it assured. However, the subprime mortgage crisis grew from their "predatory inclusion" into the promised land of real estate.[26] Decades of deregulation counteracted civil rights legislation in the 1960s and 1970s, allowing lending schemes to despoil borrowers without breaking the letter of the law. Many borrowers were women of color who qualified for standard loans but were systematically steered toward subprime mortgages, which were then tranched and sold as securities. Eventually, "securities based on the subprime market ceased overnight to be convertible into ready cash or other assets," having lost "credible claims to real-world value."[27] Fictions were uncovered. Crisis ensued. As policymakers and stakeholders accounted for its differential impact, borrowers were often blamed for living beyond their means and for their financial illiteracy. Crumbling infrastructure, educational inequities, and incentivized customer profiling went uncritiqued. Normative frameworks for subjecthood as economic agents, as citizens, and as adults reproduced racial difference as the cause of racial subjugation, as if culturally informed behaviors impeded normative attainment. In the context of the Homestead Act, the conjunction of citizenship and homeownership must contend with the displacement of Indigenous communities: seizing land and turning it into private property as a cornerstone of the new American nation involves destroying many nations and severing their ties to the lands they had long inhabited. In the context of the 2008 financial crisis, the notion of the homeland had an especially powerful allure post-9/11, when it had been rejigged to refer to nativist notions of the rural American heartland instead of to the places where people lived before immigrating to the United States; however, the global nature of the crisis emphasized that money, information, resources, and other material had become hypermobile.[28] Accordingly, its roots in securities tied to financialized subprime mortgages prompted many to think about the "cruel optimism" of the American dream, to reconsider what kind of future the systems and structures of homeownership actually realized and for whom they continued to forestall the much promised "good life."[29]

This is not to say that a future that looks different from that promised good life has no value. Far from it, the imaginative activity of speculation activates its emancipatory potential when it reveals the fictions and paradoxes of capitalism in the present. Envisioning alternative futures begins the work of materializing them.[30] The divergence of the two communities at the end of the play should alert us that finance does not have a monopoly on speculative activity, just as the market is not the only route for self-making. Critiquing the logics of value underlying one of America's most powerful collective fictions, *Wars* makes room for imagining ways of being in the world that continue effecting liberation in the face of always newly emerging forms of anti-Black racism.

"Rep and rev" in *Wars* thus bears upon how change and/in the future can be theorized. Parts 1, 2, and 3 contain numerous doubles and permutations.

These include biological and surrogate fathers, rival suitors, a bifurcated chorus, two different choruses, and paired Black men at either end of the colorist spectrum. Discrepancies between these pairs and further triangulations allow repetition to explore revision and its consequences. Moreover, by implanting doubles within different ecosystems of the dramatic world, Parks resists linear plot development.[31] Moving forward in *Wars* involves reconsiderations if not restagings of the multiple pivot points along the way and reuniting figures whose paths seemed to definitively diverge in previous scenes or mere moments before. The audience thus witnesses material forms, whose seemingly objective "meaning" and fixed value naturalized hierarchical social relations, like precious metal and organic flesh, at one moment become less determinative across these trajectories. When they have been denaturalized and rematerialized, their "meaning" and value more obviously depend on cultural performance and therefore remain open to interpretation, alteration, and misrecognition.[32] Such an approach affects the intertextual link between *Wars* and Homer's *Odyssey* as well: misrecognizing *Wars* as a retelling of Homer's poetic narrative entails affixing meaning and value to a poem aware of the constraints that space and time place on its vision of the social order and its recognizability as a bulwark of that order.

Idealized Endings and the *Odyssey*'s Postponed Futures

Homer's *Odyssey* ends marvelously. In the final sections of Book 24, the hero, Odysseus; his father, Laërtes; and his son, Telemachus, stand arrayed against a group of men seeking vengeance for their recently murdered kinsmen. One of these men, Eupeithes, lost his son, the suitor Antinous, in the events recounted in Book 22. He explains his grievance in a speech that doubles as an alternate summary of the poem: Odysseus once left Ithaca with a bunch of ships and a group of their countrymen as his companions but he came back alone; he has just killed another group of Ithacans who had to be buried; he would disgrace himself and his descendants to let all of Odysseus's brazen insolence go unpunished (*Od.* 24.421–38). Seized by both pity and a desire for retribution, several Ithacan men are persuaded to follow Eupeithes, and they set out to find the recently returned war hero. As they grab weapons, making their way to Odysseus's homestead, the epic, which seemed to have been so neatly resolved at the end of Book 23, recommences narrating a battle that threatens to nearly destroy another generation of Greek men (527–28).

Odysseus has faced such threats to his life before. Numerically, Odysseus knew he would be outmatched in the fight against the suitors. In that case, in addition to skillfully testing the loyalty of those he left behind, he teaches his as yet untested son to react to the abuse he will witness by hardening his heart to endure the suitors' mistreatment of him (17.274–75) and to recognize Odysseus's signal for hiding the weapons they will need to wreak vengeance upon their enemies. Telemachus will have to store these lessons in his mind and then apply them at the most opportune moment so that he and his father can stand a chance of surviving the altercation (281–86). Reforming his heart and training his eye, Telemachus will make himself into the person he was born to be, Odysseus's son and heir.

In the scene with the suitors' avengers, Athena will more directly intervene to protect the family of her favorite hero. Earlier in Book 24 she beautified Laërtes's body, once worn down by age and neglect, to resemble that of an immortal (234, 367–71). She reappears now in the shape of Mentor, a sight that emboldens the hero for battle. Then, hearing Laërtes's prayer as he rejoices in fighting side by side with his son and grandson, the goddess endows him with strength (513–20): as a result, the old man manages to land a shot with a javelin that instantly kills none other than Eupeithes. Having grown more confident of his abilities, Telemachus assures his father that his martial prowess will not dishonor the family legacy (510–12). At this moment, because of the favor of the goddess, all three members of the house of Arcesius stand together, each at their prime, ready to defend the honor of their house against the representatives of Ithaca's other households.

It isn't just that Athena's intervention means that Odysseus, Laërtes, and Telemachus are all, marvelously, at their physical and psychological best in this scene. As Simon Goldhill has observed, the tradition that prizes the realism of the *Odyssey,* especially once the hero returns to his fatherland from the spaces marked as exotic, fails to recognize just how much the text incorporates "normative ruses and feints," blending realism and idealism as part of its ideological force. Even if Athena did not intervene to strengthen Laërtes in the epic's final scene, the survival of Arcesius's house could still be considered one of these normative ruses.

In Book 16, the narrator emphasizes this remarkable characteristic in Telemachus's account of how Zeus has "singlified" his paternal line by repeating the infrequently used verb μουνόω (to make single, to isolate) anaphorically: his great-grandfather Arcesius had a single son and heir in Laërtes, and Laërtes had only Odysseus, who has had only one legitimate son, in turn (16.118–20).[33] The odds of a line of only sons surviving large-scale war, disease, and high rates of infant mortality—let alone a twenty-year journey and a crowd of young men conspiring against it—would have been incredibly low. Archaic Greek poetry testifies to an ambivalence about children and therefore to the trouble that plagues the opposite circumstance. Internecine conflict afflicts households that have several sons within a single generation, as they become rivals for both property and power. Tales abound about sons who kill their fathers, hastening the substitution for which patriarchal inheritance destines them. Yet, here, as the remaining members of the house of Arcesius draw weapons to defend their family honor and their family's future, the poem gives us an idealized picture of heteropatriarchal descent within and across generations where competition in martial prowess always turns outward.[34] The poem thus nurtures an optimism about this sociopolitical structure, that it is poised to provide stability, to preserve power, and to prepare future generations to do the same. Conversely, those who threaten this divinely sanctioned arrangement earn the reputation of "fools" and ruin their chances to return home from the ravages from the war (*Od.* 24.469–71; also 1.7–9).[35]

Though the poem eventually affirms this model of descent, it hints at the potential for things to (have) turn(ed) out differently. On the one hand, the poem obscures the curious coexistence of Laërtes and Odysseus. Anticleia, Odysseus's mother, revealed that Laërtes has left the homestead only recently. When he moved to the countryside, he also excluded himself from civic life. Though worn down by age and despair, through Odysseus we see him taking dutiful care of the orchard that contributes to his son's patrimony. This focalization emphasizes that Laërtes remains just as loyal as he is capable, aged but not incapacitated. Since this poem devotes a whole book to the conspicuously aged Nestor who still rules as king in sandy Pylos amid his many sons, it is unlikely that age alone would disqualify Laërtes from the same position in Ithaca.[36] It never relates the process that installs Odysseus as king of a land that already had a king without any bloodshed or ill will. On the other hand, the poem does address Telemachus's status as an only child. It repeatedly dangles the possibility that Telemachus will die at the hands of the suitors before the audience. And each time it does so, the poem generates narrative suspense by threatening the young hero *and* the significance of Odysseus's return. For if Odysseus returns but Telemachus has been killed, the family that Penelope and Odysseus have created will still come to an end and with it Arcesius's entire line.[37] Penelope's trick, weaving and unweaving Laërtes's burial shroud, buys her time with the suitors by postponing what she has framed, suspiciously, as the imminent death of Odysseus's father. However, as a signal of her willingness to remarry that presumes Odysseus's death, the ploy also involves (and, as the assembly in Book 2 makes clear, escalates) the conflict between Telemachus, a one-time heir, and whoever would be chosen as new husband. In each of these cases, the events of Book 24 sidestep these hazards to portray an image of patrilineality that maintains the social order and peace on Ithaca (24.546).[38]

This last "normative ruse" remains persuasive because the narrative realizes other, less consequential risks. The poem's opening verses inform the audience that Odysseus will fail to secure the return of the men with whom he set out for Troy (1.5–9). Though the crew's pains and travels are many, Odysseus alone will survive his homecoming. Anticipating the aforementioned charge Eupeithes will levy against Odysseus, the proem redirects the blame for the crew's death to the men themselves. Blame aside, the deaths of the crew import danger to the seafaring that will dominate the first half of the poem, connecting Telemachus to his father (and the generations of men involved in the Trojan War) through shared experience. The death of Argos in Book 17 likewise highlights the dangers of Odysseus's reintegration into his household. When Odysseus approaches the threshold of the house, still in disguise as an aged, weak beggar, he catches sight of his dog, similarly aged and lying among the dung heaps (17.291–327). Because the plight of Argos strategically recalls that of Laërtes, Telemachus, and the hero himself, his especially vivid and detailed death has an affective pull that has been remarked upon for centuries. These connections allow the dog's death to reflect the vulnerability of Arcesius's descendants at a time when the plot to ambush the suitors makes it most topical.

Indeed, Argos's performance of canine fidelity combines a realistic sense of loss with its own idealism. As many others have commented, the scene repeatedly marks Argos as singular: this is the sole moment of mutual recognition in the poem that involves neither speech nor a visible sign.[39] Argos is not only the only dog to have a personal name, but his name also appears next to Odysseus's in the genitive case, which "determines the animal's identity like a high-sounding patronymic." Mentioning how Odysseus hand-reared the pup, the scene emphasizes the role that food plays in engendering loyalty from domesticated canines and thus recalls by contrast the suitors whose never-ending feasts deplete the comestible resources of Odysseus's house and corrupt its human "resources," too. Argos is "good" because he remains true to the ideals of canine behavior that underlie this "pact of food," to use Cristiana Franco's phrase, whereby the realization of canine autonomy and strength provokes human anxiety about reciprocity in their relationships with dogs. The mutuality of Odysseus and Argos recognizing each other attests to the resolution of this anxiety since Argos's suffering demonstrates that that rearing has produced "more than just cold obedience": Argos has elected to remain near the house though others have left him starved and on the verge of death for decades.[40] Moreover, after making this connection with his master, he finally dies, channeling the dregs of his energy toward communicating in a sly manner befitting his master. Argos even dies as Odysseus said he would have liked to die (326–27).[41] With Odysseus's disguise, the narrative plays with the abjection of poverty, homelessness, and social marginalization, manufacturing a sense of relief when the aristocratic male householder is reinstalled. With Argos, the pity evoked by the dog's death is not simply a matter of his humanization: his bodily degradation plays rather vividly with the prospect of loyalty *not* sufficing for survival, with the anxieties that accompany a change in regime and the paralyzing desire for things to remain the same.

And yet, things simply cannot remain the same. When Athena ratifies the pacts forged between the family of the suitors and the hero, the text looks to the future of civic life on Ithaca beyond the poem's verses (24.545–46). Although Telemachus has received an education in Odyssean tactics, plenty of evidence reveals that he will not perfectly replicate his father as a man, a leader, or even as a speaker, that his future on Ithaca will be different from the heroic past that men like Odysseus lived through and represent. There is a limit to the reproductive futurity that motivates Odysseus's return. Furthermore, Book 23 refers to a future in the offing as Odysseus recounts to Penelope the prophecy that Tiresias revealed to him in the underworld. He will have to go on yet another journey. He will know that journey is over when the people he encounters calls the object he knows is an oar a winnowing fan because they are unfamiliar with seafaring. Odysseus should plant the oar in the ground, and he will die in this space that marks the limit of the semantic world in which the hero exists.[42]

While the prophecy suggests that he will die among people whose foreignness threatens the hero with a type of oblivion that runs counter to the memorializing function of epic, it also looks to both the shift from seafaring to agriculture that Greek communities engaging in colonial resettlement negotiated in the Archaic period and the growing interest in long-distance trade. Trying to make sense of how "themes of mapping and travel that dominate the narrative of Odysseus' travels help the Greeks . . . make sense of the spatial, temporal, social, and representational crises of early archaic Greece," Carol Dougherty has explained how Homer's *Odyssey* does not simply tie novel or strange activities to radically different outsiders—its ethnographic accounts of isolationist Phaeacians and Cyclopes, rapacious pirates and Phoenician traders, and monsters all resonate with Odysseus's restoration in Ithaca.[43] Commercial trade, colonialism, and the new networks of power that such activity creates will rearrange the social order of Greek-speaking communities of the period in which Homer composed his epics. Such rearrangements breed cultural anxiety. Odysseus's navigation of the world out there and the reinstallation of his power as patriarch on Ithaca model a successful transition to this new order of things and suggests that not everything needs to change, even if some things (e.g., writing, coined money) are bound to.[44] For those loyal to the prevailing system because it empowers them or simply because they cannot imagine otherwise, remembering that model from the *Odyssey* may diminish the uncertainties that always trail the sense of the future, especially when that future is imminent or already underway.

Dawn's Speculations

Entitled "A Measure of a Man," the first act of *Wars* begins with members of the chorus standing before their lodgings trying to calculate just how much time remains before sunrise. In addition to setting the play's plot in motion, the opening introduces this drama's engagement with the temporal frameworks of its Homeric intertexts within the context of American chattel slavery and racial capitalism. As the chorus of the enslaved hold their fingers up to the horizon, those familiar with Homeric epic will no doubt recall the phrase used to signal the beginning of another day, "rosy-fingered Dawn." The phrase, frequently repeated in both the *Iliad* and *Odyssey*, serves various functions. For the audience, it can mark the passage of time, providing an anchor amid the overwhelming details that accumulate between individual scenes and the poem's constituent books. The phrase also refers to a recurrent phenomenon that places the epic's human characters *in* time, thereby distinguishing mortal ephemerality from the gods' immortality. Likewise, the movement that commences Parks's play invites our study of the power dynamics of the plantation economy and how they structure the lives of the enslaved.

In this first act, Boss-Master's offering Hero the opportunity to accompany him into battle has disrupted how the community normally spends its free time together and prompts speculation about what is to come. Excited by both the prospect of Hero's decision and the gain to be had from it, the chorus admits that "there is a kind of sport to be had / in the consideration of someone else's fate" (11). As they prognosticate about Hero's decision, the chorus repeatedly utters the imperative "mark it." Indicating the accountability one bears for a speech act, emphasizing the treatment of enslaved human beings as chattel, and anticipating the play's interest in the racialized technology of literacy, the phrase "mark it" increasingly sounds like "market," a pun actualized when figures put up collateral to back their wagers (6–10).

The figures who believe Hero will choose to join Boss-Master, named Second and Third, put up a brass button and a metal spoon, respectively. Reckoning that Hero will turn Boss-Master down, Leader bets his shoes and Fourth his banjo. The spoon and brass button are small, decorative objects that possess use-value, but the material of their manufacture makes them more precious than their size or purpose suggests. In contrast, the banjo and pair of shoes derive more value from facilitating autonomy than from the materials of their manufacture. In Part 2, the banjo will become a tool of Black resistance to exclusionary norms of artistic production, rationality, and literacy through its connection to improvisational musical genres like jazz; within Part 1, the shoes metonymically recall the freedom of mobility that plantation-based slavery forbade. Unlike the autonomy these objects index, Second and Third treasure the metal spoon and the brass buttons because possessing them grants virtual proximity to whiteness. As objects from the dining room and the dressing room, this collateral supposes an intimacy between slaveowners and slaves that confers further prestige.

Futurity is implicated in these divergent logics of value. The faction led by Leader imagines that Hero's duties on the battlefront will be identical to or worse than those on the plantation. Even if Hero should gain a measure of respect in exchange, his activities will see him constantly reperforming his subservience to Boss-Master. Leader thus reasons that the offer will be turned down since it doesn't guarantee that Hero will improve his station and could very well cause him to lose what he already has in Penny and Old Man. In keeping with the logic of his collateral, Leader extends technologies of white superiority into the future, highlighting the risks that will come from forfeiting the bonds that have helped Hero to persevere thus far and to escape some of slavery's psychological damage. Envisioning that war offers Hero a chance to be valued in the ways that white men are valued, Second speculates that Hero will demonstrate that he has overcome the privations of Blackness enough to "prove up" to subjecthood, even if his duties remain the same. Second latches onto the possibility of Hero receiving medals, wearing the same uniform as Boss-Master, and specifies that his name "Hero" will be written in the "Big Book of History" as a hero instead of as an object in the bookkeeper's "counting-book" (8).[45]

When Hero appears onstage for the first time, he emphasizes his apparently innate abilities and glories in his reputation. He boasts about his promotion to domestic work and to caring for Boss-Master's horse, implying that Homer has been given the assignments best suited to his (dis)abilities. Homer limps because of a missing foot and has been relegated to working outside with the disfavored equid instead of performing the duties of a valet inside the Big House. To Hero and Second, who mocks Homer's appearance, Homer's disabled body makes apparent his inherent mental limitations and justifies his unequal treatment.[46]

Homer's narrative about the day Hero mutilated his foot reveals their rivalry's roots in the plantation's racialized power structure. Homer learned the truth from Boss-Master who drunkenly mistook him for Hero on another occasion. Since the pair were initially self-emancipating together, Boss-Master promised Hero freedom in exchange for betraying Homer's whereabouts.[47] Changing the terms of trade, he then coerced Hero to cut off Homer's foot in exchange for his life. Far from freeing him, Boss-Master used Hero as a tool and object of domination. In addition to the verbal contract between Boss-Master and Hero, the story reveals that Homer can substitute for Hero as valet adequately enough to go unnoticed, despite the fact that they do not look alike. With regard to Hero's assumed essential value, honesty—if not also bravery—must be removed from the list of qualities Second claimed he possessed unchanged from birth. The chorus has attached specific futures to particular bodies based on inaccurate information and assumptions that have long structured the dynamics of their community. In light of the story, Hero's unmaimed and therefore unchanged body could rightfully be considered symptomatic of cowardice and fickleness.

As foils, Hero and Homer are not just interpreted differently by others; they attach different logics of value to the material objects around them as well. Figuring self-emancipation as stealing and the self-emancipated as contraband, Hero associates Homer with deficiency: how Homer chooses to escape enslavement and his status as chattel emphasizes that he does not own property like maps or contracts. Hero's attachment to the prevailing social order means he can only see self-emancipation leading to continued inferiority and thereby ignores the significance of Homer's many exercises of choice (47).[48] Homer reckons himself otherwise: ignoring how others evaluate him using ableist, racist, or colorist criteria, he has continued to "invest" in himself. Reclaiming the time spent outside the house, he has learned to navigate by the stars and tracks on the ground (43). Essentialist norms devalue Homer's ability to read the land and sky because the knowledge this literacy imparts is less subject to white surveillance or accounting.

Notably, this exercise of intellectual autonomy gives Homer new skills eerily similar to those the play has associated with a dog, Oddsee. References to dogs recur throughout *Wars* as part of its consideration of the racializing ideals of domestication and docility. We learn that Hero was unsure what his parents named him, that he answered to this name when Boss-Master assigned it, that the chorus unnamed him to punish his dishonesty, and that he threatens to do the same to Oddsee in response to his presumed disloyalty. Hero animalizes his formerly constant companion as a "wild thing" for wanting to "go running here go running there," a label that recalls both Oddsee and Hero's "wild thing" father, lynched for trying to escape the plantation sometime prior to the drama's action (125; 45–47). When "mild" Hero counters with a claim that Boss-Master, a rational being by virtue of race, gender, and property, will have to recognize Hero's humanity through his performance of obedience, Homer responds by explaining how Hero's racial performance then mimicked Boss-Master's canines. Compelled to track Homer down and point him out alongside Boss-Master's hunting dogs, Hero has been "become against" Homer's boundary-transgressing then, and happily carries the scraps of Colonel's old uniform like a table-fed pet now (23, 47).[49]

Rather than revealing an essential quality of Hero, Black people, foreigners, canines, or animals, this backstory about Boss-Master's bad faith emphasizes how the conditions of coexistence reinforce the performance of certain gestures, duties, or behaviors that can be understood as the Odyssean attributes par excellence, fidelity and cunning, in order to maintain the status quo. Because it revises the accepted account of the day, Homer's ability to effectively narrate this story complements the information it conveys and confounds the essentializing that made Hero his superior. In terms of futurity, his narrative also suggests that investing in Boss-Master's truthfulness is risky, unlikely to pay off in terms of legal emancipation.

Throughout the first act, Hero changes his mind about what he will do come sunrise, a facet of his characterization that nods toward Odysseus's many twists and turns, and the theme of fidelity. Hero is alternately swayed by his affections for Old Man, on the one hand, and Penny, on the other. His particularly conservative "faux-father" takes pride in the privileges Hero's presumed excellence affords and attempts to coopt some of that excellence for himself: reassessing the absent "luxury of blood" between the two, he figures their relationship as a "double blessing" through an arithmetic of elective kinship which adds the sum of Hero's existence to an imagined liaison with a woman who he figures would have had to be a goddess to produce such a son. Old Man transforms Hero into a demi-god and a "real son through and through" via a pluperfect counterfactual act of sexual reproduction. Mixing financial metaphors and 1990s Black American slang, he reminds Hero and Homer that their "words are their bonds," that "both words and deeds" form part of their record (20, 48). Though he dismisses Boss-Master as foolish, bound to a racially inclusive permutation of the patriarchal, capitalist social order, Old Man demeans Penny as too full of "superstitious nonsense" to "grow out of" enslavement, too female to understand the inherently male desire for war, and too independent-minded for liberation (12, 28–30). Hero's relationship with Penny offers a more flexible mode of being. Their intimacy is most evident in their shared secrets, a morning ritual that has them "sharing the same breath," and an on-stage greeting where they manipulate each other's bodies so that Hero dances and Penny flies like a bird. Whereas Old Man still trusts Boss-Master's ability to weigh Hero's service as worthy of emancipation, Penny sees the honor of the life they currently lead and values a future where they continue to live life by working *together*, whatever else might happen.[50]

Reminded of the vulnerabilities of intimacy, Hero retreats to the hierarchies that he believes empower him as a man and a human being. In Old

Man's presence, Hero tries to stifle Penny's talk about values and addresses her only as "girl" (28–29). He takes the same tack with Oddsee, wondering if Oddsee "ain't nothing," just a "dime a dozen," after the dog fails to return home when called (17). Whereas Homer understands that choosing to go with Boss-Master to the front or to remain on the plantation is nothing more than "two sides of the same coin . . . over and over," Hero chooses to go on believing he can regain his former reputation in the community by performing some great feat and being emancipated by their enslaver (42). Instead of reevaluating Boss-Master's trustworthiness or the value system that props him up, Hero seems bound to repeat without revision, forging a pact unlikely to turn out as he had hoped.

Hybrid Futurity

Parks revises all of these issues in Part 2. In this section, set in the "wilderness," the stage no longer includes a cabin, but the idea of home still exerts its ideological power over those figures off the plantation at war. Facing one's attachments to the past entails speculating about what the future might bring and the shape "civilization" could take.

Although there are only three figures on stage in Part 2, the captive man, called a Yankee and by the name Smith, is a Black soldier passing as a white captain. Historically Smith recalls the situation of Private Charles R. Pratt, who served in the 11th Ohio Infantry; though he could pass, he chafed at the exposure to anti-Black racism.[51] Within the play, Smith functions as a double for both Hero and the Colonel. In the first half of Part 2, Smith reveals essentializing beliefs in Yankeeness that mimic the Colonel's white supremacist views. But he too changes his mind, worrying that the persistence of anti-Black racism will make it impossible for those who had been enslaved to be fully incorporated into society even if the Union were to win the war. His final speculation posits a solution of hybrid self-making that reappropriates the discourse of metal in order to resist persisting white supremacist systems and structures. His experience confounding the visual regimes of white supremacy through passing has influenced the form of resistance he imagines. Because he and Smith occupy opposite ends of the color spectrum, Hero cannot simply duplicate Smith's example. He needs to heed Smith's cautious, however subtle hedging: Hero must "rep and rev" if he is to avoid the pitfalls of hybrid futurity, remaining attentive to the normative ruses that could prolong his subjugation long after being legally emancipated.[52]

Part 2 begins with a scene that rehearses the ogre motif of the Cyclops's cave in the *Odyssey,* with the drunk Colonel hosting his captive(s) in remote isolation.[53] The Confederate officer attempts to bond with Smith, letting him walk freely outside the cage and teaching him song lyrics as he plays the banjo. But Smith refuses to reciprocate and, when forced to sing along, extemporizes, saying that he will decapitate the Colonel when he is free. Animalizing Smith as a "dirty-wounded-flea-bitten-pus-oozing Yankee," Colonel decries his insubordination (58). Eventually forcing him back into the cage, attaching him to a leash, and demanding that he follow orders, he dominates Smith as if he were a pet, offering him goodwill in exchange for submissiveness, just as we saw and heard about with Hero. Eventually we learn that Hero actually taught Boss-Master how to be "musical" (80). Fixating on performing this song exactly as he learned it effectively institutionalizes the ditty, attempting to standardize this coopted practice and thereby revalue it for the purpose of whiteness; Colonel's willingness to teach Smith, a white(-looking) man, this institutionalized version of the song reprises the play's consideration of literacy as a technology of exclusion and not as self-evident proof of human intelligence. Smith's knowing improvisation can be understood as a technology of Black resistance to literacy's monopoly on meaning in turn; it is, after all, improvising that allowed him to don the jacket of his dying captain on the battlefield, thereby preserving his life upon capture.[54] As Smith refuses to ratify Colonel's version of whiteness on principle and not because, as remains unknown to Colonel, he is not white, Colonel ties their lack of homosociality to his anxieties about being a "self-made" man without much education. He surmises Smith must have been raised with a "silver spoon in his mouth," using the discourse of metal to adumbrate intraracial class antagonism (68).

The Colonel's speculations about a future in which Hero has a measure of autonomy reveal deep paternalistic anxieties about the future if the Confederacy should be defeated. Smith's proclaimed lack of interest in owning Black slaves rebuffs the terms of white solidarity with the Colonel. In response, the Colonel prods Smith into guessing how much Hero is worth in Confederate "dollars and cents" to demonstrate that there is "fun to be had" in speculating on the life of a Black man. By promising Hero to Smith if he were to guess accurately, the Colonel intends to prove that, despite presumed class differences, the two men are actually racially and affectively united. Colonel makes Hero stand on a tree stump and inspects him as if he were on the auction block. "Counting-book" in mind, Colonel discloses that Hero can read, write, play music, and faithfully obey. But when Colonel reaches for Hero's genitals, Hero resists him, and the Colonel responds by striking him with a whip. As Hero falls from the tree stump, Boss-Master's lynching of Hero's father haunts this "weighing", to use Old Man's words (23). The Colonel recognizes that Hero would leave the plantation, given the opportunity:

> **COLONEL** . . . What will you do once you're free?
> *(Rest)*
> **HERO** I couldn't say.
> **COLONEL** I know what I would do. I would be sorry to see you go . . . And Missus. She would stand on the porch crying and I would put a brave face on it while you went off down the road, heading who knows where to do who knows what . . . Once you rounded the bend, out of sight, gone never to return, we'd have supper. Missus crying in her soup and me, making too much conversation. Then would come night fall and . . . Missus would have the bed covers pulled up over her head and I would be sitting on the bed, unable to lie down. Cause I'd be feeling like my good life had left me. Just like I felt when my son died but worse, cause you wouldn't be dead, Hero, you'd just be gone. And I'd weep.
> *The Colonel breaks down crying. Real tears.* (82)

Much of this scene's bookkeeping and racialized speculation occurs in the subjunctive mode: enumerating how Hero *should* now be worth more than his purchase price; *presuming* community between Smith and Colonel based on racial classification; imagining the *possibility* of Confederate defeat leading to Hero's departure; voicing the uncertainty about where Hero *would* go and what he *would* choose to do after leaving the plantation. More interestingly, the Colonel exposes his dependence on Hero as a laborer, a confidant, and a better version of his now deceased son. He thus recounts and forces himself to confront Hero's price*less*ness at a time when Confederate "dollars and cents" would be fluctuating in value and on the verge of worthlessness. The inability of price to perfectly capture value and meaning pushes the paradoxes inherent in the monetization of enslaved human beings to their most sentimental breaking point.[55] Amid all the accounting in the subjunctive and imagined pretending, stage notes indicate that the actor portraying Colonel should shed "real" tears.

When the Colonel expresses gratitude for his whiteness in a striking speech, he takes comfort in the futurity of white supremacy:

> I am grateful every day that God made me white. As a white I stand on the summit and all the other colors reside beneath me, down below. For me, no matter how much money I've got or don't got, if my farm is failing or my horse is dead, if my woman is sour or my child has passed on, I can at least rest in the grace that God made me white. And I don't ever have to fight the Battle of Darkness. What difficulties I may encounter will at least never be those. Life might bring me low but not that low. And I know that I will be received in most any quarter. And if the Lord should choose to further advance my economics, then I will be received in all the great houses. Not so with the lower ones. The lower ones will always be lowly. No matter how high they climb. There is a kind of comfort in that. And I take that comfort. For no matter how low I fall, and no matter how thoroughly I fail, I will always be white (83).

Thinking about life after the war, the Confederate officer here broadcasts a patently essentialist view of racial identity whereby intrinsic differences between the races grant him the privilege of immutable white superiority. Whiteness is an asset whose value relative to nonwhite groups securitizes any mistakes he might make. Aware of his deficiencies as a husband, officer, father, and farmer, Colonel here doubles down on his investment in American racism and financializes white supremacy.

Colonel's long- and short-term speculations yoke the concept of intrinsic white superiority to items made of metal. At the prodding of the Yankee captive, Smith, Colonel admits that according to the remuneration system for both armies he will not earn a promotion or be given property befitting men of higher station—a medal, a golden goblet, land, or a sexually "wild" mistress—in exchange for capturing Smith. He will more plausibly receive an expression of thanks from his direct superior, making even the golden goblet from General Lee's house a token of his inferiority (59–60). Consequently, when Colonel reimagines receiving each hypothetical prize, a third term mitigates the reality of his subservience to the higher-ranked officers handing them out (a Black slave, docile mules, and kindness that decreases the danger of the imagined mistress's sexuality). These insecurities complicate his speech's homogenizing stance on whiteness.

Rather than identifying racially, Smith identifies as "Yankee through and through" with "Yankee blood . . . ways and notions," materializing and essentializing social bonds in much the same ways that Old Man did (64). His conversation with Colonel suggests that this essential Yankeeness does not preclude the owning of slaves but instead prohibits egregious displays of wealth and power. Later, Smith tells Hero how "crafty" Ulysses S. Grant removed his medals and his golden aiguillette to become more familiar with his men (90). The details of the story emphasize the Odyssean intertext of Ulysses's off-the-cuff improvisatory cunning and anonymization. They also give the distaste for ostentation a practical merit that further distinguishes the Union from the Confederacy: because Smith is also in disguise, wiliness unites these two under the Union banner.[56] But General Grant could become anonymous because the army was racially segregated and so he was not hyper-visible without distinguishing paraphernalia. Moreover, by describing General Grant's desire to pass as a soldier, the story highlights hierarchies within the Union. Indeed, Smith's spontaneous donning of his deceased captain's coat works as a *racial* disguise because Black men can only be privates in his regiment. Since the Confederacy did not allow Black men to enlist, that rank does distinguish one side from the other. Nevertheless, as rank has been partially racialized, Smith's story discounts the stark juxtaposition of the Union and the Confederacy on which his speculative future depended. For much of the war, the Union Army and the Confederate Army, like the areas considered the South and the North, merely prized different performances of whiteness, different expressions of white supremacy.[57]

Initially, in their conversation, Union victory seems to inaugurate radical equality, and Smith promises Hero he could own a farmstead, populate it with a wife and children, or get anything else he wants. When Smith further speculates that "freedom might be coming soon," he specifies it will bring bodily autonomy and wages that level the playing field between landowners and others. Hero's conservatism probes this rosy vision of the future. Hero cites the vast number of poor soldiers of both races (94–95).[58] When Smith extolls no longer being someone else's property, Hero asks what will happen when patrolmen try to harass him. Smith's optimistic answer about belonging to oneself falls flat against Hero holding up his hands. Parks's note specifies that the gesture should be "reminiscent of hands up, don't shoot," with its aforementioned associations.

Smith eventually concedes that Black people may never be fully enfranchised, that Freedom might be more process than punctum.[59] Dispensing with essential Yankeeness, he champions hybrid self-making in Odyssean fashion and in keeping with his assumed name:

> **SMITH** . . . Sometimes I get the feeling that the heart of the thing won't change easy or quick. Cause of the way we were bought and brought over here in the first place. Maybe even with Freedom, that mark, huh, that mark of the marketplace, it will always be on us. And so maybe we will always be twisting and turning ourselves into something that is going to bring the best price. That's the way we were born into this, so is it always gonna be like that for us, slavery or not? Freedom or not? Are we ever going to get us a better place in the marketplace?
>
> **HERO** You're talking like you wanna burn something down.
>
> **SMITH** I'm just saying: if you say you're broke, I say you're double-broke—snapped in two without a penny to your name and hoping someone'll pay more than 800 dollars for you, but goddamnit, God willing, some day we'll have a place besides just the auction block. And maybe that starts by stealing yourself. Steeling yourself, making yourself like metal on the inside. Maybe it'll get better from there. But, I don't know.[60] (98–99)

Repeating the language of Hero's charge against Homer's self-emancipation as "stealing," Smith revises the metaphors of liberation. His plan tries to capitalize on the dynamics of misrecognition to evade white surveillance, and in so doing his instruction to make themselves "like metal on the inside" replays Odysseus's advice to Telemachus in *Odyssey* 17.[61] Rather than a superficial change, Smith suggests an internal transformation that would hybridize them so that they were not strictly human "through and through," a departure from the logics that operated in Part 1. An alloy of iron and carbon that superficially resembles silver, steel is significantly less costly than the precious metals referred to in currency debates.[62] It is precisely this low production cost, coupled with its strength, that made it indispensable for the construction of American cities. Metaphorically, it is this same strength, the same ability for it to be misrecognized, and the same availability of this conceptual resource that could make it useful for strategizing about how newly emancipated Black people will survive this next phase of anti-Black nation-building.

Smith's new stratagem acknowledges that life after Union victory could still entail "twists and turns," and that this hybridity only begins the journey toward liberation. His repeated hedging ("maybe . . . maybe . . . I don't know") highlights the precarity of the situation, the very precarity suppressed by the epic's marvelous ending.[63] If in the present Hero and Smith exist in poverty, then, given the persistent "stamp of the marketplace," Smith speculates they could become even more financially insecure when Freedom comes rather than less so. Instead of creating despair, this fear motivates Smith to try to invent a more radical strategy than he had first imagined. To use the fearful and nearly metallurgic language Hero does, Smith "burns something down" insofar as it goes beyond the parameters of subjecthood Smith first imagined his future operating within to at least try to start something that challenges existing structures.

The audience does not have to wait too long to see how all of this speculative activity about hybridity and Black resistance could play out: the end of Part 2 and the beginning of Part 3 both "rep and rev" Smith's suggested version of self-making. Part 2 concludes with Hero secretly unleashing Smith from captivity. Before Smith departs, he gives Hero his Union jacket, forcefully swears him in as a private in the 1st Kansas Colored Regiment, and orders Hero to quit the Colonel's makeshift camp with him. Eventually putting the Union jacket on beneath his Confederate "scraps," Hero thus reperforms an Odyssean ruse, the trick Smith once improvised to save his life. Imposed upon him, the trick does not, in itself, attest to Hero's willingness to challenge authority. In contrast to the passivity involved in his acceptance of the coat and pseudo-enlistment, Hero refuses to move when Smith attempts to drag him along as he exits the camp.

Moreover, in keeping with Argos's late appearance in the *Odyssey*, Oddsee finally appears on-stage in Part 3, which represents the short-term future from Part 2's timeframe. Right before Oddsee enters the scene, Penny looks to the horizon and spots "someone—or something . . . a wild thing" coming (125). Directors and costume designers approach the figure's appearance variously; many opt for a furry overcoat or jumpsuit as the sartorial reminder that the presence onstage is (partly) canine. Parks's script includes two behavioral elements that complement this costuming. First, she instructs the actor to circle Penny "giggl[ing] and wiggl[ing] then boldly lick[ing] [Penny] on the face." (126) Second, because Oddsee will speak in English, the figure crosses one of the lines conventionally demarcating "brute" animality from humanity. Both Oddsee's speech and his bodily comportment can be understood as "bold." Whereas Homer begs Penny for a kiss without success in public, Oddsee simply licks her face without invitation and with only mild recrimination. While the audience never sees the interior of the cabin and does not know the status of Homer and Penny's fledgling relationship, Oddsee's keen canine sense of smell alerts him to Homer's hormonal response to Penny and to Penny's pregnancy.[64] His disclosure flouts conventions of privacy, propriety, and shame that often apply to sexual relationships and inform ideals of domesticity.

Because he has left the plantation—the very exercise of autonomy that cost Homer his foot and Hero his father, Oddsee has, like Odysseus, gotten to see and know much more about the outside world through his travels. The community members try to glean some advantage from Oddsee's roaming, seeking to fill in gaps in their knowledge about the front. However Oddsee goes well beyond answering the questions asked of him: he talks excessively, circuitously, and with non-sequiturs. Sometimes he indulges stereotypically canine interests (food, play). At other times, he muses on the nature of power to specify that while the Colonel was Hero's Boss-Master, when he talks about his master he alludes to Hero. In one aside, he breaks the fourth wall to explain how compassion breeds secrecy: he knows that Hero has broken a promise of fidelity to Penny and hesitates to disclose that. He thus exercises "higher orders" of rationality (critical reflection and speech) to weigh self-control against the more recognizably canine demonstration of intelligence through obedience to human demands. Given the history of Blackface minstrelsy, a performance of racial boundary-crossing, Oddsee's conspicuous hybridity enjoys a license articulated by the dynamics of the cyno-human relationship with its racializing and racist entanglements. The signifiers of that license are not "radically open."[65]

Though Hero is feared dead, like the Colonel, Oddsee heralds his return, stating that he has "distinguished himself." Because this phrase signals the coupling of corporeal disintegration with recognition from a white supremacist institution in *Mutabilities,* its appearance at this point of *Wars* doesn't bode well.[66] Now calling himself Ulysses after the Union general, the one-time favorite comes back to a different community: his surrogate father, Old Man, has died sometime after Part 1, and the chorus of the enslaved has been replaced by a chorus of self-emancipators using this plantation as a pit stop. Bragging that he chose the name "for himself," unlike any of his peers, Ulysses kisses the ground twice. Doubly reperforming a gesture he has observed others perform, repetition that "feels right" to him, the gesture allows him to belong to the Union or even the still emerging nation via an affective script (141).[67] This gesture complements the performative force of that speech act since the provenance of his new name, Ulysses—itself an English transliteration of an ancient Greek name that had been translated into Latin—from General Grant, contradicts straightforward claims of originality.[68]

Ulysses's attempts to mend the relationships reveal his attachments to both power and property. He commands everyone to gather around "like a king graciously holding forth" (144–47). If, in Part 1, Hero claimed Boss-Master dangled freedom before him "like a carrot" for his horse, in the final scene, he reperforms this trick with the Proclamation in his pocket as the carrot (21). Rather than read the document immediately, he stalls and uses gift exchange to ingratiate himself with the community. Unfortunately, in this instantiation of "rep and rev," every item could be understood as a costlier but dreadfully insensitive upgrade of an item from Part 1. A string of brass buttons multiplies Third's wagered button. The alabaster shoe mold for Homer is no doubt luxurious, but, being white and in the shape of a foot, it reminds Homer of Ulysses's betrayal and the white supremacy that prompted his mutilation. The silver-tipped spade given to Penny, itself a hybrid object, is the enlarged, horticultural version of Second's spoon in Part 1, the silver spoon Colonel refers to in Part 2, and the new shiny spoon Ulysses takes from his satchel.[69]

Ulysses's attachment to power and property has also influenced what love means to him. The spade comes with rules about what vegetables Ulysses thinks Penny should plant and an unexpected item. In a nod to Odysseus's infidelity and the precarity of Odysseus's household, Ulysses married a woman named Alberta before returning to the plantation because he had blamed Penny for their childlessness:

> ULYSSES Alberta. She's a nice gal. Real nice.
> PENNY Who is she aside from nice?
> ULYSSES She's my new wife.
> . . .

PENNY I'm—But I'm—

ULYSSES You and me, Penny, we don't have no kids. Can't, right? You're still just as pretty still just as strong, but I was thinking it would be good to have children. I was thinking—I know you'll understand. You're good and true like that. Alberta, she'll help you around here. When planting time comes she'll do her part and work right along beside you. And with Homer heading out, we'll need an extra hand. She'll be a help to both of us.

PENNY But I'm—me.

ULYSSES And I'm giving you the better part of the deal, Penny. You can't say that I'm not.

PENNY Hero. I mean—

ULYSSES I'm giving you the advantage in this. You're getting the upper hand. I haven't told her about you. . . . You got the upper hand on it. So you can prepare yourself. And by the time she gets here, Lord, you'll have it all figured out. What her chores are and and and, and all the rest. (148–49)

Ulysses transforms himself in Boss-Master's image, introducing unpaid and gendered labor that he controls to work the land he intends to pass on to an heir. In response, "repping and revving" on "I'm me," Penny eventually utters "I mean." Referring, simultaneously, to Ulysses by his deadname (Hero) and to her one-time unique significance in his life, the slippage "physicalizes" Penny's more directly expressed fear that she has misrecognized this man as the man she loved as a stammer: "Now you're back. But you're not back, are you?" (150). Ulysses's matching stutter ("and and and") physicalizes both Odyssean likemindedness and duplicitousness. Ulysses's speculating has plotted capitalist heteropatriarchal norms so firmly in the future that he undermines the most important relationship he has in the present. In betraying Penny for the mere possibility of children, he also "reps and revs" on the attitude of Old Man in Part 1 whose imagined liaisons trumped most of his actual relationships.

Of course, "rep and rev" also makes it so Oddsee and Ulysses do not provide the only models of hybridity in the scene. At some point after the events dramatized in Part 1, the former chorus disbanded. Parks's Brechtian casting means that an actor from that chorus performs the role of Oddsee, while the others perform as members of the self-emancipating group. This chorus might have familiar faces but it operationalizes a different set of ethics. Though Homer had once been treated as Hero's devalued alter ego, this chorus appreciates his wherewithal. Early in the scene, Homer laments that he was not born a lizard since humans do not have the natural ability to regenerate lost limbs. In response, the chorus reminds Homer of the skills he has acquired through hard work on and for himself, insisting that he could reframe this aspect of his character as his "nature" as well. Though they are literate enough to counterfeit proof of their emancipation and possess numeracy, they view Homer's literacy of the ground and the sky as crucial for their journey northward.

This chorus likewise appreciates Penny. Just like her Odyssean analogue, she is often awakened by vivid dreams. Rather than belittle these dreams as "superstitious nonsense," as Old Man once did, the chorus recognizes that oneiromancy undoes literacy's monopoly on meaning through a temporal metaphor ("You're reading a page that ain't wrote yet") and explains that her "value . . . would be better spent in a better place" (119). Penny's form of literacy can escape white surveillance in part because it does not depend on fixed forms for its performance. In addition to making writing's belatedness more apparent, equating her talents with traditionally conceived literacy elevates Penny and the ephemerality of dreams without resting the authority of interpretation in a patriarch or his substitute.[70] Considering the man she loved as effectively dead, Penny accepts Homer's love and the chance for a restart with the new chorus.

The self-emancipating chorus uses the discourse of metal to think more creatively about how their exercise of physical autonomy should influence other aspects of their way of life. They cautiously speculate that the streets elsewhere might be "paved with gold."[71] Still, the conditions of "Freedom-ville" could dismember and debilitate, "burst[ing] brains to madness." The group recognizes it ought to continue speculating about "where is Freedom, really?" even after arriving in the North. So, they preserve Black oral traditions, "old stories," in order to make sense of what that new place will bring (151; compare "keep this plan in your mind," *Od.* 16.281). They become their "North Star," replacing a geographic telos with a shared mode of inquiry capable of sustaining an intergenerational quest and building something different and more beneficial to their well-being. These old stories—and the social supports that ensure their continued transmission—constitute their wealth in common and feed their resilience.

In comparison with the new chorus's approach to the future and freedom, Oddsee dramatizes the limits of hybridity as his final words and actions affirm the status quo that has cost his master everything. Abandoned, Ulysses first frustatedly kicks Oddsee after the dog mentions his infidelity to Penny. Because it was a kick that caused Oddsee to run away before the play began, this moment replays that earlier one. Instead of running away, Oddsee offers consolation this time: "For me, faithful is easy. It's easy for a dog to be faithful. Don't ask me why but it's true. Faithful for a dog comes natural. Like to a man such as you comes walking upright. Faithful is in a dog's bones. We're all born to do it. Can't be broke. But for a man or a woman person, faithful comes extra. Like speech comes extra for me. It's not a given" (153). Asserting that certain characteristics and behaviors are "natural" to dogs but come "extra" to human beings doubles down on the kind of essentialist logic that has continually resurfaced in the play and been used to exclude certain bodies from their due portion of citizenship, economic and physical well-being, and "humanity," and to pardon the failure to directly address racism. By uttering the same participle used by Smith, "broke," the essentializing intratextual allusion suggests that hybridity is not in itself incompatible with espousing dangerous logics of value.[72]

Picking up the spade Ulysses brought home for Penny, Oddsee substitutes for a spouse, the underling Hero has always needed for his own self-esteem, and the heir whose future existence justifies his decisions in the moment.[73] As Ulysses admits to having done for Boss-Master since he used to "feast" on his promises of emancipation that remained unfulfilled up to Boss-Master's last breath, Oddsee begins to live for Ulysses, as "good dogs" tend to (155). Consequently, his ability to speak should be understood more as affording his conformity with human ideals about dogs than as liberating him from canine inferiority by way of humanization: there is more than a touch of irony involved in listening to a talking "dog" delivering a lecture on "natural behaviors." Once a model for being and seeing otherwise, Oddsee realizes the hybridity Smith speculated about as a deferral rather than a revolution.[74]

Ulysses's continued overinvestment in property and power at the end of the play engages Eupeithes's complaint in *Odyssey* 24 and the model of futurity the final phalanx supports. Though he ends up punished by Athena via Laërtes, Antinous's father points out Odysseus's complicated relationship to sociality, the price others and other groups pay for coming into contact with the Trojan war hero. The men he left the island with never came back. The poem works hard to legitimize their deaths. It likewise works hard to legitimize the deaths of those that hinder the success of the house of Arcesius (that is, the suitors) as well as the misfortunes that those who help Odysseus suffer (that is, the Phaeacians). As a rejoinder to the poem, *Wars* lingers on the question of success. Ulysses prized his ability to read as the ultimate proof of his intelligence, evidence that he could "prove up" to whiteness and be worthy of Freedom, and lords it over his peers. However literate he may be, his failure to notice the theme running through almost every story he has heard has revealed the folly of his loyalty (*Od.* 24.469–71; compare 1.7–9). The Grant legend, Smith's plans, Old Man's imagined liaisons, and Boss-Master's breakdown all expressed a deep desire for community.[75] Grant wants to be among not above his soldiers; Smith does not mind losing his feet so long as he can embrace his family; Old Man relishes surrogacy; and Boss-Master can't fathom life without Hero. Trying to secure a physical house and heirs at any cost, this Ulysses's conservative speculations have cost him Penny's love and membership in a collective whose practical skills he already values or could benefit from learning (such as community-building). At the end of Part 3, with the Emancipation Proclamation still in his pocket unannounced, Hero is, as Smith predicted, "without a penny to [his] name" (99).

Cultures of Capital

In the history of American racism, essentializing logics of value have adhered to bodies and metal alike. These logics of value affix meaning to material objects, endowing them with intrinsic properties that affix their place in the status quo. Figuring material properties as immutable through some external authority, like God or Nature, these logics of value produce collective fictions that defend the social order as the only possible arrangement of things. When a historical event—whether the election of a president, an epoch-defining war, or a global crisis—threatens to alter the social order's trajectory, preserving collective fictions about that trajectory helps to minimize anxieties and uncertainties about the future. In this way, in addition to limiting how people imagine the future, essentializing can dissuade radical action in the present to create a particular future and its attendant social order.

Narrating why her father joined the military, Parks discourages the promulgation of collective fictions about color-blindness, equal opportunity, and the resolution of anti-Black racism, fictions especially attractive upon the election of Barack Obama but always in circulation, and the complacency they have the power to bring about. While the Bronze Star honors Colonel Parks's career in the armed forces, he never "gloried in war or his military service" as Ulysses does at the end of Part 3 of *Wars*. In conversations where she specifies how he inspired the play and in some of her earlier work, Suzan-Lori Parks makes sure that the honor does not overwrite her father's earlier attempts to secure some degree of professional respect. Her father's experience exemplifies the paradox of Black value within a culture of white supremacy. The medal distinguishes her father's heroic actions on behalf of his country: made of bronze, an alloy of copper and tin, it symbolizes how much the US Army values his service. However, he had value, even limited to the terms of the labor market, long before the medal distinguished him. Persistent, widespread, entrenched anti-Black racism denied it. Instead of setting him apart from countless other Black Americans, Donald Parks's Bronze Star serves as a poignant reminder of how many others must still search for fair treatment and livable wages, of how incremental the quest for full citizenship has been.[76]

Comparing the *Odyssey* to shrapnel, Parks draws on this same discourse of metal. Trying to "distinguish" this play through its Homeric intertexts and thereby integrate it within the narrative of that tradition's exclusive greatness runs the risk of setting *Wars* apart from the cultures of production that necessitate its intervention. This work is no hybrid that legitimates cruelly optimistic integrationist myths about American culture, that it is both the cause and the remedy for the rot at its core.[77] Framing *Wars* as a retelling could extend the unnuanced prioritization of these texts well into the future. *Wars* asks its audience to speculate otherwise.

CHAPTER 4

Afterwards

OCEAN VUONG'S COLLECTION OF LYRIC POEMS *NIGHT SKY WITH Exit Wounds* was first published in the United States in April 2016. Vuong had already written two chapbooks and seen individual poems appear in well-respected journals and literary magazines. But *Night Sky with Exit Wounds* (hereafter, *Night Sky*) was the writer's major debut. Some of the poems in the collection revisit collective memories about and impressions of historical events such as the Kennedy assassination ("Of Thee I Sing"), the Vietnam War (especially "Aubade with the Burning City"), and 9/11 ("Notebook Fragments" and "*Untitled (Blue, Green, and Brown)*: oil on canvas: Mark Rothko: 1952"). Others look at incidents that pertain to smaller groups, such as relationship-defining moments ("The Gift"), the immolation of a couple in a homophobic hate crime ("Seventh Circle of Earth"), and sexual encounters ("Devotion"). In the world of the collection, violence, pain, love, war(s), displacement, marginalization, care, and tenderness coexist and affect one another, in sometimes unpredictable ways.[1] Individually, poems experiment with a distinct form or technique. But themes, images, and words frequently recur across poems, continuously shaping the lyric persona. Through this recurrence, the poet allows the postmemorial ruminations and reminiscences to resonate with a particular attentiveness to language.[2] In the years since *Night Sky* appeared, Vuong has earned many prestigious awards—a T. S. Eliot Prize, a Whiting Award, and a MacArthur grant, to name a few—and has followed up his debut collection with a novel titled after one of *Night Sky*'s poems (*On Earth We're Briefly Gorgeous*) and another collection of poetry (*Time Is a Mother*).

Only a few months after the release of *Night Sky*, in November 2016, Maya Lin's decades-long career in architecture and design was being celebrated at the White House. A member of the jury for the design of the National September 11 Memorial, Lin has a vast portfolio including the Civil Rights Memorial in Montgomery, Alabama; the Langston Hughes Library in Clinton, Tennessee; and Women's Table, a memorial sculpture for female alumni of Yale University in New Haven, Connecticut.[3] Still, it is Lin's first commission, the Vietnam Veterans Memorial in Washington, DC, that remains her best known project. A self-described "Greek mythology nut" who designed the memorial with the myth of "Orpheus and Eurydice" in mind, Lin hoped its "litany of names" would evoke an "epic Greek poem." Lin also describes it in surgical terms: "I imagined taking a knife and cutting into the earth, opening it up, an initial violence and pain that in time would heal. The grass would grow back, but the initial cut would remain a pure flat surface in the earth with a polished, mirrored surface, much like the surface on a geode when you cut it and polish the edge . . . It would be an interface, between our world and the quieter, darker, more peaceful world beyond."[4] Submitted to an open competition while she was still an undergraduate, the *katabasis*-inspired design was controversial at the time of its selection. Lin was subjected to sexist, ageist, and racist scrutiny; when another, more traditional work was commissioned to offset her memorial, she was even paid at a lower rate than her white male counterpart.[5] Now, some thirty years later, her vision for the memorial and its interaction with other classicizing sites on the National Mall is routinely applauded as a masterpiece of public architecture that exemplifies American excellence. That the memorial was her debut work has made it all the more remarkable. President Obama remarked upon it in the East Room of the White House that November as he awarded Lin the Presidential Medal of Freedom in a cohort that included billionaire technology philanthropists Bill and Melinda Gates, the actor Robert DeNiro, and the athlete Michael Jordan. Obama focused on how the memorial, one of Lin's "physical acts of poetry," helped Americans "heal" from the divisive wounds of the Vietnam War.[6]

Though Vuong and Lin stand at different stages of their respective careers, memory and care characterize both of their bodies of work. In *Night Sky* some poems refer to the Vietnam War, which occurred before Vuong's birth, and the displacement he experienced in that war's ongoing wake. Others center large-scale historical events that occurred on American soil, likewise before and during the poet's lifetime. Still other poems gesture at the experiences of racial capitalism, heterosexism, addiction, and social isolation occurring every day in places that dot the national map but are infrequently called on to represent the United States. While many of the spaces that appear in Vuong's collection may be described as cloistered—bedrooms, apartments, shower stalls, and car interiors—the world of *Night Sky* is above all social: "loneliness," one poem tells us, is still "time spent with the world" (83). Consequently, the private always provides a route to understanding larger publics and the "structures of feeling" that link the two routinely hierarchized realms.[7] Lin, in contrast, often designs memorials that are in spaces explicitly demarcated as public and are intended to constitute an authoritative history (or History). Facilitating the reperformance of grief that made the physical space necessary, these interactions signal an emotional resolution perceived to be just on the horizon, if not yet actualized. And by bringing this resolution into being and marking a defeat or war, for example, as past, Lin's plans contribute to an institution's or a nation's understanding of itself as an entity capable of providing care and crafting community for those it deems worthy of embracing as its own. In this way, the Vietnam Veterans Memorial's granite slabs are conspicuous and conspicuously costly products of care that interrupt the destabilizing trajectory of past violence and disregard. They attempt to alter both physical and psychohistorical landscapes, as President Obama's remarks highlighted. Sites of national importance enmeshed in circuits of historical and educational tourism, these memorials and the memories they curate are the privileged antithesis of the neglect and elision *Night Sky* repairs.

The near coincidence of these milestones in the artists' careers refracts outside the bounds of their professional biographies. Symptomatic of inverse memorializations of the Vietnam War, this coincidence highlights the nuances of how this war continues to be historicized. Some forty years after America ostensibly ended its military intervention in Vietnam, the United States still grapples with what the war meant for its national identity and geopolitical ambitions. These questions grow in complexity considering the refugee crisis that followed and America's approach to subsequent "waves" of immigrants into the country. They took on additional meaning during the second decade of the War on Terror, a war whose diffuse objectives, mostly undefined duration, and Orientalizing rhetoric were haunted by the Vietnam War from the moment President Bush declared that it would be necessary for the restoration of American security and global peace after the September 11 attacks.

The Vietnam War has been recuperated by narratives of American exceptionalism as, in the words of President Reagan, "a noble cause" that went awry.[8] Once a polarizing war that spawned now iconic protests, widespread draft evasion, and generational schisms, the Vietnam War saw American troops both disenchanted with their welcome home and traumatized by their time abroad. The veterans' experiences and the erosion of public faith in American institutions combined to elevate the trauma of individual members of the armed forces into a collectively felt and therefore nationally unifying "ailment" labeled "Vietnam Syndrome." This syndrome tallied the number of American casualties, the sting of defeat, and the unrest it produced on the domestic front only to find the cost of intervention unreasonably high.[9]

The revisionism so well encapsulated by Reagan's rhetoric has persisted over the last four decades. Military, political, and cultural leaders during multiple administrations hoped that an imminent victory would finally put the syndrome to rest.[10] As the United States began fighting the global War on Terror, some officials and public intellectuals referenced both Vietnam Syndrome and the Vietnam War as cautionary tales for American interventions in Iraq and Afghanistan.[11] At the same time, documentaries such as *Last Days in Vietnam* (2014) and *The Lucky Few* (2011), newspaper articles, awards (for example, Nguyet Anh Duong's 2007 National Security Medal), Hollywood films such as *Rescue Dawn* (2006) and *We Were Soldiers* (2002), and other cultural entities continued to tell tales about America's global leadership and its correlate tropes.[12] Framing military involvement in Vietnam as a matter of humanitarian care instead of politics, these entities gathered enemy combatants past and present (whether North Vietnamese communists, radical Islamic terrorists, or Arab geopolitical rivals) under the banner of antidemocratic threats that American leadership was morally compelled to bring to order. Caution morphed into cowardice.

When he chose psychomedical rhetoric alongside multiculturalist imagery in his 2016 remarks, President Obama and his administration joined a chorus of those who remember the Vietnam War as a trauma first and foremost of the American people. The president's reference to Lin's memorial healing a united multicultural body politic, during that November 2016 medal ceremony, was certainly on brand. The reference is also consistent with the presidential proclamation issued by the Obama administration declaring a thirteen-year period of commemoration of the Vietnam War. Declaring that this period would conclude at the fiftieth anniversary of the fall of Saigon in 2025 and citing the Vietnam Veterans Memorial's humanizing force, the presidential proclamation sought to remind Americans of the awe-inspiring dignity of the service members who "pushed through jungles and rice paddies, heat and monsoon, fighting heroically to protect the ideals we hold dear as Americans . . . [and] upheld the highest traditions of our Armed Forces."[13] In so doing, the proclamation elides that the American military's primary foes were not the abstracted forces of climate and geography. Like the American soldiers and officers deployed across Southeast Asia, they were human beings charged with taking and defending lives to achieve *political* goals. Overriding the war's political aims, Obama's rhetoric, like the rhetoric of previous administrations and the memorial complex that developed around Lin's installation, looks away from the grim and sizeable tally of Vietnamese war deaths.[14]

This chapter considers what it means to come "after" in Vuong's 2016 collection, in light of this articulation of the Vietnam War's legacy in the post-9/11 period. Yen Le Espiritu's research in critical refugee studies has documented how the "before and after" temporal framework has well served the recuperation of the Vietnam War and the accompanying legitimization of the global War on Terror: biographical profiles repeatedly adopt it to efficiently render Vietnamese refugees fungible objects of study and figures of crisis. Robbing refugees of full personhood, this framework exculpates the nation from the stain of warfare and exploits stories about "good refugees" to construct the US as an exceptional provider of global care. The preponderance of reviews invested in details about Vuong's life as the background for his rise to literary fame emplot the writer into the "good refugee" narrative arc, even if only to query his assimilation into American culture and the "Western" tradition.

A conspicuous strand of Greco-Roman mythology runs throughout the collection's fabric, with poems bearing titles like "Eurydice" and "Odysseus Redux." Critics frequently praise Vuong's interweaving of these mythological intertexts with images of Vietnam or queerness, for example. The biographical fascination that treats "ethnic literature" as a window into the author's personal life or as an avenue for the performance of racial authenticity can overlook the sociopolitical salience of Vuong's approach to Homeric mythmaking after the Trojan War.[15]

Because the English word "myth" derives from ancient Greek *mythos* (plural, *mythoi*), meaning, in Greek epic poetry from the archaic period, an utterance with something at stake, discussing the term may help frame Vuong's writing in the context of both the ongoing commemoration of the Vietnam War and hotly contested policies about immigration and asylum.[16] Biased by Plato and other authors, classicists once defined *mythoi* as the primitive and/or fictitious forebears of rationalistic accounts called *logoi* (historical narrative, philosophical discourse). The history of ancient Greek thought is messy and fraught with competitions over power and cultural influence for which ahistoric oppositions often provide more utility than accuracy.[17] The English word runs the risk of connoting similarly (that is, that myths are falsehoods dispelled by the truth of science or economics), but can more productively signal this contest over what counts as a master or authoritative narrative under different sociohistorical conditions. In the case of Vuong's poetry and its stakes, adapting the temporal and spatial conditions of well-known ancient Greek myths locates power in the struggles that normative American narratives often efface as failure.

In particular, *Night Sky* wrests caregiving from the disenfranchising clutches of American hegemony to endow the postmemorial projects of those whom hegemony has forcibly displaced with both agency and authority. By thinking about the poetics of *Night Sky* in relation to duties of care, I elaborate upon a trend Rosemarie Ho observed in her review of Vuong's novel.[18] "Care" refers to the existence of needs and desires as well as to their recognition, satisfaction, prolongation, augmentation, or neglect at the individual, interpersonal, or community level and in analogous macro-contexts (imperial, transnational, global): caregiving of the intimate and personal kind relates to the kind of care promised by governments, empires, and transnational corporations. "Poetics" encompasses the full spectrum of creative acts both in and outside of the culturally determined realm of literature and pays attention to activities like maintaining a relationship or organizing a life, as well as to song-making, storytelling, and artistic performance. To inquire into a "poetics of care" entails thinking about how creative acts respond to needs and desires, and, just as important, acknowledging how particular acts of and approaches to care bring about political philosophies, critical epistemologies, and ethics.

Accordingly, if we consider Vuong's stated approach to Homer, details about the Trojan Horse and warrior heroes matter, and not because Vuong's handling of "Western material" demonstrates his successful assimilation into multiply minoritized American life. *Night Sky*'s mythmaking does not classicize in order to emplot the poet into his own before-and-after story. Rather, its cleverly audacious acts of imagination redefine what it means for those ignored by nationalist narratives to come "after" and thereby performs its most Homeric gesture.

Good Refugees, Model Minorities, and Other National(ist) Myths

Describing American intervention in Vietnam in measured terms as a "murky crusade against Communism," *Daily Times* writer Taylor Goebel profiled Thinh Pham, a Vietnamese American restaurant owner who retired to Rehoboth Beach, Delaware.[19] The title of the 2018 article betrays Goebel's approach to Pham's life-story: "Rehoboth Restaurant Owner Escaped Vietnam under Communist Rule, Now Thanks Veterans." The writer describes Vietnam in terms that Americans steeped in American films and photojournalism about the era will recognize: "The Vietnam War was saturated in monsoon rain and the blood of countless people who died in the 20-year conflict. It stung children screaming from napalm burns and North and South Vietnamese citizens covering their loved ones with conical hats, enemies indistinguishable in the face of death." Goebel's emphasis on rain and the murkiness of American objectives here dovetail, making the region's landscape contribute to the atrocities she glosses without attribution. The next vignette typifies the voyeuristic strategy of "poverty porn": the journalist quotes Pham describing the "backbreaking" labor of loading "black market produce" for his mother before attending a school for "four hours" where he was reprimanded for thinking independently. Though the author claims to observe glimmers of that same young man before her as a "resilient and undaunted" business owner and American citizen, the profile emphasizes that the food Pham prepares, redolent of "the perfumes of [his] country," were unavailable to him because "after American troops left" his family only had access to "minuscule bits of meat." For realism's sake Goebel mentions the My Lai massacre as part of the "traumatic presence" American troops had in Vietnam "at times." But she quickly pivots from mass murder to Pham's memory of troops building structures that would benefit the Vietnamese and feeding young Vietnamese children "so they could one day contribute back to society." Pham's contributions are spelled out: once he "got the chance to immigrate to the United States," he worked as an electrical engineer before turning to the restaurant business, and successfully supported his family. Now, every Wednesday US service members and their family enjoy a discount on their meals at his restaurant, as a "small token of his gratitude" that "he could still go to school when they were stationed" in his town. No longer breaking his back, Pham exerts himself to thank the American troops who enabled the life he leads now in America.

Despite incorporating a few gory blips of warfare, the profile traffics mostly in heartwarming scenes that depoliticize the war. The well-constructed narrative commences with scenes of precarity endemic to "developing" nations and the physical economic and intellectual violence of communism, only to end with entrepreneurial ingenuity and multiethnic sustenance Stateside. Goebel's profile flattens out the Vietnamese, but makes certain to disambiguate the few bad apples in the American military from the mostly humanitarian-minded ones. Industriously "restless," Pham seems to embody the American ethos of hard work paying off. The concluding quote, "I thank you all that I'm here . . . I have my family here," ostensibly refers to the presence of Pham's biological family. The details furnished in the article's final subheading make it so that quote could also refer to the soldiers whom gratitude compels Pham to feed and, through them, the country that allowed all of this to happen.

Goebel's framing of Pham's life-story contributes to an ever growing archive of newspaper profiles of Vietnamese refugees who have successfully acclimated to American life. Studying coverage of the anniversaries of the fall of Saigon and the end of what Americans know as the Vietnam War, Espiritu identified the recurring trope of the "good refugee" in profiles of Vietnamese Americans. Because America initially understood itself to have lost the Vietnam War, Espiritu surmises that the war actually "ha[d] the potential to unsettle the master narratives of World War II—in which the United States rescued desperate people from tyrannical governments and reformed them." Memories of this defeat would have acted as a powerful "antidote" to the liberationist myths that facilitate American imperialism. Her research uncovered the opposite reality: Vietnamese refugees have been figured by various cultural agents—including the academy—as grateful beneficiaries of American intervention and therefore capable of resolving the moral and political predicaments of that involvement, in the first instance, and American imperialism, more generally. Like all other displaced and dispossessed communities in American history, the Vietnamese refugees to America were considered *and studied* as figures of crisis. They were "problems that needed to be solved" in order to preserve the priority of the nation and the safety of the American people.[20] As such, refugee populations spurred the creation and institutionalization of ethnic studies in the American academy as a means of finding those solutions. The successfully assimilated and grateful Vietnamese refugee does not flag the multi- and intergenerational complexities of resettling in a new country. These complexities would remind intended audiences of these recuperative and assimilationist narratives of American violence and disregard for human lives marked as others—whenever and wherever they may be. And so, Espiritu observes, as figure, the grateful Vietnamese refugee is generally deprived of full personhood in order to be folded within a racialized subjectivity. Thus (ac)counted (for), the good Vietnamese refugee erases the messy drag of war and American inequality to reinforce the model minority myth.

Because the twenty-fifth (2000) and thirtieth (2005) anniversaries of the fall of Saigon fell on either side of 9/11, Espiritu could chart the impact of 9/11 and the global War on Terror on the deployment of this trope in projects that historicize the Vietnam War. Carefully crafted glimpses into the lives of Vietnamese refugees satisfy that sociological impulse to learn about and therefore domesticate these figures of statelessness. Whereas Vietnam Syndrome reflects on failure and thus admits the potential pointlessness of violence, the good refugee makes it so America wins even if it loses or, going one step further, even if there are no set objectives to determine what winning and losing might mean.[21] Occurring during the Second Iraq War, the thirtieth anniversary received significantly less coverage than the anniversary five years earlier; Espiritu noticed that by 2005, there was a sense that America had been cured of Vietnam Syndrome. Profiles moved past the harrowing tales of traumatized veterans—innocents deposited in a disorienting and exotic land by the currents of war—placed alongside those of refugees saved from the primitive perils of the jungle and communism by modernity, capitalism, and democracy. Rather than admitting that Vietnam provided the United States with difficult lessons about war, they stressed the country's now flourishing economy and deep ties with the United States. By shifting toward the happy resolution of what had once been considered a questionable political and military intervention, these thirtieth-anniversary profiles subtly heralded what was to come for Iraq and other countries in the (Middle) East that America was planning to "free" from the despotism of Islamic governance.[22]

Building on Espiritu's field-defining research, Mimi Nguyen has focused on the refugee patriot, a more specific iteration of the good refugee that emerges in the post-9/11 period. In *The Gift of Freedom,* Nguyen documents how the United States frames warfare as bestowing freedom upon those it deems unable to properly govern themselves. Because of their endemic deficits, liberal warfare's targets cannot exist in modernity on their own: granted freedom, they are ushered into modernity, but they remain forever indebted to the imperial power for this privilege. Stridently anticommunist and procapitalist like the good refugee, the refugee patriot zealously demonstrates their (newly secured) worthiness in relation to the war machine reconceptualized as the engine for humanitarian peace.[23]

The public personas of Tony Pham, the senior official "performing the duties of the director" for Immigration and Customs Enforcement (ICE), and Nguyet Anh Duong exemplify this trope. Profiles of Duong, a weapons engineer, occupy a chapter of Nguyen's study. Pham's 2020 appointment to the agency that works under the Department of Homeland Security bears traces similar to the articles celebrating Duong's achievements in the global War on Terror. In a quote on his personnel page, the appointee draws on financial metaphors to reflect on his new role in ICE: "When we came to this nation seeking hope and opportunity as refugees, I signed a promissory note to America. I owe a debt for my freedoms and opportunities which must be repaid. I do so by committing to my community as a dutiful citizen and to pass along my experiences and opportunities to serve those around me."[24] Steeped in the language of indebtedness, gratitude, and a selfless commitment to service, Pham cuts the figure of the ideal citizen-leader who understands America's role in the preservation of freedom and as the purveyor of opportunities and therefore embraces policies that punish people who have not followed the rules as well as he has. His self-description recalls the words George Will used in *Newsweek* to describe the scientist Duong a decade earlier. Declaring her "debt paid with interest," Will's profile emphasized her diminutive size and her skills as a nurturing mother to reassure his reader that the so-called "bomb lady" is not herself a "weaponized woman."[25] In addition to mentioning her aspirations to write poetry and her antiviolence stance while raising her children, Will harps on this reassuringly heteronormative gender performance when he frames her work in terms of protecting

American troops, ensuring that they could return home. If in the recuperation of the Vietnam War, America's biggest regret remains the total number of American causalities, Duong's designs for an extremely efficient thermobaric bomb respond to one narrow lesson from the war—preserve American life above all—and extend maternalistic caregiving from her children to members of the American armed forces and the nation they represent. As profile types, these Vietnamese American refugees surpass the good refugee's eager participation in the free market as consumer or entrepreneur to dedicate their public *and* private life toward engineering war and US imperial expansion as efficient global care. In this way, as Nguyen argues, the refugee patriot's repeatedly signaled gratitude and debt to America abet the manufacture of liberal warfare's peculiar brand of freedom in the form of a transnational biopolitical regime.[26]

Each trope operationalizes specific temporalities to make the case for American exceptionalism. In the book *Body Counts* and related articles, Espiritu observed the extent to which profiles of the good refugee depended on the framework of "before and after." Indicative of a dramatic transformation, these profiles often accompany their narratives with striking visual images and descriptions. The before-and-after split-screen is as familiar to those who read Victorian print media as it is to those who watch the reality makeover shows that have dominated American television programming in recent decades. In the archive she studied, Espiritu identifies the juxtaposed shots of "thatched huts" from the refugee's past in Vietnam with the luxury vehicles of the successfully assimilated person's present. On the surface, thoughts about what would have been or could have been if the interviewee had stayed in Vietnam deepen the article's biotemporal reach and, by incorporating more information about the family who remained in Vietnam, accommodate (a fuller) personhood. Yet, as Espiritu observes, these "postulations" incorporate family separation only to celebrate American life, prosperity, and modernity: all the pain and anguish of separation remains over there, in the conceptual past that "underdeveloped" countries are consigned to and that derives from being denied the opportunity to live under freedom.[27] Instead of adding complexity to the figure being profiled or to the conception of the war and its long wake, then, these glimpses into what could have been foreclose the potentiality they seem to indulge. Relying on stereotypes of deprivation, as we saw in the profile of Thinh Pham, they carve their objects of study into more recognizable and easily consumed units of empire. Such easy consumption blunts the uncertainty that once accompanied the Vietnam War and that haunted the Bush administration's description of the War on Terror as a campaign whose duration and cost exceeded reckoning.[28]

The refugee patriot's unflinchingly promilitary stance removes the moral stain from the violent past and present of liberal peace, creating an optimistic trajectory for American hegemony that begins in death-dealing warfare but ends in a secure and fulfilling way of life eventually being provided for everyone everywhere. Whereas Espiritu thinks about the afterlives of those displaced as refugees in the United States, Nguyen's figuration of the refugee patriot emerges from the "gift of freedom" analytic and thus delves into the temporality of exchange. Liberal warfare promises to help its target nations transition from forms of governance and economic activity (communism, monarchy, caliphate) incompatible with modernity. Conspicuously welcoming them into its seemingly homogeneous time, modernity's ambassadors bemoan their targets' ability to "catch up."[29] As a result, though a war may be very publicly declared "mission accomplished," the "cultural deficits" of the target end up necessitating a prolonged period of transition to independence, a transition the imperial hegemon must regulate and constantly monitor.[30] In terms of the temporality of these operations, the target's freedom is both given at the war's conclusion and deferred to a perpetual horizon, leaving the target indefinitely indebted and subject to recurring acts of force.

The production of the "good refugee" within domestic media derives from the deferral of the trans- and international gift of freedom. The effects of American geopolitics cannot be demarcated neatly across national lines: the governmentality and Foucauldian biopolitics that suffuse Nguyen's study do not require territory to enact sovereignty. Rather, profiles of the good refugee and the refugee patriot betray a logic that acts as if those conditions were in fact the case. Relocating the Vietnamese refugee to the United States, freedom's ostensible homeland, exposes them to unadulterated modernity and socioeconomic freedom, and allows them to learn what those who remained could not. The cultural arms of liberal warfare—magazine articles, documentary profiles, and so on—figure those who stayed behind or who are unsuited to rescue as existing in a nebulous time. They are always being granted freedom and perpetually incapable of taking full possession of it, occupying a period of well-publicized transition that could be more accurately described as independence-averse stasis.[31] That is, "before and after" suits the good refugee trope because it conceives of nations in hierarchical relation to one another, rendering the radical improvement the framework supposes as evidence of the essential difference between "developed" and "underdeveloped" countries.[32] Leaving the murky truths of warfare and geopolitics out of frame, the logic of the before-and-after framework naturalizes the stasis that renders periods of transition so ironically disempowering for those being granted freedom.

From Biography to Mythmaking

Critiquing *Night Sky* for *New Criterion*—a magazine that bills itself as "engaging with those forces dedicated to traducing genuine cultural and intellectual achievement whether through obfuscation, politicization, or a commitment to nihilistic absurdity"—William Logan finds fault with what he believes to be a growing cultural obsession with the "oppressions of biography" that has led to what he labels as identity politics too often substituting for merit.[33] As the poet Paisley Rekdal spotted in an article for a literary nonprofit organization, Asian American Writer's Workshop, despite a professed distaste for a biography of oppression, Logan yearns for *more* of it.[34] Logan first establishes Vuong's refugeehood and birth on a rice farm, and notes that his first collection winning the T. S. Eliot Prize is a rare achievement, before claiming that the poems in *Night Sky* seem ready-made ("assembled for a kit") for sentimental legibility ("heartfelt cry for understanding"). Logan complains about not getting transparent enough glimpses into Vuong's feelings, not having full access into the ravages of war, and not becoming privy to affecting vignettes of doubly orphaned "immigrant" life. Simultaneously claiming to be unmoved by Vuong's rendering of the war and emotionally distracted by his approach to the war's wake, Logan deems *Night Sky* little more than a sentimental biography with line breaks.

Logan's review invokes two approaches to temporal drag that, in tandem, recall the temporalities and hierarchies deconstructed by critical refugee studies. The first looks to the past and the transhistorical value of the ancient Mediterranean classics. It includes familiar talking points about the stultifying effects of identity politics. Logan buttresses these points with queries about Vuong's relationship to the Vietnam War, only to then lament the underexplored *gravitas* of ancient Greek and Roman poetry by infantilizing

Vuong ("he fools around with the Greeks as if they were action figures," "toying with a tradition"). Whereas Vuong's poetic immaturity makes it so he never gets out of the "long shadow" of the classics, the wake of the Vietnam War is insufficiently long for his attachment to it.[35] As a result, Vuong's refusal of now, that is, his trauma from a war he did not experience, smacks of ethnic inauthenticity and lacks the truth of immigrant feeling or experience as Logan knows it: "Little in Vuong's work conveys the immigrant's wrenching dislocation or permanent sense of loss."

The other facet of temporal drag pertains to the ever moving future horizon of assimilation and obligation. In a statement surely meant to read as racial and intellectual generosity but that demonstrates how literary and aesthetic hierarchies can racialize masculinity, Logan praises the Saint Lucian Nobel laureate poet Derek Walcott for grappling with the seriousness of the classics as an "outsider" by means of "main force" even if only to realize that the classics can only provide insufficient comfort. As a path toward a full investigation of who Logan thinks is not an outsider with respect to an ideologically, temporally, if not also geographically distant culture, note the consequences of opposing Vuong and Walcott. Vuong is racially feminized, enfeebled, and infantilized through Logan's signposting of his "soft focus" and his inability to "embrace" Greco-Roman texts: as Logan puts it, "when Vuong touches on the horror of the war, the touching isn't quite enough. The debt incurred should demand something like *Heart of Darkness.*" Failing to assimilate into this tradition and this "new world," Vuong marshals only "minor graces," touches too gently, as queer Asian men are assumed to do, and remains *indebted* to the tradition to which he has been granted access.[36] This same failure indefinitely prolongs the period that Logan's use of the adverb "yet" implies Vuong needs to properly take up the Western tradition of poetry.[37]

Accordingly, Logan leans into the comfort of canonically authoritative narratives, like Conrad's *Heart of Darkness,* and the homogenizing aspirations he assumes motivates engagements with them. In its retrograde way, the review nods to the fact that *Night Sky* has been lauded as an exemplary specimen of minority literature. Its accolades, the publishing industry's approach to marketing "ethnic literature," and the misconception of lyric voice as sincerely and straightforwardly autobiographical conspired to reinforce the tendency for minoritized writers like Vuong to be treated as "anthropological conduits," as Vuong himself put it, for the edification of the racially unmarked public.[38] Though spoken with reference to his decision to write a novel instead of a straightforward memoir, the writer's comment is no less salient for the industry around his breakthrough poetry collection. Indeed, articles, interviews with the author, and reviews of *Night Sky* frequently rehearse the same few facts about Vuong's life—his father abandoned the family; his late mother worked at a nail salon and was mostly illiterate; his grandfather was an American soldier deployed in Vietnam; he himself struggles with dyslexia and did not have a straightforward path through college—before identifying verses and poems that allude to these facts. By juxtaposing these details about his life before his book's success with those after Vuong's meteoric rise to the heights of the literary world, favorable profiles shoehorn the writer's family into a narrative about success, equal opportunity, diamonds in the rough, and the banishment of the ghosts of Vietnam. With the book so personalized, *Night Sky*'s readers seem to gain access to the inner workings of various communities of which the author is part and the readers of high-profile publications are assumed not to be. These profiles less readily steer readers toward the collection as poetry. While certainly less complimentary than these, Logan's review similarly struggles to comprehend the value of these racialized experiences for understanding Vuong's poetry as poetry and, more simply, for thinking about the Vietnam War. Using white Euro-American canonical authors and one model racial outsider as comparanda for Vuong's project, Logan leverages a conveniently elastic tradition to rewrite what has usually been a good refugee story into an instruction manual for a parvenu who needs (Logan's) help with artistry proper.

Rekdal, in contrast, considers how Americans have tended to learn about war. Drawing on the work of memoirist-scholar Viet Thanh Nguyen, her own poetic practice, and critical knowledge of the texts Logan so reveres, Rekdal specifies how Conrad and the Conrad-inspired Coppola film, *Apocalypse Now,* provide a "dubious aesthetic standard" for Vietnamese and Asian American artists.[39] Rather than represent their experiences and the praxes they help develop, this aesthetic originates from the memories and viewpoints of "Western and American veterans' experiences . . . filtered through white-helmed Hollywood and television studios." It is therefore not enough to "know the narrative of war because we have read our Homer and then our Conrad and then our Hecht." These facets combined with, as Rekdal diligently outlines, Logan's conflation of immigrant experience with refugee experience highlight the illogicality of his concerns about how steeped in war Vuong and his collection actually are. The version of reality to which he thinks Vuong's account ought to conform was always a fictionalization of what the Vietnamese and those in a diaspora created by forced displacement thought and experienced, even as it granted its white (or whitened) protagonists a semblance of greater facticity. It is this viewpoint and its authority to silence those privy to war's drag, its slow "corrosive effects," that allow a military mission to be so neatly accomplished: to echo Rekdal's response to Logan's citation of the twelve-year gap between the fall of Saigon and Vuong's birth, "wars rarely have cultural end dates that align with their political ones."[40]

As a poet whose own writing engages both explicitly and deftly with Greco-Roman mythology (poems from her collection *Nightingale* include "Philomela," "Io," "Marsyas," and "Astyanax"), Rekdal rejects the limits Logan imposes on myth's ability to address the full scope of warfare, pain, and minoritized life.[41] The disparate set of texts Logan selects could have been put in fruitful dialogue with one another beyond the "insider/outsider" binary he concocts as a screen for the supremacy of the so-called Western tradition.[42] His take on the reverberations of war misunderstands Vuong's classicizing as enfeebled because it discounts Vuong's writing as the biography of an outsider alone. It never considers the kinds of knowing that racialized and ethnic experiences, in particular, impart. Vuong himself has observed that this familiar bias with its yearning for transparency and transcription always denies minoritized writers the "musculature of imagination."[43]

Vuong's comments indicate a more creative mode of engagement with Homeric poetry. He has been open about having to invent what he does not know about the past. In a profile of the poet titled "War Baby," an interviewer for *The Guardian* wonders how he could write a "collection . . . so full of fathers when [he] grew up in a household of women."[44] Vuong acknowledges his experience and Greek mythology's preoccupation with fathers only to then muse about mythmaking: " 'Western mythology is so charged with the father,' he says. 'Personally, I'm always asking who's my father. Like Homer, I felt I'd better make it up. The Japanese have a word for it: *yugen,* when you have so little you have to imagine it.' " There is a bigger point in this: " 'I was thinking about Homer particularly, who wrote those two epic poems out of a historical event that happened nearly 400 years in the past. I admired that audacity to invent. In inventing he preserved history.' " The poet highlights the authority that Homeric epics enjoy despite Homer not being an observer of the war with which his name has become nearly synonymous. Characterizing this move toward inventing history as audacious, Vuong reorients the rhetoric of deprivation that adheres to refugeehood (and to minoritized bodies more generally) in order to make temporal separation a spur for creativity instead of disengagement. In so doing, he also complicates the East/West binary that the phrase "Western mythology" seems to introduce: Homer, the so-called father of the Greek literary canon and Western literature, exemplifies a concept that English has no single word or concept for but which in Japanese is known as *yugen.* While the interviewer signals Vuong's sleight of hand ("there is a bigger point"), the profile quickly defaults to the biographical as it resumes painting a portrait of the artist as a young man and onetime "war baby."

Night Sky's prefatory poem initiates its abiding interest in postmemorial *mythopoiesis,* or the creation of authoritative narratives about events you have learned about and trauma you experience at a spatiotemporal remove. Placed before the collection's three sections, "Threshold" introduces a host of images and words that will lend *Night Sky* its signature texture and also will characterize other poems: the emphasis on bodies, animals, and postures; imperfectly audible voices and other types of sound; a respect for ephemera; frequent enjambment; and the particularly clipped phrasing. It also clarifies the stakes of crafting poetry under the aforementioned conditions. In "Threshold," Vuong endows the figure of the poet with an authority independent of autopsy and other firsthand sense impression, rejigging distance and loss of various kinds to the poet's and the reader's advantage.

What begins as a primarily visual scene with sexual undertones eventually concentrates on the penetrative and transformative power of song:

> In the body, where everything has a price,
> I was a beggar. On my knees,
>
> I watched, through the keyhole, not
> the man showering, but the rain
>
> falling through him: guitar strings snapping
> over his globed shoulders.
>
> He was singing, which is why
> I remember it. His voice—

it filled me to the core
  like a skeleton. Even my name

knelt down inside me, asking
  to be spared.

He was singing. It is all I remember.
  For in the body, where everything has a price,

I was alive. [. . .] (3)

Here, for the first time but certainly not the last, the posture of the narrator reads as both sexual and religious; the initial identification of the target of this voyeurism simply as "the man showering" further imbues the posture with homoeroticism. Soon the man's actual body begins to fade as metaphors counterbalance the poem's quality of direct reportage; by describing the shower as "rain / falling through him" and "guitar strings snapping over his globed shoulders," the body functions as an aperture much like the sound hole of a guitar. With his voice filling up the narrator "to the core / like a skeleton," this act of penetration turns further from the sexual to the constitutive, and the two become inversely related to one another—the outpouring of the figure's voice flows into and becomes the narrator. The switch from the physical body to the metaphorical body impacts the revelation that the man in the shower is the narrator's father: as much as it complicates the sexual undertones of the entire scene with the biology of genetic inheritance, it is just as important to note that the song's transference occurs as a result of a desire for and curiosity about crossing boundaries—not through genetic and familial inevitability. Likewise, the powerfully postponed statement, "I was alive," reroutes the life-giving power of paternity to the song's ability to permeate the various materials that are separating the narrator from his showering father.

By the poem's halfway point, the narrator has mentioned memory twice in an explanatory mode: the limiting phrase "it is all I remember" jars initially because the previous images had seemed so rich with detail rather than lacking in context. Though it reads nearly as an excuse, the statement's concessive tone helps attune the reader to the advantage of the spatiotemporal remove over the impression of direct sense perception, especially given the ephemeral nature of the song. If there had not been this other crafted sound, the entire memory would have faded entirely. As it stands, the narrator realizes that the song has given shape and structure to the memory as if it were his own body as well. Ephemerality has not robbed the song of meaning—the song has accessed memory according to ephemerality's affordances and been memorialized in the poem.

In turn, the narrator prioritizes memory over autopsy when he describes his transformation into a poet. In the previous instance, likening the father's body to that of a guitar emphasized the play with absence, presence, and shape through poetic recall. In the next section, calling his father "a dark colt in a downpour," the narrator once again includes a vivid metaphor:

> That one morning, my father would stop
> —a dark colt paused in downpour—
>
> & listen for my clutched breath
> behind the door. I didn't know the cost
>
> of entering a song—was to lose
> your way back.
>
> So I entered. So I lost.
> I lost it all with my eyes
>
> wide open. (3–4)

Switching to the metaphorical register emphasizes that the father figure is no longer singing: mirroring the poem's opening scenario, he is listening to the sound of his son on the other side of the door. What begins as the son's nervously clutched breath develops into the narrator actively choosing to "enter a song" and thereby taking up his father's role as the singer. Equating "entering a song" with "losing it all," the narrator at first associates singing with unsuccessful homecomings ("lose your way"), poverty, and the limits of mortality: the phrase "the cost of entering a song" recalls the narrator's observations that "everything in the body" has a price. As a work that repeatedly draws on metaphor to render things occluded by various kinds of barriers retrievable and vivid, the poem's imagery demonstrates what the craft associated with this creative medium that enjoys a different kind of materiality than the mortal body can overcome.

The clever enjambment of "eyes / wide open" allows for a significant reappraisal that affects how we conceive of the poem, the poet, and, no less important, the figure of the reader. The poem's focus, up until the end, remains fixed on the transition rather than the viewer (before) and the singer (after). By the end of the scene portrayed in the poem, the son has not yet begun to sing himself; his eyes—not his mouth—remain wide open in the final lines.[45] The process that will lead to that singing, that opening, has only begun. For the reader *about to* enter the collection, there is an obvious cost to revisiting traumas both personal and public—in the present time, the difficulty of exposing oneself to pain, to reconsider things that seemed to have been resolved in ways that serve present purposes, can be most apparent. Through its play with metaphorical vividness, "Threshold" also asks for the reader to be open to seeing things differently, to rid themselves of the familiar accounts and explanations in order to perceive things differently than before. Of course there is risk involved. To do so could, in a nod to the story of Orpheus and Eurydice, lead one to be lost in and to the pain of the past without a clear route back to the present. It could also bring into focus an unforeseen path to healing. And in time, as the backward glance of "Logophobia" will attest ("I enter / my life / the way words / entered me— / by falling / through / the silence / of this wide / open mouth," 81), another song could come, this time from a reader.

"Notebook Fragments" exemplifies the combination of duties of care, spatiotemporal remove, and memory as it relates to the creation of poetry, thereby instantiating what "Threshold" envisions. The poem is frequently cited in reviews because it is replete with biographical details that can be verified and traced. But "Notebook Fragments" also functions as cultural criticism that connects the memorialization of 9/11 to that of the Vietnam War and the domestic opioid crisis. Topicalizing the remembrance of 9/11 victims, Vuong's poetics of care deprioritizes the biographical in order to emphasize the urgency of mythmaking for those considered less "deserving" on the transnational stage.

The poem's content centers memory and caregiving. Worry about and affection for an aged relative abuts guilt about inattentiveness to a friend in crisis; the disregard for life considered collateral and dismembered decades ago vies with the unidentified remains stored at Ground Zero; repetitive strain from masturbation meets the pain that lingers after a lover comments on the ravages of war with ironic indifference; the unlikely odds of one's birth respond to the hope that a garden will survive winter and the pleasant shock of daffodils ushering in the spring. In the poem's first stanza, the narrator remembers his wish to be "a scar's width of warmth on a worn man's neck," a comfort that emanates from a preserved trace of past wounding rather than its erasure (68). This wish coincides with other types of bittersweet memories as it continues. Some lines index moments when the narrator seems to have failed to live up to the duty of care created by friendship and membership in a wider community. Others confess behaviors that the narrator would like to change in order to take better care of himself. In still others, by etymologizing Vietnamese vocabulary words, Vuong troubles the way everyday language inserts violence into life-sustaining activities like eating and thereby threatens to normalize its toll.[46]

Form follows content. "Notebook Fragments" takes shape through a series of brief, discrete, journal entry–like stanzas. This form renders the parts or limbs of the poem especially visible and allows entries from different moments of the narrator's life (or moments from different lives, it is impossible to say) to accumulate over its four pages. It also reveals the process through which the narrator becomes who he hoped to be at the poem's outset, someone defined by a concern for care in its many guises. With "here / That's all I wanted to be," the poem's second-to-last line echoes the first stanza's second sentence. Understood only with respect to each other, these antipodean phrases chart the narrator's movement from the desire to be of comfort to another toward finding individual self-confidence. But the successiveness of short, sometimes even one-word entries supports a different interpretation; cascading nonchronological entries inform what "here" means, in terms of both readerly space and time. Having experienced this roll call of vignettes and emotional responses, Vuong's reader arrives at the penultimate entry well attuned to the fact that we know this otherwise unidentified narrator mostly through his relationship with others. Throughout the collection, remembering and care grant an integrity usually understood as part of a unitary individual lyric voice. As this particular poem nears its final sentence, the reader grasps how "Notebook Fragments" has been crafted as a work of both remembering and continued care that is greater than the sum of its individual parts.

Stanzas acknowledge biography without dwelling on it in isolation for too long:

> An American soldier fucked a Vietnamese farmgirl. Thus my mother exists.
> Thus I exist. Thus no bombs = no family = no me. (70)

As mentioned in this poem and repeatedly cited in interviews, Vuong is not only a refugee from South Vietnam; he is also the grandson of a white American serviceman who began a relationship with a Vietnamese woman while he was deployed. On the one hand, this fact further complicates Vuong's relationship to the United States, its military, and its construction of race and ethnicity. On the other hand, the poem's narrator considers his ancestry with two unsentimental constructions in one rather clipped entry. Rather than romanticize his grandparents' sexual relationship, Vuong's narrator recalls the fact with the indelicate expletive "fuck," one he will use again in connection with his grandparents in "Self-Portrait as Exit Wounds," and as a formula with equal signs that will recur in the section's etymologizing stanzas (for example, " 'Eggplant' = cà pháo = 'grenade tomato' "). The narrator reacts to the facts that lead to his birth with a flippant "Yikes." The slightly cartoonish, monosyllabic colloquialism doubling as a line of verse ironizes the data while ceding poetic space to the next entry and the memory it recalls: one entails the realization that the narrator loves his mother, while another sketches a casual sexual encounter. Amid these varied glimpses, biological descent becomes one factor among many structuring the social world these memories index, with short-term and long-term relationships reflecting back on one another.

Prioritizing the bonds forged by care over biological kinship, the poem leverages form, repetition, and imagery to juxtapose different memorializations of violence. In a quick succession of lines, the narrator follows the recounting of a memory his grandmother has shared with him about Vietnam with a fact about Ground Zero:

> Grandma said *In the war they would grab a baby, a soldier at each ankle, and*
> *pull . . . Just like that.*
>
> It's finally spring! Daffodils everywhere.
> Just like that.
>
> There are over 13,000 unidentified body parts from the World Trade Center
> being stored in an underground repository in New York City. (68–69)

Quantifying the remains as "over 13,000" and specifying that they have been collected in an "underground repository," the narrator communicates the diligence of this national project. Because the 9/11 attacks were immediately considered historically significant, the victims received conspicuous care. As part of the nation's promise to "never forget" that day, great pains were taken to name those who had died and to describe their lives. Unidentified remains provide a painful reminder of the random destruction violence causes as well as the limits of such activities to fully represent those they seek to memorialize. If collecting, quantifying, and preserving unidentified remains requires a scrupulousness that can become monumental in its own right, the memory about a baby being dismembered signals a conspicuous disregard for life. Vuong's use of punctuation accentuates the contrast between this disregard and the consecration of the 9/11 victims at what was once Ground Zero. An ellipsis after the verb "pull" inserts a lapse between this line and the next that allows the reader just enough visual space and time to reflect on the soldiers dismembering and murdering a baby. The memory as it is reported in the entry sees the soldiers turn these unidentified babies into unidentified body parts. While the reflective phrase "just like that" signifies the ease with which such a brutal act was done, Vuong's italicizing of it in its first iteration clarifies that the reflection belongs to the grandmother's memory of the event. It is not an editorialization. As such it influences how these unidentified remains correspond to those 13,000 body parts stored in the repository in New York. Though the poem suggests that the children have not been memorialized in the same way the victims of 9/11 or even those who have died of natural causes in peacetime have been, the description's emotional if not also visual vividness counters the sense of material deprivation and the possibility of these babies being entirely forgotten, especially at the temporal remove: though there is no ostensible biology linking her to these infants, the grandmother figure has retained this memory for decades in the inconspicuous repository that is her mind. By virtue of being included in this poem, if only as victims of wartime violence whose all too brief lives included *other* ephemeral moments, these children have also been accounted for and can continue to be remembered. Further transmitting this memory, the narrator is able to provide them a modicum of afterlife care. This care derives from the kind he gives his grandmother who has had to witness the ease and disregard of such violence herself. Hinting at the concerns for grandmother's advancing age a few lines later, this transmission grows more urgent, lest grandmother's memories pass away with her.

For these reasons, when Vuong's narrator repeats the phrase "just like that," the echo prompts further reflection on the intentional labor that living with such memories requires. Through repetition, the text imitates postmemory as intergenerational transmission: no longer italicized, "just like that" recurs as the narrator's own utterance. The phrase has entered his personal lexicon. In terms of imagery, the phrase appears in a line that deploys the arrival of spring trope, and so, like other instances of the trope, it remarks upon the cycles that connect life and death. The sudden appearance of daffodils above ground also reveals the various processes necessary to sustain that cycle, especially those processes that can elude the human eye. As "Into the Breach" will make clear with "a field turns / its secrets / into peonies," the daffodils only *appear* to return suddenly and effortlessly (39). Later in the poem, the narrator will recall his grandmother fretting about her garden as a blizzard passes through:

> *God must be a season,* grandma said, looking out at the blizzard drowning
> her garden.
>
> My footsteps on the sidewalk were the smallest flights.
>
> Dear god, if you *are* a season, let it be the one I passed through
> to get here.
>
> Here. That's all I wanted to be.
> I promise. (72)

The recalled memory manages to communicate the labor it takes to care for something, the fear of seeing it threatened by violence, and the hope that it might survive the next onslaught. Though we are not sure the daffodils in the poem's first half exist in *this* garden, because this memory comes later in the series of stanzas, it is impossible to read about the anxieties of winter without thinking of spring's reassurances. "The smallest flights" operates similarly through an intertextual reference to the collection's other 9/11 poem, "*Untitled (Blue, Green, and Brown):* oil on canvas: Mark Rothko: 1952," where the narrator connects personal grief and suicidal thoughts to the license of patriotic mourning. In that case, though once tempted to jump to his death, returning his footfall to the concrete grounds, literally and metaphorically, the speaker's struggle to continue and to make a misrecognizable place within a "structure of feeling." Spoken here, these flights may inform the sense of survivorship that suffuses the prayerful entry immediately after it. Even so, this reference would simply complement the dynamics Vuong has already set in place intratextually—when daffodils (re)surface, their survival consoles in no small part because they remind the reader that the energy and diligence required to care for life against powerfully destructive forces may not be fruitless or go unnoticed forever. In the context of postmemory this means that those exposed to difficult memories, who recall them, and who share them with others need not only inherit trauma; they can also learn to thrive through the collectivity that such memory work supports. And, as the final ring composition demonstrates, having taken the time to recall this, the narrator not only finds strengths in the challenges that have shaped his life amid others, but also enlists the reader as witness to this coming into assurance. This is how, within the space of a poem, Vuong's poetics of care imbues the lyric voice with an authority that refuses to elide struggle and inconvenient narratives from History.

Whereas the title "Threshold" drew on a spatial referent to announce its role as preface and metaphor's contribution to the power of poetry, "Notebook Fragments" signposts this poem's sensitivity to the ideological implications of dismemberment and memory within the post-9/11 context. Its form does not act as a mere vehicle for the empty sentimentalizing of an oppression fetish, as Logan would have *New Criterion*'s readers believe. As a result of that form, readers experience the narrator coming into being over the poem's duration. Vuong incrementally fashions a narrator whose care *for* memories moves memories *of* care outside the private world into the realm of the social—and the actionable. Moreover, by drawing attention to the poem as a product of design and labor, the poet thus contests the flagrant disregard the poem recalls with its own conspicuous form of care.[47]

To put it another way, realizing poetic form *as form* is an achievement of Vuong's writing, not an unfortunate byproduct of it. Throughout *Night Sky*, other forms, constraints, and devices appear in individual poem titles ("Immigrant Haibun," "Aubade with Burning City," "Anaphora as Coping Mechanism"). Assorting forms and devices so obviously suggests that while familiar "containers" might accommodate a facet of lived experience, one persistent, preexisting form (or narrative) does not suffice for communicating the totality of those experiences. Titles like "Odysseus Redux" and "Eurydice" similarly move an aspect of the collection's constructedness from the background to the foreground.

Greco-Roman Myth and the Authority of Postmemory

With the words, "I seal my father's lips / & begin the faithful work of drowning," "Telemachus," the first of four poems scattered across *Night Sky*'s three subsections whose titles explicitly refer to ancient Greek mythology, ends paradigmatically (8). The poem portrays a son rescuing his father from their former home as it is being destroyed, caring for his father "like any good son" would. Managing to drag him from the ocean, the son still fails to save his father's life: the gunshot wounds piercing his back will prove fatal. Apertures abound in the poem's visual imagery. Bullet holes, lips, and eyes open bodies up to the external world. The poem suggests that time may also be opened up, unlocking different possibilities than the present affords. Bombs have ruined a cathedral of wood and stone, but a cathedral of trees still remains. Though his father has died, the narrator interprets the kiss that bids him goodbye as a portent of the intimate gesture that he will perform with lovers in the future. Rather than denoting death at sea or the overwhelming snow of a blizzard, as in "Notebook Fragments," the "drowning" that ends this poem (and reappears in "On Earth We're Briefly Gorgeous" as the act of sinking into a lover's arms) refers to seeing oneself deepened by the care one provides to others as a moment of closure and finality transforms into an opportunity for further becoming.

A son rescuing his father from a city on fire might more obviously belong to the *Aeneid*'s protagonist than the *Odyssey*'s, but "Telemachus" applies the Odyssean recognition motif to a wider range of connectivity. The poem hits its most Odyssean stride when the son asks to be recognized, "*Do you know who I am, / Ba?*" (7). Comprehending that his efforts at rescue have not succeeded, the son compares his father lying on the beach to a green glass bottle washed ashore from sea. On the one hand, objectifying the body this way marks the sad transformation of the living body into a corpse that will not receive a formal burial and the father's subsequent anonymization—"anyone's father" echoes the poem's first words, "any good son." The remainder of the poem makes the case for accepting this loss with a now familiar hopefulness. For the narrator's analogizing of his father's body with a green bottle foresees that bottle arriving at a young man's feet, connecting him to a "year / he has never touched." Adding a temporal layer to the poem's haptic focus resists a sense of futility or inertness. The bottle counteracts the threat posed by the waves "rushing in to erase" the trail the body made in the sand as it was dragged along.

The poem's focus on the figure of the good son rather creatively plays with the etymology of Telemachus's name—in focusing on the connections possible over time and space, it rewrites the effects of a war that is spatially and temporally far away. In this vein, the reader witnesses duties of care switching register from the heroic to the quotidian as the homoeroticism of the kiss to come emends Odyssean domesticity. Consequently, the "faithful work of drowning" does not so much concern a likemindedness that guarantees the prevailing order as it does the hope of connecting across time and space irrespective of that order's constraints. Read this way, the hopefulness of "Telemachus" entails the sort of activity telescoped in "Threshold." After washing up on the beach, the bottle remediates the intergenerational separation symbolized by the father's corpse when it lands at the otherwise unidentified boy's feet. A product of craft, the glass bottle resembles poetry, generally, and this poetry collection's ambition in particular. It attempts, like that bottle, to initiate contact with a "year / he has never touched."

Reading these lines of the poem closely against Homer's, Kelly Nguyen has argued that its focus on the father's death and the subsequent absence of a truly Odyssean recognition scene between father and son point to one of the suppressed scenarios facing the house of Arcesius: "Vuong asks what would happen to Telemachus if Odysseus had not returned home from war," a future that could very well include his fleeing Ithaca and becoming a refugee.[48] Indeed, as mentioned earlier, the first two books of the epic explain (and the latter books reinforce) that the men courting Penelope threaten both the life and livelihood of Telemachus, Odysseus's sole (legitimate) heir. On his own, Telemachus would not be able to fend off their pursuit of her much longer, and so he would either be forcibly displaced from his homeland and disinherited or be killed as a holdover of a previous householder. Homer's narration of Odysseus's return, his education of Telemachus, method of killing the suitors, punishment of the unfaithful members of the household, and reconciliation with Penelope, all while minimizing conflict between the men of the family, consistently displaces that tension onto others marked as outsiders. Nevertheless, the poem cannot completely ignore the fact that Telemachus did not fight in the Trojan War himself and that the cursory education he receives from old man Nestor and from Odysseus in the epic's latter books is meant to compensate for the dearth of memories of the father who left him to participate in it and of Laërtes, the grandfather who has been avoiding social and civic life on the island: Telemachus is simply not equipped to reproduce the feats of his father or his father's generation.[49] Moreover, Nguyen reads the inconsonant memories of Odysseus that Menelaus and Helen share with Telemachus in *Odyssey* Book 4 as a "reflection of the process of creating postmemories" that contribute to one's account of themselves. Relying on these incomplete narratives alone, a son's attempt to perfectly mimic his father would certainly fail. Nguyen thus sees Vuong's Telemachus figure striving to "differentiate himself from his father rather than emulate him," a choice that frees him from fulfilling the poem's heteronormative imperative.[50]

This imperative and its circumscription of gender expression take center stage in "Trojan." In it, a wallpapered room sets the stage for a boy twirling in a dress before a mirror. As light glints from the mirror onto the picture frames, the narrator portrays the boy's dancing casting a shadow that "cracks" the glass that encases family portraits. His movements cause the dress to "petal" and a reference to shut eyes anticipates the predictions that close the poem: "How like / the wind, they will see him. They will see him / clearest / when the city burns" (9). The narrator's final words shroud the boy's joyful experience of his beauty and power in a kind of isolation.

"Trojan" includes multiple motifs from Homeric epic that revolve around visibility: daybreak as a temporal marker, a dressing scene, and, most obviously, the Trojan Horse. With "a flame the width of a coffin," "a flash," "a white asterisk," and perhaps even the tiny fracture that cracks the glass in the picture frames, we get a hint of the gleam of light that the Homeric narrator associates with vitality and movement, generally, and, particularly, with the sight of a warrior armed for battle as light bounces off the metal that protects and accessorizes his body.[51] In fact, as Nguyen's comparison of the poem's first few lines to *Odyssey* 2.1–3 makes clear, the sword that Telemachus dons as he dresses to leave home to speak publicly before the assembly anticipates the "steel glinting" in the figure's mouth.

Nguyen connects clothing's contribution to Telemachus's performance of elite male householder to the tension surrounding this celebration of the figure's sexuality.[52] Instead of donning elite masculine drag, the red dress in this poem seems freighted with the boy's vulnerability, not because the dress feminizes and thus weakens him, but because, as it moves, the narrator pairs its reveal of the boy's skin with a metaphor that looks inside him:

> . . . his horse
> -head shadow thrown on the family
>   portraits, glass cracking beneath
> its stain. He moves like any
>   other fracture, revealing the briefest doors. The dress

petaling off him like the skin
of an apple. As if their swords
aren't sharpening
inside him. This horse with its human
face. This belly full of blades
& brutes. As if dancing could stop the heart
of his murderer from beating
between his ribs. How easily a boy in a dress
the red of shut eyes
vanishes
beneath the sound of his own
galloping. How a horse will run until it breaks
into weather—into wind. How like
the wind, they will see him. They will see him clearest
when the city burns. (9)

In his imagining the boy as the Trojan Horse amid another burning city, Vuong's play with light and visibility in "Trojan" turns out, like "Threshold" before it, to limit the power and knowledge associated with sight. Hypervisible as a gift, invisible as a stratagem, the wooden horse allowed inside the walls of the Trojan citadel with a "belly full of brutes" was poised to destroy the city and to turn the tide of the war. The Trojans have been observing the horse all along, but they understand the horse's dual purpose most clearly when the Greek warriors open up its belly and exit in order to ransack their city. Though not a warrior, the boy here harnesses his power in motion, embracing a bodily capacity whose destructiveness (cracked glass) might also open up possibilities. Moreover, it is sound and other sensations, not sight, that tap the boy's, for lack of a better phrase, inner strength. Others fail to see him and this power in full; they observe secondary effects, the shadow he casts on surfaces and the destruction he causes. "Aubade with Burning City," which immediately follows "Trojan," takes up the language about intruders already within a city's borders to imagine the capture of what used to be known as Saigon. In this poem, "insiders" and "outsiders" might pertain to the family unit itself and, as Nguyen sees it, the homophobia constraining the figure's relationship to it.[53] "Trojan" recalls "Threshold" insofar as its overt focus on visual detail highlights vividness—in metaphor and in description—while deprioritizing autoptic experience's special purchase on knowledge. In fact, that poem's "dark colt" might forecast the young boy as horse here.

Limiting visuality matters in the case of identities deemed to be self-evident and understood through visual regimes—like race, gender, sexuality, and ability—and the voyeuristic access literature can provide to the inner life of those subject to the knowledge those regimes purport.[54] If Telemachus going to the assembly is this scene's primary Homeric intertext, it is striking that the boy in this poem does not speak, does not (yet) have a public. This silence provokes wonder about which projects he will support with his speech and what kinds of knowledge they will advance.

"Eurydice" handles the issues of a public, poetry, and connectivity slightly differently. Among the conspicuously classicizing poems in this collection, this poem alone bears no direct relation to Homeric poetry. Though Eurydice and the beloved lyre player, Orpheus, belong to a prior generation of heroes, their myth has still enjoyed a varied and long afterlife across various media: when Eurydice dies shortly after the two are wed, the musician whose power to charm men, animals, and even inanimate objects tries to rescue her from death. The poet Virgil's adaptation of the myth alters the trajectory of the story, associating Orpheus's journey to the underworld with failure: on the cusp of returning to the upper world, Orpheus cannot resist turning around to look at Eurydice and so loses her again in death. Before this version, Orpheus succeeded, and the singer's myth celebrated the ability of things to reincarnate.[55] Subsequent versions, like the one told by Ovid in *Metamorphoses,* develop around this failure. Because, as a lyre player, Orpheus can be conflated with the lyric poet, poets often use the character to reflect on their own practice, especially as it relates to the salvific potential of writing.

One of *Night Sky*'s more challenging poems, Vuong's "Eurydice" strikes a Rilkean pose because it is narrated from the point of view of an unidentified figure.[56] The poem names neither Orpheus nor Eurydice directly, though the ending suggests the pair. There the narrator laments in a callback to "Threshold": "Silly me. I thought love was real / & the body imaginary. / I thought a little chord / was all it took" (47–48). Describing a "Him calling for the girl. The girl beside him," the narrator expresses the failed recovery through the tantalizing closeness of the figures.[57] If this is the point where the poem hails the mythological figures most clearly, the rest of the poem makes it just as difficult to parse the narrator's identity from the opening analogy:

> It's more like the sound
>   a doe makes

when the arrowhead
        replaces the day
with an answer
    to the rib's hollowed
hum. [...] (47–48)

Teasing the reader with proximity, the narrator's short, clipped phrases progressively specify the terms of the analogy as she initially attempts to describe the sound of Orpheus's music. Then as the narrator shifts toward the second person plural, the reader learns that the thrall of life-affirming foliage ("green")—not a sound, not the danger in the offing ("the pink brushstroke" of fire)—pulled them through a hole in the garden closer to the core scene. In the next three sentences, where details of the myth come into focus, the proximity of both sight and sound is framed in terms of gravitational relativity, allowing Vuong to incorporate the image of a figure on its knees once again. It becomes increasingly clear that the narrator's identity is not necessarily fixed—like a stream or a rock enchanted by Orpheus's music; it is defined in relation to the other entities and moving targets of the poem. For these reasons, the analogy, a rhetorical device that puts objects in relation to one another, cleverly introduces one of the poem's central concerns.

Its *other* concern, the long wake of longing and trauma, emerges in the poem's second half as a facet with intertextual and intratextual significance. Enjambing "again," Vuong alerts the reader to the fact that the unidentified figure, the boy, and the girl have all been in this situation before. This doubly postponed adverb changes how the reader could interpret the narrator's question about being involved in the recurrent scenario. Asking "Why did we / keep saying *Yes*— / even with all those birds. / Who would believe us / now?" the narrator reflects on how longstanding connections may, from hindsight or a similar distance, be misunderstood, how the openness to those connections flies in the face of prior evidence and experience. Intertextually, Vuong's move on this front follows Rilke by dislodging the permanent mourning that defined Ovid's elegiac version of the Orpheus myth from the hero-poet to include the narrator: it is, after all, the narrator's voice that we learn has begun to fail, not Orpheus's ("My voice cracking / like bones inside the radio.").[58] It is this same figure that we understand to have returned to this space, to have done what prior Eurydices did not. The thrall that brings the narrator back to the field might not be the sound of

Orpheus's playing or the sight of fire alone but an affective bond between all of the figures, one that the aforementioned question worries will not suffice as explanation to those looking in from the outside. Intratextually, "Eurydice" could also comment on the marked recurrence of tropes—radios, fields, brief spans, and even downrange does—within *Night Sky* that testify to the thrall of certain images and sounds in the wake of events that shape a life bonded with other lives as well as the hope, failure, fear, beauty, frustration and poetic inspiration that accompany them.[59]

While the term "redux" has a particular resonance in Hollywood's memorialization of the Vietnam War, the scene "Odysseus Redux" narrates comes closer to moments of reunion in the epic than to Coppola's reissue. Nguyen argues that both the poem's title and details about honoring one's ancestors in Vietnamese culture suggest that the father or a similarly paternal figure has entered the room.[60] Mentioning the boy's yearning for contact could also resonate with Odysseus's futile attempts to embrace his deceased mother during his journey to the underworld. Furthermore, temporal details couple with the scene's intimacy in ways that also recall the hero getting to finally talk to Penelope, his wife, as himself after two decades of separation. In the penultimate book of the epic, the goddess Athena halts the sunrise, keeping the sun just at the horizon, in order to indulge the couple's desire to spend that night narrating what has happened since they've been apart and making love. The supernatural favor that has helped his family survive against all reasonable odds implicates the natural limits of mortal beings: moving the boundaries of night and day reminds the audience of the limits of human knowledge—the impossibility of understanding any one story synoptically and the impossibility of transmitting that same story to others. Indeed, Odysseus's recounting of the prophecy in which he travels to the ends of the earth and reaches the limit of his fame looks to a future beyond the poem's limits as well. Vuong does not have his narrator appeal to a goddess, though the arrival of dawn once more looms over a pair's night together:

. . . I waited

for the night to wane
into decades—before reaching

for his hands. Then we danced

without knowing it: my shadow
deepening his on the shag.

Outside, the sun kept rising.
One of its red petals fell

through the window—& caught
on his tongue. I tried

to pluck it out
but was stopped

by my own face, the mirror,
its cracking, the crickets, every syllable

spilling through. (78–79)

While the varying level of indentation continues to move the edges of each line, the boundaries of night and day remain fixed: the narrator specifies that, unlike the Odyssean source text, the sun has continued to rise as this pair unites. The narrator's focus initially remained on the other figure in the poem, attaching"decades" to the longing to make physical contact and seeing the red rays of dawn on his tongue. However, when the narrator's gaze falls onto the mirror, his attention shifts onto himself. Instead of the sun stopping at the behest of Athena, it is the narrator's own face that shifts the momentum of the scene and that eventually fosters the connection between him and the man whose hands he yearned to touch. Familiar images signal that the narrator's personal boundaries mimic those on the page as syllables "spill" out of him.

These images and these ideas about connectivity reappearing in one of *Night Sky*'s poems inform what "redux" means. The collection frequently reminds readers that connections with others deepen the connections one experiences with oneself and with the world at large and are therefore an inverse of the isolation of "Trojan." Blending a scene between parent and child (like Telemachus and Odysseus, Odysseus and Anticleia, or perhaps even Odysseus and Telegonus), a pair of lovers (like Penelope and Odysseus), and of someone, literally, facing themselves recapitulates the collection's study of interconnectedness and care without renarrating detail by detail what other poems already have shared. One of the final poems of the collection, it might therefore function similarly to the nuanced and curtailed narration of Odysseus's journey in Book 23.[61]

These connotations of "Odysseus Redux" also spill over into the poems that follow it. Appearing immediately after "Odysseus Redux," "Logophobia" begins with the word "afterward," continues by setting the scene in "the red dark" of early morning, and then describes the narrator's impulse to write (80–81). The adverb thus encourages us to think about the content of this poem and title, a fear of words, in the context of all that preceded it.

Writing down the Vietnamese word for family on a pad initiates a series of allusions to both "Telemachus" and "Threshold," the collection's opening poems. "Drilling ink" into a period on the page and thus re-creating the bullet hole in his father's back, the scene reiterates the various chains of transmission that occurred in the prefatory poem from sight to sound to written speech, from eye to mouth to hand, from family to self to the world. The bullet wounds in "Telemachus" function as both punctuating end-stops here and, once again, apertures that allow the narrator to "climb inside . . . life" and for words to enter him in turn.

The poem's final sentence ends sans punctuation in keeping with this focus on openings and opening up. The collection's final poem, "Someday I'll Love Ocean Vuong," complements this focus by reorienting the spatial concerns of "Odysseus Redux" toward self-affirmation:

> . . . Ocean,
> are you listening? The most beautiful part
> of your body is wherever
> your mother's shadow falls.
> Here's the house with childhood
> whittled down to a single red trip wire.
> Don't worry. Just call it *horizon*
> & you'll never reach it.
> Here's today. Jump. I promise it's not
> a lifeboat . . .
> . . .
> You asked for a second chance
> & are given a mouth to empty out of.
> Don't be afraid, the gunfire
> is only the sound of people
> trying to live a little longer

> & failing. Ocean. Ocean—
> get up. The most beautiful part of your body
> is where it's headed. & remember,
> loneliness is still time spent
> with the world. Here's
> the room with everyone in it.
> . . .
> . . . Yes, here's a room
> so warm & blood-close,
> I swear, you will wake—
> & mistake these walls
> for skin. (82–83)

Vuong cleverly expands upon the meaning of the horizon, putting the Odyssean context from Book 23 in dialogue with his name. When tempted to recall only the difficulties of childhood, the narrator enjoins himself to reimagine the danger of it, symbolized as a red trip wire instead of the red light of the dawn, as the horizon, one that remains perpetually out of reach. This is not a horizon of perpetual dependence, as in the case of the gift of freedom: inserting this space between himself and that trip wire allows for other memories to enter, for the narrator to inhabit new ways of seeing things like loneliness, violence, displacement, and intimacy.[62] All of these things resonate in the collection; it is hard to read the narrator's hope that the walls of an isolating room will turn to the comfort and protection of skin and not think of "Trojan," for example. Consequently, "Someday I Will Love Ocean Vuong" extends that same gaze we read about shifting the momentum of "Odysseus Redux." It encourages the reader to look back at the collection as a reimagining of the events it has recalled and, shifting from intimate connections to larger socialiaties, to look toward a future horizon, one of which we will discuss in closing.

Night Skies and Other Memorabilia

In the poem "Always & Forever," the narrator's father instructs him to open a shoebox hidden beneath his bed if he should ever be needed. Seven years later, when the narrator opens it, he finds a gun, a Colt .45. The discovery prompts an image that partially explains the name of the collection: "I hold the gun / & wonder if an entry wound in the night /

would make a hole wide as morning" (17). No longer a horse in the rain, the father's association with colts now involves a gun, a weapon with a potential to wound. As in the many other cases we have discussed, Vuong quickly reasserts that a wound is a particular kind of opening, even if minuscule like a keyhole, and challenges the narrator and his reader to see through it to something at a distance on the other side of it, beyond the violence it seems to presage so clearly and to remind him of so painfully: "That if / I looked through it, I would see the end of this / sentence."

Rather than a pat healing that comes from the passive acceptance of time's progress, Vuong's conflation of stars as wounds in the night sky demands the kind of postmemorial curation his poems have consistently demonstrated. In "To My Father / To My Future Son", the narrator reimagines several moments, especially that moment with the gun, with a significant alteration:

> You move through me like rain
> heard
> from another country.
> Yes, you have a country.
> Someday, they will find it
> while searching for lost ships . . .
> . . .
> Quick. Can you see the red dark shifting?
> This means I am touching you. This means
> you are not alone—even
> as you are not.
> If you get there before me, if you think of nothing
> & my face appears rippling
> like a torn flag—turn back.
>
> Turn back & find the book I left
> for us, filled
> with all the colors of the sky
> forgotten by gravediggers.
> Use it.
> Use it to prove how the stars
> were always what we knew

they were: the exit wounds
                                        of every
      misfired word. (57–59)

Vuong here transforms the shoebox into a book as the narrator offers both his father and his son a different archive to account for displacement, separation, and disenfranchisement.[63] Importantly, the book reminds readers of what has otherwise been "forgotten" and offers other ways of perceiving light in keeping with the movement of twilight ("red dark shifting"). Like the search for "lost ships" earlier in the poem, the book aids the retrieval of what has become less visible. Like that search, too, this retrieval requires exertion, and that is the force of the imperative, repeated anaphorically, "Use it."

This book is not merely an inherited object, a possession; it has the force to change preconceptions and "to prove" to others what they already knew, if it is used. In the 9/11 poem, "*Untitled (Blue, Green, and Brown):* oil on canvas: Mark Rothko: 1952," the narrator reminds us: "They say the sky is blue / but I know it's black seen through too much distance" (49). Likewise, when the gun as metaphor has appeared elsewhere, such use changes the mouth from a gun that can misfire and wound to a tool that reveals and repairs, even if this revelation and repair can only be seen from a distance.[64] After all, as "Immigrant Haibun" clarified, stars are "Little holes. Little centuries opening just long enough for us to slip through" (14): to consider the night sky a place with exit wounds entails the recognition that looking at the stars is not only to see those visible objects of light but also to see a glimmer of the past. Offering this tool to both his father and his son, the narrator thus offers a way for thoughts and memories to come not merely *after* an event but as a meaningful supplement to it, to recognize it in a way that alters the nature of the relation.[65]

Imagined as a piece of memorabilia, *Night Sky* participates in another aspect of the competing memorializations of the wars in Vietnam. Though it was not part of Lin's original design, it is now routine to bring items of remembrance to the Wall during a visit: the Vietnam Veterans Memorial fund estimates that nearly 400,000 objects have been left since the Wall was opened to visitors in 1982, and the museum collection whose curation it supports financially includes 250,000 items.[66] This objects in this ever growing archive run the gamut from the militaristic and patriotic, like medals, dogtags, and POW/MIA bracelets, to the more obviously personal and sentimental, like teddy bears, cowboy boots, and locks of hair. The pattern of objects left behind has changed over the years, as the ritual has become regularized, and the task of curation has grown more systematic in response.[67] These objects, both the assortment and the metamorphosis of a funereal ritual at the public site, also reflect an important truth about memorializing: that the process—even within the nationalizing context of the Mall, the intentionality of the design, and the bureaucratic patina of an official archive—cannot be fully anticipated or even controlled.[68] The peacefulness Lin associated with black granite and death ends up reflecting the dynamism of this process as engaging the memorial serves different needs.

Though the Vietnam Veterans Memorial helps us appreciate this dynamism and, by comparison, the ingenuity of Vuong's engagement with ancient Greek and Roman texts, *Night Sky with Exit Wounds* as memorabilia bears even more in common with *Explosions in the Sky*, Hồng-Ân Trương's 2006 video installation that prompts its viewers to reconsider the periodization of history and warfare. Truong's art installation loops black-and-white found footage of artillery fire in the sky from the Battle of Điện Biên Phủ in 1954 and an English-Vietnamese upbeat adaptation of "Sounds of Silence" playing in the background. The black-and-white footage of explosions comes from a battle commonly understood to end French imperial control over Vietnam and to begin Vietnamese sovereignty.[69] But as Mimi Nguyen has observed, the date could also be considered an important reference for the seriality of war and political violence rather than strict demarcations: after the French left the region, the United States intervened in the region more directly.[70] From the point of view of the South Vietnamese diaspora displaced in the wake of America's Vietnam War, Viet Thanh Nguyen explains, the rock-and-roll–influenced audio recalls the "yellow music" that would have been popular in South Vietnam. As such it speaks to the need to recognize multiple types of loss involved in warfare and regime change: recording the South Vietnamese perspective on the joys *before* exile has not been especially useful for the national(ist) memories of either the United States or Vietnam. Texts, centers, online archives, and associations that honor this perspective have proliferated in the last decade—even as nationalist memories have continued being institutionalized.[71] Coupling issues of sequentiality and seriality with the dynamics of the song as not-quite cover, Truong's assemblage of archival material recalls Rekdal's observation about war in her response to Logan inasmuch as it contrasts the clean breaks

Fig. 4A. Still from 00:27 of French artillery fire during the Battle of Điện Biên Phủ. Hồng-Ân Trương, *Explosions in the Sky (Điện Biên Phủ 1954)*, 2006, still image, from *Adaptation Fever* video quartet. Courtesy of the artist.

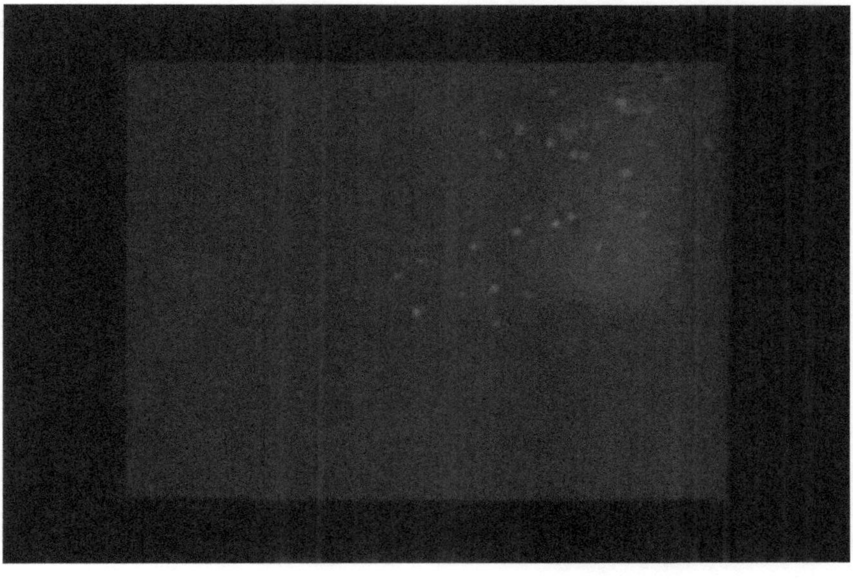

Fig. 4B. Still from 01:03 of the sky dotted with stars and artillery smoke during the Battle of Điện Biên Phủ. Hồng-Ân Trương, *Explosions in the Sky (Điện Biên Phủ 1954)*, 2006, still image, from *Adaptation Fever* video quartet. Courtesy of the artist.

of historical periodization with the reality of temporal loops and unwieldy temporal drag.

Explosions in the Sky, as assemblage, demonstrates the agency of postmemorial *poiesis* while encapsulating how postmemorial projects do not simply come after; in preserving aspects of the past otherwise overlooked, they add something that could not be so easily perceived up close. Given these nuances of Trương's work, we can read Vuong's observation about the blue sky on 9/11 in "*Untitled*" better attuned to its promise: the media-rich footage from 9/11 will also be found and reconsidered one day when technologies will far outpace those of this era, a discrepancy that could contribute to a reframing of the event's epochal and affective significance.

In the years since he published the poetry collection, Vuong has further allowed the duties of care that acknowledge the transgenerational impact of forced displacement and war to spur his creative acts. He has recently cofounded the Center for Refugee Poetics. In a collaboratively authored 2020 article for *Verge,* Lawrence-Minh Bùi Davis reflects on the conversation that led him and Vuong to begin working on the center. Davis feared that their dream for giving the center a physical space would be perpetually deferred, postponed by the quagmires of funding and bureaucracy. They and a group of other artists heeded Espiritu's call to reconsider the refugee "as a site of social critique" rather than as a unit of imperial governmentality alone. In this context, that meant imagining what not having a physical space or a fixed institutional home allowed rather than prohibited, identifying what needs such a space served beyond the settler colonialist impulse to use space to acquire respect and power. Allowing "the conversation to spool outward" meant acknowledging "the forces that perpetually reproduce [the global refugee condition]" as the cofounders reached out to other communities that have been forcibly displaced and dispossessed, and having pop-up events and digital exhibitions make the center's ethos manifest.[72] As to how the center operates on future occasions, that will be up to the community to decide.

End Times, An Envoi

THIS PROJECT BEGAN TO TAKE SHAPE IN 2016 SHORTLY AFTER I started reading Vuong's *Night Sky with Exit Wounds* while rereading Lerner's *Angle of Yaw* and Cyrus Console's poetry collection, *The Odicy.* I had been thinking about and with Console's *The Odicy* for some time, but mulling on it and *Night Sky* simultaneously united formerly disparate strands of thought. Coming across other texts, deepening my interest in contemporary art, conversing with a range of practitioners, and other developments all influenced what eventually became *Epic Events:* analyzing temporal rhetoric took second place to investigating the feelings and experiences of citizenship as an extension of time.

However, nothing has had a greater effect on the arguments this book advances, the texts it includes, and the methodologies it uses than the COVID-19 pandemic. Pandemic-related lockdowns prohibited me from visiting multiple sites and thus substantially changed the plan for this book. Furthermore, because the virus changed how many people conducted their lives, individually and as part of social groups, it no longer felt so strange to research the politics of time. Beforehand, because reception so often gets labeled as "not real Classics," some senior scholars and peers voiced concerns about the project in its infancy; they worried that choosing to complete it as a first book would endanger my career as a Black scholar on the tenure track, not just proving I had failed to assimilate into the discipline but also acting as a mechanism for excluding me from it. After COVID-19, though, the project seemed unquestionably timely.

In "Afterwards," I argued that Vuong's reception of ancient Greek and Roman material advances a poetics of care responsive to the before-and-after framework American culture uses to craft a grateful refugee and to imagine benevolent imperial hegemony. That same framework, I reasoned, haunts how the Obama administration planned for the Vietnam War to be commemorated in 2025, recapitulating a medicalized discourse of Vietnam Syndrome. Marking the years since the Vietnam War "concluded," the US government claims to heal a wounded populace, while continuing to wage costly and deadly wars. I do not want to lose sight of the particular challenges facing those who came to America after experiencing the Vietnam War firsthand or whose lives had been shaped by it on a second- or third-hand basis. That context matters.

However, reviewing the matter of care in *Night Sky* during a worldwide health emergency and, in 2020 and 2021, as a well-publicized epidemic of racist violence by law enforcement officials surged spotlighted aspects of other texts I had been analyzing and the sociopolitical realities they represented. In place of care, Hero/Ulysses offers, or thinks he offers, economic opportunity; the Batistes need to more consciously care for another and their neighbors since their state and national citizenship has been so devalued; and like Vuong, Spahr carefully sutures the erotic to a yearning to respond to and to satisfy the needs of all her beloveds. These texts repeatedly proclaim a remarkably persistent deficit of and desire for care in the United States.

The pandemic allowed for types of care to be normalized or at least made more common, interpersonally and institutionally. These extraordinary extensions of care had temporal components: larger populations were benefiting from everything from student loan repayment pauses and vaccines with time limits to flexible work hours, asynchronous teaching, and overtime pay for essential workers. These changes may have been instituted in response to the novel coronavirus, but cultural conversations repeatedly demonstrated that the problems they solved predated the pandemic. Americans had been in dire need of these kinds of care before the pandemic; the rapid, extraordinary, and extremely dangerous spread of COVID-19 taxed an already barely tenable status quo.

The introductory chapter of this book explained how chronopolitical analysis focuses on the circulation of power rather than simply noting temporal rhetoric or the multiplicity of temporal experiences. During the pandemic, arguments universalizing the pandemic were frequently and productively complicated by biopolitical realities: each person had different risks of exposure, risked being treated differently by medical institutions, had different formal and informal labor power, all of which configured what the pandemic meant for them.[1] One's temporal experience of the pandemic depended on one's access to and the circulation of power before it. The temporal components of those extensions of care must be considered accordingly.

The chronopolitics of care in *Night Sky* and of preparedness in *Salvage the Bones* in particular inform my concerns about declaring the pandemic over. When the Centers for Disease Control and Prevention (CDC) announced that the public health emergency would end on May 11, 2023, it did not mean that the novel coronavirus no longer posed a threat: the announcement repeatedly reinforces the importance of preventing severe COVID-19 and the priority of creating sustainable long-term public health infrastructure.[2] However, the CDC's declaration comes months if not years after other institutions, companies, and organizations had curtailed policies meant to ameliorate the pandemic's impact on members, employees, patients, beneficiaries, and customers. Rather than advocating something radical, the agency's announcement echoed a widely expressed desire for a return to normalcy. Still, by drawing attention to the kinds of information the CDC would no longer collect or have access to, to the kinds of intervention it would no longer be able to enforce or to fund, the announcement encourages us to note the information other organizations no longer had to gather or to furnish and the needs organizational policies would no longer have to acknowledge. Recalling the way emergency and the everyday are imbricated, I think about how disabling moving to a post-pandemic frame of mind can be for the untold number of people suffering from "long COVID," given the state of healthcare, labor rights, voting rights, and so on across the United States: whose suffering will be acknowledged and remedied, and whose will be accepted as the cost of maintaining the economy? Whose health and leisure time will dangerous and risk-filled overtime labor (continue to) secure? With regard to crumbling social institutions and safety nets, I wonder how the formal end of the pandemic overlapped with, responded to, or encouraged a loss of hope in changing how we relate to each other as vulnerable creatures on a vulnerable planet, within any one nation's borders and beyond. For whom was the end of the public health emergency, returning to business as usual, supposed to feel good?

These big-picture questions relate to ancient Greek and Roman studies in multiple ways. In terms of classical reception, this book set out to expand the scope of the subfield by explaining how adaptations of and responses to ancient Greek and Roman material negotiate the *tempus quo* of American citizenship. It has detailed how the authors and artists under consideration expose the temporal heterogeneity of the present and thus contest the temporal homogeneity and affective uniformity that are germane to discourses of national unity, patriotism, and American exceptionalism. By explaining how these contemporary works emphasize, elaborate, or invert temporal details from ancient texts, it has sought to chronograph the cultures animating American society and the cultures out of which these source texts emerged. Consequently, getting to grips with the chronopolitics of American citizenship by studying the reception of ancient Greek and Roman literature should be construed less exclusively in terms of timelessness—a clarifying kind of temporal alienation or estrangement from the present that gets attached to classicized material—and more critically in terms of the relational and embodied nature of being-in-time at any time.

The relational and embodied nature of being-in-time has further implications. As Sarah Sharma states in a nod to Kimberlé Crenshaw's work originating in critical legal studies and workplace discrimination against Black women, temporality is intersectional.[3] Temporal critique requires that characters, figures, authors, speakers, and artists be treated as multidimensional social actors, that is, people variously enmeshed in a host of relationships to power, rather than essentialized as atomized individuals defined and, more importantly, served by single identity categories that social systems, structures, and institutions recognize. This book has therefore investigated how various institutions, social roles, and practices impact temporal experience. It has taken deep dives into the American news media and emergency management infrastructure, and brief glances at the carceral system, the factory floor, and the publishing industry. It has probed the temporal subjectivities that radio, television, books, telephones, and the internet create and the temporal scaffolding of tourism, imperialism, and assimilation.

Becoming a member of an academic institution and field comes with temporal strictures and creates temporal subjectivities as well. In the introductory chapter, I expressed a hope that, in addition to studying the chronopolitics of belonging in the United States, this book's arguments and methods could inform discussions about belonging in the discipline of classics. The American branch of the discipline has been scrutinizing its active (and not simply historical) relationships to racism as part of an ongoing bid for relevance. I phrase this intensified interest in racial justice this way not to overlook whatever ethical shifts and changes of heart motivate this recent fervor for equity. Given the skepticism regarding sentimentality's ability to change the status quo that I have expressed in this book, such framing points to the practical fear also driving these discussions. There is concern that, should the discipline not change, it will further wither and then die as the college-age population grows less white and affluent (and therefore less likely to have studied ancient Greek or Latin before college) at the same time as institutions adopt policies more tied to quantified value or returns on investment: numbers in the form of class sizes, number of majors in the subject, and number of postgraduate applicants justify the funds allocated to classics programs, departments, and faculty. These discussions occur within a university system attempting to stay afloat amid greater financial disinvestment from the public, escalating skepticism about the cultural and economic benefits of higher education, especially when academic disciplines prioritize anything critical of the sociotemporal order, and the related devaluation of laborers and their rights.

In this context, it becomes necessary to clarify that paying attention to time as a racializing material does not endeavor to satisfy a contemporary need for projects on race and the classics that can attract a more diverse student population by proving the relevance of studying the ancient Greeks and Romans. It intends to deepen the field's understanding of how race, racism, and power actually work in American society in tandem with and across other identity categories. Conceiving of race primarily as a spectacularly visible and immediately apparent difference, as work not grounded in critical theories of race tends to do, ignores how societies racialize, that is, how they create and reinforce what that difference, or any other difference, for that matter, means. Ignoring how American racism manufactures race decreases the likelihood of effectively remediating it, even as the discipline increases the scholarships, committees, policies, and time devoted to doing so. The concerted conservative attack on racial justice, including laws that undermine affirmative action and educational policies that censor historical details in the name of preventing distress, demands that we continue strategizing against the insidious ways in which racializing systems and structures function in terms of both time and feeling while proclaiming a noble pursuit of color-blindness, equality, and freedom.[4]

Acknowledging time as an embodied relation of power while the field of classics considers restructuring and reimagining itself could entail multiple things. It could encourage the field to continue to theorize how ancient Greek and Roman communities approached, for example, specific kinds of bodies (rather than the undifferentiated body), the relationships between humans and nonhumans, those between social classes, and so on from the earliest stages of language training.[5] The field needs to assess how the time involved in conference planning, contingent labor, normative time to degree, admissions and hiring practices, course deadlines, the tenure clock, metrics of productivity, and service demands contributes to the inequities we purport to want to rectify. Reflecting on belonging, it also needs to confront disempowering affective scripts (having to *love* one's job or discipline) and to take seriously how the discipline can actually feel to the obviously minoritized (for instance, endangering), to those safely ensconced within it (for instance, disenchanting) or, crucially, to those trying to earn membership in it (for instance, frightening, mysterious). These feelings could be symptomatic of needs, deficits, and imbalances that seem otherwise untraceable, eluding preexisting forms of data collection. For those who have been forced to leave the field of classics—people who have been all but rendered invisible—and those who have chosen to remain in it but do so critically, reconsiderations of the kind I have just mentioned have been a long time coming.

Notes

Unless otherwise indicated, all translations of ancient Greek and Latin are my own.

TIMELESSNESS, AN INTRODUCTION

1. https://store.911memorial.org/products/metal-virgil-quote-keychain. See also Sturken, "The 9/11 Memorial Museum and the Remaking of Ground Zero," 487–89.

2. National September 11 Museum and Memorial, https://www.911memorial.org.

3. Sodaro, *Exhibiting Atrocity,* 157–59.

4. Wyke, *Caesar in the USA,* 181–92.

5. National September 11 Museum and Memorial, Learn-Timelines, https://timeline.911memorial.org; Sodaro, *Exhibiting Atrocity,* 146; Olick, "Collective Memory," 338–43, 346.

6. Nora, "Between Memory and History: Les Lieux de Mémoire," 12; Sodaro, *Exhibiting Atrocity,* 146; Shapiro, "Rebuilding Confidence"; Low, "The Memorialization of September 11," 336; Adler, "Design after 9/11."

7. Seider, "Allure without Allusion," 178–80; McKeown, "The 9/11 Memorial and the *Aeneid*"; Barnard, *Empire of Ruin,* 1.

8. Alexander, "Out of Context."

9. Dunlap, "A Memorial Inscription's Grim Origins"; Dunlap, "Scholarly Perspectives on Inscription at the 9/11 Memorial Museum."

10. Barnard, *Empire of Ruin,* 2.

11. National September 11 Memorial and Museum, The Memo Blog: Trying to Remember the Color of the Sky on That September Morning, https://www.911memorial.org/connect/blog /trying-remember-color-sky-september-morning.

12. National September 11 Memorial and Museum, OCME Repository at the World Trade Center, https://www.911memorial.org/connect/911-family-members/ocme-repository.

13. Allen, "Introduction," 2.

14. Sharma, *In the Meantime,* 14.

15. Sharma, *In the Meantime,* 14; Bear, "Time as Technique," 487–89.

16. Fortier, "Affective Citizenship and the Management of Unease," 17–30; Fortier, "Afterword," 1038–44; Ahmed, *The Cultural Politics of Emotion*; Berlant, "Citizenship," 37–41.

17. Bush, "President's Remarks at National Day of Prayer and Remembrance."

18. Bush, "A Proclamation, National Day of Prayer and Remembrance for the Victims of the Terrorist Attacks on September 11, 2001."

19. Sanders, "A Mighty Fortress Is Our Battle Hymn of the Republic," 65–69, 81-83.

20. Bush, "Statement by the President in His Address to the Nation."

21. The phrase comes from Shakespeare's *Hamlet* and recurs often in scholarly and public coverage of the 2001 attacks. For one approach to the relationship between Hamlet, the genre of tragedy, and the post-9/11 era, see Wallace, *Tragedy since* 9/11, 11.

22. Bush, "Statement by the President in His Address to the Nation."

23. Pease, *The New American Exceptionalism*, 158.

24. Sharma, *In the Meantime*, 14; Bear, "Doubt, Conflict, Mediation," 16; Berlant, "Citizenship," 37.

25. Fabian, *Time and the Other*, 7, 18; Chakrabarty, *Provincializing Europe;* Mignolo, *The Darker Side of Western Modernity.*

26. Said, *Orientalism;* Khalid, "Gender, Orientalism and Representations of the 'Other' in the War on Terror"; Nayak, "Orientalism and 'Saving' US State Identity after 9/11"; McAlister, *Epic Encounters.*

27. Mills, "The Chronopolitics of Racial Time," 304, 307–12; Smith, *Everything You Know about Indians Is Wrong;* Rifkin, *Beyond Settler Time.*

28. TenHouten, "The Emotions of Hope," 80.

29. Patman, "Out of Sync," 222.

30. "National Security Strategy of the United States."

31. Bush, "President Bush Delivers Graduation Speech at West Point United States Military Academy."

32. Amoore, *The Politics of Possibility*, 9; Dunmire, *Projecting the Future through Political Discourse*, 2.

33. Ericson, "The State of Preemption."

34. Stahl, "A Clockwork War," 78; Virilio, *Desert Screen*; Bray, "Aesthetics in the Shadow of No Towers."

35. Hannah-Jones et al., "The 1619 Project"; Hannah-Jones, *The* 1619 *Project: A New Origin Story*, xvii-xxxiii; Douglass, "What to the Slave Is the Fourth of July?" 66–71.

36. https://www.instagram.com; Jaffe, "The Collective Power of #MeToo," 80; Burke, *Unbound.* See also, National Women's Law Center, "Time's Up Legal Defense Fund."

37. Sharma, "Critical Time," 316–17.

38. Greenwood, "Reception Studies," 42.

39. E.g., Wyke, *Caesar in the USA;* Monteiro, "Power Structures."

40. Stavrinaki, "Fossil," 177.

41. Greenwood, "Reception Studies," 42.

42. E.g., University of California, Berkeley, https://dagrs.berkeley.edu/index.php/about/department-history; McMaster University, https://www.humanities.mcmaster.ca/stories/department-of-classics-to-be-renamed-department-of-greek-and-roman-studies.

43. Rankine, "The Classics, Race, and Community-Engaged or Public Scholarship," 353–54; Eccleston and Padilla Peralta, "Racing the Classics," 201–2 .

44. See also Hanink, "It's Time to Embrace Critical Classical Reception"; Ward and Umachandran, *Critical Ancient World Studies.*

45. Compare Grethlein and Krebs, *Time and Narrative in Ancient Historiography.*

46. Feeney, *Caesar's Calendar*, 2; compare Feeney, "Time."

47. Newlands, *Playing with Time;* Pasco-Pranger, *Founding the Year.*

48. Purves, *Space and Time in Ancient Greek Narrative*, 23.

49. Eidinow and Maurizio, "Introduction," 9.

50. For example, Rood, Atack, and Phillips, *Anachronism and Antiquity;* Holmes, "At the End of the Line: On Kairological History."

51. Postclassicisms Collective, *Postclassicisms,* 29–30.

52. Cite Black Women Collective, "Cite Black Women"; Hanink, "Not All Classicists."

53. Martin, *The Language of Heroes,* 14–22.

54. Berlant, *The Queen of America Goes to Washington City,* 1–24.

55. See, for example, Fasolt, "Breaking Up Time—Escaping from Time."

56. Sharma, "Critical Time," 316.

CHAPTER 1. INSTANTS AND REPLAYS

1. Lang, "Eric Fischl's *Tumbling Woman,* 9/11, and Timeless Time," 25.

2. Senie, *Memorials to Shattered Myths,* 134–35; Butts and Fischl, "@Risk: Risk for Art's and America's Sake."

3. Fischl and Homes, "BombLive!"; compare Balzer, "Art's Bad Boy Looks Back."

4. Feyeric, "Nude 'Ashe' raises racket at U.S. Open"; Adande, "It's Art, But It's Sure Not Arthur"; Berkow, "Sports of *The Times*; Bronze Guy Stands Tall Sans Towel."

5. On Rodin's classicism, see Vout, "Rodin's Complicated Relationship with Classical Art"; Van Schepen, "Falling/Failing 9/11," 140.

6. Dwyer, *Pompeii's Living Statues,* 14.

7. Dwyer, "The First Plaster Casts of the Pompeian Victims," 49–50.

8. Associated Press, "After Complaints, Rockefeller Center Drapes Sept. 11 Statue."

9. Young, "Memory and Counter-Memory: The End of the Monument in Germany."

10. Senie, *Memorials to Shattered Myths,* 135; Junod, "The Falling Man," 212, 216–27.

11. Fischl and Homes, "BombLive!," 2005.

12. Peyser, "Time to Let People Decide If 9/11 Sculpture Is Art or Exploitation."

13. Compare Van Schepen, "Falling/Failing 9/11," 120.

14. Berlant, *The Female Complaint,* 21; Luciano, *Arranging Grief,* 180–83.

15. Jaramillo, *Ugly War, Pretty Package,* 34.

16. Carey, "American Journalism on, before, and after September 11," 99; compare Baym, "Infotainment."

17. Bird, "Converging into Irrelevance?" 193.

18. William and Carpini, *After Broadcast News,* 232.

19. Holleran and Holleran, "Relic Steel"; Huyssen, *Present Pasts,* 6–27.

20. On the first anniversary of 9/11, advertisers remained wary of commercials because they did not want to seem to be capitalizing on the attacks. See Cosgrove-Mather, "Commercial Free 9/11 TV Coverage."

21. Auletta, "Battle Stations," 60–67.

22. Bush, "Statement by the President in His Address to the Nation."

23. Kurtz, "Journalism's Surreal Reality Check."

24. Kurtz, "The Line between Journalism and Sensationalism."

25. On the condemnation of Reuters for adhering to its rules for identifying "terrorists," see Jamieson and Waldman, *The Press Effect,* 140.

26. Brockill, "She Was the Only Member of Congress to Vote against War in Afghanistan."

27. Carter, "ABC to End 'Politically Incorrect.'"

28. Bush, "Presidential Address to the Nation."

29. Gershkoff and Kushner, "Shaping Public Opinion," 525–37.

30. Dower, *Cultures of War,* xix, 4, 8.

31. Berlant and Greenwald, "Affect in the End Times," 79.

32. Freeman, "Synchronic/Anachronic," 13, 38.

33. Spigel, *Make Room for TV,* 36–72.

34. For a description of Fordism, especially how its accumulative strategy influences and responds to other social structures, see Jessop, "Fordism and Post-Fordism."

35. Antonio and Bonanno, "A New Global Capitalism?," 35.

36. Hong, *A Violent Peace,* 10–12.

37. The United States defines ancestry as "a person's ethnic origin or descent, 'roots,' or heritage, or the place of birth of the person or the person's parents or ancestors before their arrival in the United States." https://www.census.gov/topics/population/ancestry.html. See also Omi and Winant, *Racial Formation in the United States*, 21–31, 40. See also Akram, "The Aftermath of September 11, 2001".

38. Rosenfeld, "Brokaw's 'Generation' Veneration." Compare Moore, "Tom Brokaw's 'Greatest Generation' Honors WWII's Heroes."

39. Conner Sr. and Conner Jr., "Review: *The Greatest Generation* by Tom Brokaw."

40. Kennedy, *Freedom from Fear*, 632. For similar approaches to the mythologization of this period, see Rose, *Myth and the Greatest Generation;* with regard to the memorialization of this myth, see Doss, *Memorial Mania,* 187–252.

41. See also Omi and Winant, *Racial Formation in the United States,* 40–46.

42. Rosenfeld, "Brokaw's 'Generation' Veneration," points out that in *The Greatest Generation,* Brokaw claims that those who served in and survived World War II dreamt of achieving the American dream in the form of a "wife, kids, and a few appliances."

43. Albertson, "Zenodorus's 'Colossus of Nero,'" 106.

44. Wyke, *Caesar in the USA,* 179–83. Cf. Niall Ferguson, "The Unconscious Colossus," 21–23.

45. Gaonkar, *Alternative Modernities,* 6.

46. Jessop, "Fordism and Post-Fordism."

47. Pope, "NBC Boosts Brokaw Book and Gets Boost Back."

48. Compare the use of ancient Greek etymology to define corporate synergy in Goold and Campbell, "Desperately Seeking Synergy."

49. Compare Eccleston, "Cyrus Console's *The Odicy* and Epic Ecology," 33–38; Luciano, *Arranging Sacred Grief,* 263.

50. George Washington earned his nickname as the "American Fabius" for using the strategy during the Revolutionary War; see Shalev, "Ancient Masks, American Fathers," 166; Ricks, "The Roman Character." The Viet Minh used the strategy against the French in the Battle of Điện Biên Phủ, discussed in chapter 4; Polack, "George Washington: The Guerrilla King," 167.

51. Scanlon, "Your Flag Decal Won't Get You into Heaven Anymore," 175, 178–79; compare Fisher, "Commemorating 9/11 NFL-style," 218.

52. Berlant, *The Queen of America Goes to Washington*, 1–24.

53. Compare Nickels, *Poetry of the Possible*, 1–3.

54. Spahr, "Introduction," 2.

55. Gwiazda, *US Poetry in the Age of Empire*, 107.

56. Vernant, *Mortals and Immortals*, 50–74.

57. West, *Iambi et Elegi Graeci ante Alexandrum Cantati*, 174–75.

58. Loraux, *The Invention of Athens*, 275n5.

59. Loraux, *The Invention of Athens*, 20; Arrington, *Ashes, Images, and Memories*, 110.

60. Yu, *Race and the Avant-Garde*, 1–18.

61. Spahr, "Poetry in a Time of Crisis," 7–8.

62. The poem has a geographical postscript, "Brooklyn, NY," that could seem to privilege New Yorkers as especially affected by the tragedy.

63. Marcy Borders, the woman pictured in one of the most striking photographs from the ash fallout of 9/11 in New York City, died of stomach cancer at age forty-one in 2015. While the relationship between her illness and her exposure to the ash has not been proven, the government continues to track the various illness associated with toxic exposure across all sites (see Centers for Disease Control and Prevention, *Health Effects of 9/11: An Online Exhibition*). Such findings contributed to the plea for ongoing support of the September 11th Victim Compensation Fund. See Kim, "The Battle over Extending the September 11th Victim Compensation Fund, Explained."

64. Compare Stanley, "Habits of Modernism," 853–60; also Bellini, "Rethinking the Subject through the Everyday."

65. Gwiazda, *Age of Empire*, 98.

66. Anderson, "Emergency/Everyday," 177–91; compare Adey et al., "Introduction: Governing Emergencies," 5–6; Anderson, "Emergency Futures," 463–77.

67. Spahr, "Bernadette Mayer's *Sonnets*," 111.

68. Culler, *Theory of the Lyric*, 16.

69. Jordan, "The Bombing of Baghdad," 51; Rukeyser, *The Collected Poems of Muriel Rukeyser*, 125, 445. Compare Gardinier, "On Muriel Rukeyser"; and Metres, *Behind the Lines*. On the relation between Rukeyser and Rich, see Huber, "Muriel Rukeyser 'Among Wars' "; Gwiazda, " 'Nothing Else Left to Read.' "

70. Spahr, "Bernadette Mayer's *Sonnets*," 108–9.

71. I use the simplified text from Voigt, *Sappho et Alcaeus. Fragmenta*, 41–43, without recently suggested emendations, out of concern for provenance. Moreover, it is possible that Spahr, like other contemporary lyric poets, became familiar with fragment 16 through Anne Carson's translation of that text in *If Not, Winter*; Spahr cites another work of Carson's in her article about Bernadette Mayer.

72. Voigt, *Sappho et Alcaeus*, 43; Carson, *If Not, Winter*, 28.

73. Spahr, "Bernadette Mayer's *Sonnets*," 108.

74. Power, "Sappho's Parachoral Monody," 92.

75. Kurke, "The Value of Chorality in Ancient Greece," 224, 227–31; Weiss, "Ancient Greek *Choreia*," 161–62.

76. Kurke, "The Value of Chorality in Ancient Greece," 226; Olsen, "Sappho's Kinesthetic Turn," 291.

77. Kurke, "Sappho and Genre," 98–99.

78. Voyce et al., "Poetry and Other Antagonisms." Compare Altieri, "The Place of Rhetoric in Contemporary American Poetics."

79. For one such dismissal framed in counterpoint to Language poetry, see Brill, "The Radical Syntactical Forms of Language Poetry."

80. Gelpi, "The Transfiguration of the Body," 8: "The size and range of Rich's readership indicates that her strategy is . . . at least more successfully radical than that of Language poets such as Ron Silliman or Charles Bernstein. For where the Language poets have marginalized themselves into an avant-garde elite with a small academic audience, Rich has written herself from the margins to the center without capitulating to the values of the dominant culture."

81. Demeyer and Vitse, "The Affective Dominant: Affective Crisis and Contemporary Fiction," 546: "The prevailing questions are 'How can I feel reality (myself, the other, the past, the present, etc.)?'; 'How can I feel to belong to reality?'; and 'How can I feel reality to be real?' The affective dominant manifests itself in motifs as desire, attachment, fantasy, embodiment, and identification. Formal and narrative devices that in modernist or postmodernist fiction contributed to an epistemological or ontological dominant tend to foreground questions of affectivity in contemporary fiction."

82. Jacobs, "Adrienne Rich's Countermonument," 727.

83. Rich, *An Atlas of the Difficult World,* 12.

84. Waldman, "Adrienne Rich on *Tonight No Poetry Will Serve.*"

85. A similar dynamic can be observed in Rich's book-length essay *Poetry and Commitment.* Commenting on "My verse works," a line of poetry by the South African author-activist Dennis Brutus, Rich identifies the two valences of the verb "work" in relation to writing poetry: "meaning as participant in political struggle, and at the personal, visceral level, where it's received and its witness acknowledged"; Rich, *Poetry and Commitment,* 23.

86. Weil, quoted in Rich, *Tonight No Poetry Will Serve,* 83.

87. Rich here follows Lattimore's translation in rendering μάχης ἀπάνευθεν ἐόντες (*Iliad* 17.426) as "turning away".

88. Burden, *The Other Vietnam Memorial* (1991, Museum of Contemporary Art, Chicago); see also Burden, drawing of *The Other Vietnam Memorial* (1991, Museum of Modern Art, New York City). In "Living Memory," from the collection *Time's Power,* Rich praises Lin's memorial as "the granite bulkhead / incised with names / . . . made / by the living, for the living." A scene in Section XI of "Atlas of the Difficult World" reappropriates the word "patriot" from the missiles bearing that name in the First Gulf War and applies it to the person "wrestl[ing] for the soul of the[ir] country as [they] wrestle for the soul of [their] being" and "trying to . . . remember [their suffering] land." This wrestling could occur as the patriot gazes from Tséghádoodzání (Window Rock), a natural monument in Navajo Nation, to the "sheen of the Viet Nam Wall." This section of "Atlas" seeks, as Lin's memorial did for the Vietnam era, to prioritize "our connection to place and to each other" within the nation, and so values the memorial's reparative function.

89. *The New York Times* published "Portraits of Grief" to commemorate the individual lives lost in the 9/11 attacks, first as a serial section in the newspaper and, subsequently, as a

book. For scholarship on those undocumented laborers "missing" from these portraits and the politics of memorialization here and in the official September 11 Museum and Memorial, see Edkins, *Missing,* 15–37. For coverage of these missing and unvalorized bodies in light of the twentieth anniversary of 9/11, see Garsd, "Families of Undocumented Immigrants Lost on 9/11 Continue to Search for Closure."

90. Juslin, *Unlocking the Secrets of Musical Affect,* 278–80, 282–85.

91. Ikoniadou, *The Rhythmic Event,* 71–76.

CHAPTER 2. OUT OF SYNC

1. National Centers for Environmental Information, "Costliest U.S. Tropical Cyclones," 2.

2. Freeman, "Synchronic/Anachronic," 138–39.

3. For a summary of the famous controversy involving Getty Images, the photo-sharing site Flickr, and captioning in the wake of Katrina, see Ralli, "Who's a Looter?" For a longer discussion of this incident in the context of the media, see Scheible, "Prepositioning Katrina Online," 203–5; 212–15.

4. Nixon, *Slow Violence and the Environmentalism of the Poor,* 2; Keeble, "Siblings, Kinship and Allegory in Jesmyn Ward's Fiction and Nonfiction," 41.

5. Nixon, *Slow Violence and the Environmentalism of the Poor,* 47.

6. Hartnell, "When Cars Become Churches," 205–18.

7. Compare Stevens, "Medea in Jesmyn Ward's *Salvage the Bones,*" 166–68, 172; Tulip, "Storytelling in Jesmyn Ward's *Salvage the Bones,*" 14. On Euripides's intervention in Medean myth, see Mastronarde, *Euripides:* Medea, 52.

8. Keeble, "Siblings, Kinship and Allegory in Jesmyn Ward's Fiction and Nonfiction," 42–43.

9. Keeble, *Narratives of Hurricane Katrina in Context,* 22–24; compare de Waal, "An Imperfect Storm."

10. Mastronarde, *Euripides:* Medea, 45.

11. Haley, "Self-Definition, Community, and Resistance," 179: Mastronarde, *Euripides:* Medea, 50–52.

12. Compare Wright, "Making Medea Medea."

13. Mastronarde, *Euripides:* Medea, 47.

14. Compare Aristotle, *Poetics* 1449b.

15. Klooster, "Apollonius of Rhodes," 86-88. Compare Mori, *The Politics of Apollonius Rhodius' Argonautica,* 49.

16. Mori, *The Politics of Apollonius Rhodius' Argonautica,* 216–17.

17. Boyle, *Seneca* Medea, lxxxii–lxxxvi.

18. See also Manuwald, "Medea: Transformations of a Greek Figure in Latin Literature," 117.

19. In his edition of the *Tristia*, Hall chooses *tenendus* in place of *morandus*; the sense remains the same.

20. Curtis, "Explaining Exile," 428–29.

21. Feeney, *Caesar's Calendar*, 211.

22. Curtis, "Explaining Exile," 430, citing Schubert, "Zu Ovid, *Trist.* 3.9," 161.

23. Oliensis, "Return to Sender," 189.

24. Boyle, *Seneca* Medea, lxxxvi.

25. Walsh, "The Metamorphoses of Seneca's *Medea*," 75.

26. Boyle, *Seneca* Medea, lxxxii; Walsh, "The Metamorphoses of Seneca's *Medea*."

27. Trinacty, "*Imago Res Mortua Est*," 22–23.

28. For more on the relationship between the verbs Medea and Jason use, *largire* vs. *dona*, see Boyle, *Seneca* Medea, n. 1015.

29. Mastronarde, *Euripides*: Medea, n. 1396.

30. Rimell, "The Labour of Empire," 214–21.

31. Rimell, "The Labour of Empire," 227, 231–33.

32. Rimell, "The Labour of Empire," 216.

33. On the tension between a universalized calendar and imperial subjectivization, see Feeney, *Caesar's Calendar,* especially 210–11.

34. Compare Phaethon's failure at Ovid, *Metamorphoses* 2.540–58; Medea here also refers to the yoke binding the serpents' scaly necks (*squamosa colla serpentes iugo*) to her chariots, recalling the term for spouse (*coniugem*). Rather than she herself being yoked, the serpents have submitted to her power. Her word choice might reflect the transformation that she has undergone from instrument of Jason's quest (his view) or even partner in that quest (her former view) to the helmswoman of a journey all her own. Identifying the dragons by their scales, a trait they share with fish, encourages Jason to reinstall her in the narratives involving the *Argo* and sea travel.

35. Compare Walsh, "The Metamorphoses of Seneca's *Medea*," 77, 87.

36. Walsh, "The Metamorphoses of Seneca's *Medea*," 71–73.

37. Barbour, "Remarks of Governor Haley Barbour to a Special Session of the Mississippi Legislature."

38. Schmidt, "Down around Biloxi," 135–37.

39. Sturken, "Weather Media and Homeland Security: Selling Preparedness in a Volatile World."

40. Babington, "Some GOP Legislators Hit Jarring Notes in Addressing Katrina."

41. Rumsfeld, Department of Defense News Briefing.

42. Sturken, "Weather Media and Homeland Security."

43. Fitzgerald and Clark, "Remembering A. J. Holloway"; Myers, " 'Looks like Hiroshima.' " Quoted by Garman, Prepared Statement.

44. Musquelier, "Why Katrina's Victims Aren't Refugees," 735–43.

45. Babington, "Some GOP Legislators Hit Jarring Notes in Addressing Katrina"; Hartnell, "Domesticating Katrina," 244–59.

46. Hartnell, *After Katrina,* 15, 71.

47. Dao, "The Vietnamese in Mississippi," 269–73; Yoosun et al., "Everything Has Changed," 106; Schmidt, "Down around Biloxi," 132–33.

48. Eckstein, *Sustaining New Orleans,* 211–14.

49. See Hartnell, "Katrina Tourism and a Tale of Two Cities."

50. Bibler, "Always the Tragic Jezebel," 23.

51. Trethewey, "Our Loss, Through the Eye of the Storm"; compare Schmidt, "Down around Biloxi," 135–40.

52. McAlister, "Domesticating Citizenship," 84–104.

53. Kelman, *A River and Its City*, 6.

54. On the racialized politics of dog-fighting and athletes, see Boisseron, *Afro-Dog*, especially 41–48 .

55. Epstein, Blake, and González, "Girlhood Interrupted," 4–6.

56. Keeble, "Siblings, Kinship and Allegory in Jesmyn Ward's Fiction and Nonfiction," 45.

57. Klooster, "Apollonius of Rhodes," 86–88.

58. See Mackie, "What's in a Name?", on heroism and Jason's relationship to healing.

59. Leonie, the protagonist of Ward's 2017 novel set in Bois Sauvage, *Sing, Unburied, Sing*, sees Esch and Skeetah walking with a black dog down the street "in sync, both of them bouncing."

60. Hamilton, *Mythology*, 178.

61. https://think100climate.com/katrina.

62. https://www.facebook.com/eeechogulfcoast/; https://www.pewtrusts.org/en/research-and-analysis/articles/2023/06/15/on-mississippis-gulf-coast-a-local-advocate-works-to-protect-underserved-communities-and-wetlands; https://taproot.earth/.

63. Costley, "15 Years after Katrina, a Fight against 'the Jim Crow of Climate Change' Rages on in the Gulf Coast."

64. Hamilton, *Mythology*, 7–11, 18.

65. Murnaghan, "Myths of the Greeks," 83–85.

66. Hamilton, *Mythology*, 9; Hamilton, *The Greek Way*, 14–15, 17.

67. Franklin Delano Roosevelt, "Four Freedoms."

68. Borgwardt, *A New Deal for the World*, 50–53.

69. Roosevelt, "Message to the Conference on Economic Conditions of the South"; Bibler, "Always the Tragic Jezebel," 14–16; Wright, "The New Deal and the Modernization of the South," 70–73.

70. Hamilton, *The Greek Way*, 15.

CHAPTER 3. HOME, LAND, FUTURITY

1. Hartman, *Scenes of Subjection*, 1-10, especially 7; Parks, *The America Play and Other Works*, 12: Parks prefers terms like "figure," "ghost," and "player" rather than "characters."

2. This chapter contains substantial, but revised portions of "Medals and Metals: Speculating Freedom in Suzan-Lori Parks's *Father Comes Home from the Wars*" and "Metal and Mettle: Odyssean Elements of the Racialized Body and Oddsee's Hybridity in Suzan-Lori Parks' *Father Comes Home from the Wars* (Parts 1, 2 & 3) (2015)." "Medals and Metals: Speculating Freedom in Suzan-Lori Parks's *Father Comes Home from the Wars*" first appeared in *Modern Drama* 64, no. 1 (Spring 2021): 24–46. Portions of "Medals and Metals" have been reprinted with permission of University of Toronto Press. "Metal and Mettle: Odyssean Elements of the Racialized Body and Oddsee's Hybridity in Suzan-Lori Parks' *Father Comes Home from the Wars* (Parts 1, 2 & 3) (2015)" first appeared in *American Journal of Philology* 143, no. 4 (Winter 2022): 539–66.

3. Each syncopation of Odyssey Dog to Oddsee "reps and revs" the dog's name. Signifying this way emphasizes performativity over speech as regulated communication and privileges sound over sight in a manner befitting Argos's sense perception and the play's critique of literacy.

4. Hartman, *Scenes of Subjection,* 19.

5. Harrison, "An Arrested Development," 33, 38. On this response to aspects of *Venus,* see Catanese, "Remembering Saartjie Baartman," 47–62.

6. Eccleston, "Mettle and Metals," 546–54.

7. Kolin, *Suzan-Lori Parks,* 189.

8. Nájera, "Creating Roads"; compare Brown, "Suzan-Lori Parks."

9. Kolin, *Essays,* 189.

10. For example, Parks, *The America Play and Other Works,* 189.

11. Parks, "Tradition and the Individual Talent," 27–29.

12. Norris, "Suzan-Lori Parks' New Play."

13. Parks, *The America Play and Other Works,* 6–18; Gates, *The Signifying Monkey,* 20–21.

14. Parks, *The America Play and Other Works,* 8.

15. Saal, "Of Diggin' and Fakin'," 69.

16. Compare Reed, *Freedom Time,* 156–63; Frieze, "Imperceptible Mutabilities in the Third Kingdom," 523–32.

17. Persuading Black men to volunteer for service in the Union Army in an 1863 speech, Douglass envisioned how "with one courageous resolution we may blot out the handwriting of the ages against us. Once let the black man get upon his person the brass letters U. S.; let him get an eagle on his button, and a musket on his shoulder, and bullets in his pocket, and there is no power on the earth or under the earth which can deny that he has earned the right of citizenship in the United States. I say again, this is our chance, and woe betide us if we fail to embrace it." His position will change as he realizes the entrenchment of anti-Black thought in social and political life. "Address for the Promotion of Colored Enlistments," 598.

18. Garrett-Scott et al., " 'When Peace Come,' " 19–25; Biden, "Remarks by President Biden at Signing of the Juneteenth National Independence Day Act." Biden's statement also mentions the goal of increasing Black homeownership as a route to minimizing racial discrepancies in generational wealth.

19. Reidy, *Illusions of Emancipation,* 339; Edwards, "The Homestead Act and the Struggle for African American Rights," 177, 189–91.

20. Edwards, "African Americans and the Southern Homestead Act," 107–8, 115.

21. O'Malley, "Specie and Species," 377; O' Malley, *Face Value,* 4, 2, 15.

22. O'Malley, *Face Value,* 4.

23. Hill, *Reimagining Equality,* 15–16.

24. O'Malley, *Face Value,* 213.

25. Nyong'o, "No Halvsies!" 464; Medford, *Lincoln and Emancipation,* 111.

26. Taylor, *Race for Profit,* 1.

27. Wyly, "The Subprime State of Race," 381; Hill, *Reimagining Equality,* 165–67, 181–85. For an in-depth study of how African American women were excluded from and or extorted

by traditional banking institutions during Reconstruction and afterwards, see Garrett-Scott, *Banking on Freedom*; Haiven, *Cultures of Financialization*, 171.

28. Eccleston, "Enemies, Foreign and Domestic," 172–73; Kaplan, "Homeland Insecurities," 86.

29. Hill, *Reimagining Equality*, 5–7; Berlant, *Cruel Optimism*, 1; Kamin, "Discrimination Seeps into Every Aspect of Home Buying for Black Americans."

30. Bahng, *Migrant Futures*, 21; Haiven, *Cultures of Financialization*, 5; Nilges, "The Realism of Speculation," 50.

31. Parks, *The America Play and Other Works*, 15–16.

32. Compare Reed, *Freedom Time*, 160.

33. Goldhill, "Idealism in the *Odyssey* and the Meaning of *Mounos* in *Odyssey* 16," 116–17.

34. Goldhill, *The Poet's Voice*, 20.

35. "Eupeithes led *the fools* (νηπιέῃσι), intending to avenge the death of his son. He wasn't fated to *make his way back home* (ἀπονοστήσειν) again—but to meet his death instead" (*Od.* 24.469–71). Compare "For the *fools* (νήπιοι) died because of their own recklessness—the ones who ate the cattle that belonged to the god Helios; he robbed them of their day of *homecoming*" (νόστιμον, 1.7–9).

36. Morris, "The Use and Abuse of Homer," 116-120, 126-129.

37. Post-Homeric tales about Telegonus, one of Odysseus's sons with Circe, complicate this picture of patrilineal descent and once again challenge the borders of the poem. For more on Telegonus and other heroes' sons, see Sammons, "The Space of the Epigone in Early Greek Epic." For more on Telegonus's disruption of the text's perceived unity, see Purves, *Space and Time in Ancient Greek Narrative*, 87.

38. Compare Scodel, "The Suitors' Games."

39. de Jong, *A Narratological Commentary on the Odyssey*, 421; compare Mueller, "Recognition and the Forgotten Senses in the *Odyssey*," 1–20.

40. Franco, *Shameless*, 37, 41, 123. Compare Fulkerson, "Epic Ways of Killing a Woman," 344-47: Telemachus' murder of the disobedient, conspicuously mobile, and sexually active enslaved women covers up any suspicion of disloyalty and weakness in his parents' marriage.

41. de Jong, *A Narratological Commentary*, 422.

42. Martin, "Telemachus and the Last Hero Song," 239–40; Purves, *Space and Time in Ancient Greek Narrative*, 80.

43. Dougherty, *The Raft of Odysseus*, 5, 14–16.

44. Compare Silvermintz, "Unravelling the Shroud for Laertes and Weaving the Fabric of the City," 38–42; Kurke, *Coins, Bodies, Games, and Gold*, 11–23.

45. Compare Douglass, *Selected Speeches and Writings*, 615–16.

46. Baynton, "Disability and the Justification of Inequality in American History," 33–57.

47. Compare Franklin and Schweninger, *Runaway Slaves*, 103-09, 164.

48. Compare O'Malley, *Face Value*, 15.

49. Boisseron, *Afro-Dog*, 23. Compare Frederick Douglass's discussion of men of the Union functioning as slave watchdogs in order to emphasize the necessity of abolition: "The Mission of the War," in Douglass, Foner, and Taylor, *Selected Speeches and Writings*, 627.

50. See Hunter, *Bound in Wedlock*, 7.

51. Berlin, Reidy, and Rowland, *Freedom's Soldiers*, 25n44.

52. Nyong'o, *The Amalgamation Waltz*, 7.

53. Rankine, *Ulysses in Black*, 43–50.

54. Barrett, *Blackness and Value*, 55–93.

55. O'Malley, *Face Value*, 15.

56. An anecdote about Ulysses Grant hiding like a "fox in a hen house" (90–91) relates him to Odysseus while in the Cyclops's cave attempting to save his crewmates. It anticipates the ruse on the battlefield that saved Smith's life and Hero's own donning of the jacket at the end of Part 2. It could also be inverted with Hero's internalization of Boss-Master's model for his postemancipation life. Odysseus's dedication to his crew and his return without them will be significant for how Parks chooses to end the play.

57. Reidy, *Illusions of Emancipation*, 53-57.

58. On the discrepancy in payment between white and Black soldiers in the Union, see Berlin, Reidy, and Rowland, *Freedom's Soldiers*, 2; "Address for the Promotion of Colored Enlistments," in Douglass, *Selected Speeches and Writings*, 595–600.

59. Compare Douglass's sentiments in "Men of Color, to Arms!" to those in his letter of August 1, 1865; Douglass, *Selected Speeches and Writings*, 585–88 and 601–2.

60. Smith's name is so generic that it functions as the equivalent of Odysseus's anonymizing pseudonym, "nobody," and an allusion to the discourse of metal running throughout the play and the *Odyssey*: Smith is a Black private passing as a white officer that advocates for self-making as metalworking and thus plays the role of a Black Smith and a blacksmith in this scene.

61. Fagles translates this passage using the same metal imagery: "If they abuse me in the palace, steel yourself / no matter what outrage I must suffer" (*Odyssey*, 347). This might be coincidental, as Parks claims regarding the names Penny and Homer, but seems more likely to be a case of indirect transmission.

62. In the *Odyssey*, characters frequently refer to a heart made of iron to talk about the ability to tolerate more than one should, and therefore it can also signal a lack of human(izing) compassion (*Od.* 4.292, 5.190, 23.172). If within the Homeric discourse of metals, iron looks just beyond human capacity, then choosing an iron alloy to effect hybridization here can dislocate humanity as the ultimate aim of Black aspiration. Since Black people are *already human*, aspiring for the recognition of what you already are reinscribes the validity of one's own denigration.

63. Goldhill, "Idealism," 127.

64. Mueller, "Recognition and the Forgotten Senses," 20.

65. Sullivan, *A Critical Introduction to Queer Theory*, 88.

66. Parks, *The America Play and Other Works*, 132.

67. Ahmed, *The Cultural Politics of Emotion*, 12.

68. Rankine, *Aristotle and Black Drama*, 71.

69. The spade has at least three other intertexts: (1) the racist slur for a Black person; (2) Lorraine Hansberry's *A Raisin in the Sun;* and (3) *Odyssey* 24 when Odysseus finds Laertes working in the orchard that forms part of Odysseus's patrimony.

70. Barrett, *Blackness and Value*, 110–11.

71. Compare Parks, *Venus*, 10, 15.

72. Compare Nyong'o, "No Halvsies!" 464.

73. Edelman, *No Future*, 6.

74. Nyong'o, *The Amalgamation Waltz*, 6–7.

75. In an 1863 speech, "Our Work is not Done," Frederick Douglass enjoins, with reference to Lincoln and the continued need for Black enlistment as part and parcel of abolition and the re-creation of the nation: "We are not to be saved by the captain, at this time, but by the crew." Douglass, *Selected Speeches and Writings*, 6.

76. Lawson, "Interview: Suzan-Lori Parks." Compare Medford, *Lincoln and Emancipation*, 111-112.

77. Nyong'o, *The Amalgamation Waltz*, 5.

CHAPTER 4. AFTERWARDS

1. Schwartz, "Review of *Night Sky with Exit Wounds* by Ocean Vuong," 647–51.

2. Hirsch, *The Generation of Postmemory*, 8. Coined in the context of Holocaust studies to account for trans- and intergenerational trauma, Hirsch understands the prefix "post" to refer to both to the phenomenon's "belatedness" and its supplementary nature in relation to the more readily recognized trauma of firsthand experience.

3. Kapp, "Of Stone and Steel: The Story behind the 9/11 Memorial."

4. Lin, "Maya Lin on the Challenges and Triumphs of Designing the Vietnam Veterans Memorial"; Lin, "Making the Memorial," 33–35.

5. Sturken, *Tangled Memories*, 47–56.

6. Obama, "Remarks by the President at Presentation of the Presidential Medal of Freedom."

7. Williams, *Marxism and Literature*, 133–34.

8. Reagan, "Peace: Restoring the Margin of Safety."

9. Herring, "The Vietnam Syndrome," 409–12.

10. Herring, "Reflecting the Last War," 38; Rowe, "The 'Vietnam Effect' in the Persian Gulf War," 124.

11. Schneider, "The Vietnam Syndrome Mutates"; Snepp,"The Vietnam Syndrome"; Kalb, "It's Called the Vietnam Syndrome, and It's Back."

12. Boyle, "Naturalizing War," 175–92.

13. Obama, "Presidential Proclamation."

14. The National Park Service, charged with maintaining the memorial complex, explicates: "The purpose of this memorial is to separate the issue of the sacrifices of the veterans from the U.S. policy in the war, thereby creating a venue for reconciliation." For a discussion of this tally and the politics surrounding it, see Hirschman, Preston, and Loi,"Vietnamese Casualties during the American War: A New Estimate."

15. On the tropes and "straitjackets" facing Vietnamese diasporic literature and other "ethnic literature" in the current literary marketplace, see Viet Thanh Nguyen, "What Is Vietnamese American Literature?" 50–63.

16. Fowler, "Mythos and Logos," 53; Martin, *The Language of Heroes*, 54.

17. Fowler, "Mythos and Logos," 45, 48, 65.

18. Ho, "Love, Cruelty, and Grace."

19. Goebel, "Vietnam Refugee, Restaurant Owner Thanks Veterans."

20. Espiritu, *Body Counts,* 12–16.

21. Espiritu, "The 'We-Win-Even-When-We-Lose' Syndrome," 329–52.

22. Espiritu, *Body Counts,* 99–100.

23. Nguyen, *The Gift of Freedom,* 31–38, 151.

24. Pham, "ICE Leadership." Compare Wang, "Interim ICE Director, a Vietnamese Refugee, Draws Fire from Asian Groups"; Aleaziz, "ICE's Controversial Leader Plans to Resign after Five Months on the Job."

25. Compare Nguyen, *The Gift of Freedom,* 170–73; Will, "Anh Duong, Out of Debt," 84.

26. Nguyen, *The Gift of Freedom,* 175; compare Blumenfeld, "Spurred by Gratitude, 'Bomb Lady' Develops Better Weapons for US."

27. Espiritu, *Body Counts,* 111–12.

28. Since 2010 the Costs of War Project (https://watson.brown.edu/costsofwar/) has been tracking and debating the wide, often unacknowledged variety of costs incurred by American warfare post-9/11.

29. Nguyen, *The Gift of Freedom,* 17.

30. Nguyen, *The Gift of Freedom,* 51–52.

31. Nguyen, *The Gift of Freedom,* x.

32. Espiritu, *Body Counts,* 112–15.

33. Logan, "Old Wounds."

34. Rekdal, "Wounded Elders."

35. Compare Sharpe, *In the Wake,* 11-18.

36. On Asian American queer men and their feminization in American culture, see, among others, Eng, *Racial Castration,* and Nguyen, *A View from the Bottom.*

37. Compare Sharpe, *In the Wake*, 14.

38. Gonzáles, "Be Bold: A Profile of Ocean Vuong."

39. Rekdal, "Wounded Elders."

40. Compare Nguyen, "Refugeetude," 113–14.

41. Rekdal, *Nightingale.*

42. Compare Liu, "Looking for Parnassus in America," 89: "In America, as an Asian American, I am among another things a model minority, an *eternal outsider.*"

43. Gonzales, "Be Bold."

44. Armitstead, "War Baby."

45. "To My Father / To My Future Son" duplicates this sense perception: "Do you understand? I closed my mouth / but could still taste the ash / because my eyes were open" (58).

46. Nguyen, "What Is Vietnamese American Literature?" 55–56: bilingualism and etymology is a familiar trope in Vietnamese-American literature.

47. Compare Jeon, *Racial Things, Racial Forms,* 110–14.

48. Goldhill, "Idealism," 117; Nguyen, "Queering Telemachus," 435–46.

49. Martin, "Telemachus and the Last Hero Song," 238–39; Eccleston, "Cyrus Console's *The Odicy* and Epic Ecology," 40.

50. Nguyen, "Queering Telemachus," 438–43.

51. Redfield, *Nature and Culture in the* Iliad, 174.

52. Nguyen, "Queering Telemachus," 442–43.

53. Nguyen, "Queering Telemachus," 443–44.

54. Jeon, *Racial Forms*, 112.

55. Liveley, "Orpheus and Eurydice," 292.

56. Rilke, "Orpheus. Eurydice. Hermes."

57. Another poem, "A Little Closer to the Edge," incorporates a detail closer to the myth, complementing the tone of "Eurydice." Describing a couple about to have sex in a bomb crater in a field, the narrator hints at violence to come in their relationship away from the tenderness of this moment (13). He first alludes to the domestic violence that will mar their relationship and then specifies: "In this version, the snake is headless—stilled / like a cord unraveled from the lovers' ankles." The snake that bit Eurydice after her wedding to Orpheus disrupted their romance—here the narrator acknowledges that he has introduced a variant to the story to make the snake less an animal and more an abstract force let loose over time. As the poem continues, the narrator begs for the euphoria and tenderness of the present moment to be protracted so that the violence will be postponed. This wish to delay the intrusion of violence recalls the words spoken by the American service member in "Aubade with Burning City" and the scenario found in "Odysseus Redux."

58. Because, in Ovid's narrative, birds feature prominently to describe Orpheus's power and then to describe the Maenads who will kill him (Ov. *Met.* 10.143–44, 11.20–28), their appearance in Vuong's poem shrouds the scene with danger. On the politics of aligning Orpheus with elegy instead of lyric, see Young, "Inscribing Orpheus." See Liveley, "Orpheus and Eurydice", on the politics of revision in the myth's reception.

59. In "The Smallest Measure," Vuong's narrator describes himself as a doe downrange from a father coaxing his son to take a shot. The narrator stays focused on the scene just long enough to catch the instant when the coaxing recedes and the father, observing that the boy is being overwhelmed, helps him lower his gun, a gesture that turns on the movements that separate predator from prey and violence from tenderness. Even though the smallest measure first refers to the doe's distance from the pair, by the end of the poem it also refers to the perceived distance between (or, more positively, the proximity of) these two types of relationships.

60. Nguyen, "Queering Telemachus," 445.

61. de Jong, *A Narratalogical Commentary on the* Odyssey, 562–63, note to 23.310–41.

62. "Afterward" heralds a similar reorientation via the poet's intervention in "Detonation": "There's a joke that ends with—huh? / It's the bomb saying here is your father. / Now here is your father inside / your lungs. Look how lighter / the earth is—afterward. / To even write father / is to carve a portion of the day / out of a bomb-bright page" (60).

63. Other details further suggest a connection between the two objects: in the box, the Colt .45 sits atop "yellowed newspaper"; in "Logophobia," the narrator writes "gia đình on this yellow pad."

64. In "On Earth We're Briefly Gorgeous," "Self-Portrait as Exit Wounds," and "Ode to Masturbation," Vuong also suggests a connection between guns and penises, likening the shooting of a firearm to ejaculation.

65. Hirsch, *The Generation of Postmemory*, 8.

66. Vietnam Veterans Memorial Fund, "Items at the Wall"; Vietnam Veterans Memorial, "Vietnam Veterans Memorial Collection."

67. See Curtis, "Stewarding a Living Collection."

68. The National Park Service forefronts the six categories it uses to organize the archive to demonstrate a measure of uniformity and authority, but the narrative also suggests that the archive is rather unwieldy. Available at: https://www.nps.gov/orgs/1802/vive.htm.

69. On the significance of black-and-white footage in light of the departure of the French imperial apparatus and the televised nature of the Vietnam War in America, see Nguyen, "Seeing Double"; Truong, "Explosions in the Sky (Điện Biên Phủ 1954)."

70. Nguyen, *The Gift of Freedom*, 187–88.

71. Nguyen, "Seeing Double." Compare Hong, "Reframing the Archive," 35.

72. Davis et al., "On the Center for Refugee Poetics," 104.

END TIMES, AN ENVOI

1. Rose, "Biopolitics, Essential Labor, and the Political-Economic Crises of COVID-19," 213–14; Suckert, "The Coronavirus and the Temporal Order of Capitalism," 1165–69; Wright et al., "Equalities in Freefall? Ontological Insecurity and the Long-term Impact of COVID-19 in the Academy," 163–66; Malisch et al., "In the Wake of COVID-19, Academia Needs New Solutions to Ensure Gender Equity"; Lorenzini, "Biopolitics in the Time of the Coronavirus," S42–44.

2. Centers for Disease Control and Prevention, "End of the Federal COVID-19 Public Health Emergency (PHE) Declaration."

3. Sharma, "Temporality," 194.

4. Compare 600 U.S. 20–1199, J. Thomas, concurring, 48; Florida State Legislature, Individual Freedom Act (HB 7), 4.

5. E.g., Bostick, "Not for All"; Dugan, "The 'Happy Slave' Narrative and Classics Pedagogy"; Churchill, "Is There a Woman in This Textbook?"

Bibliography

Adande, J. A. "It's Art, But It's Sure Not Arthur." *Los Angeles Times,* August 30, 2000.

Adey, Peter, Ben Anderson, and Stephen Graham. "Introduction: Governing Emergencies: Beyond Exceptionality." *Theory, Culture & Society* 32, no. 2 (2015): 3–17.

Adler, Ben. "Design after 9/11." *Architect Magazine.* September 1, 2011.

Ahmed, Sara. *The Cultural Politics of Emotion.* New York: Routledge, 2013.

Akram, Susan M. "The Aftermath of September 11, 2001: The Targeting of Arabs and Muslims in America." *Arab Studies Quarterly* 24, nos. 2–3 (2002): 61–118.

Albertson, Fred C. "Zenodorus's 'Colossus of Nero.' " *Memoirs of the American Academy in Rome* 6 (2001): 95–118.

Aleaziz, Hamed. "ICE's Controversial Leader Plans to Resign after Five Months on the Job." Buzzfeed News. December 10, 2020. https://www.buzzfeednews.com/article/hamedaleaziz/ices-leader-plans-to-resign.

Alexander, Caroline. "Out of Context," *New York Times*, April 6, 2011.

Allen, Thomas M. "Introduction." In *Time and Literature,* ed. Thomas M. Allen. Cambridge: Cambridge University Press, 2018.

Altieri, Charles. "The Place of Rhetoric in Contemporary American Poetics: Jennifer Moxley and Juliana Spahr." *Chicago Review* 56, nos. 2–3 (2011): 127–45.

Amoore, Louise. *The Politics of Possibility: Risk and Security beyond Probability.* Durham, NC: Duke University Press, 2013.

Anderson, Ben. "Emergency/Everyday." In *Time: A Vocabulary of the Present,* ed. Joel Burges and Amy Elias, 177–91. New York: NYU Press, 2016.

———. "Emergency Futures: Exception, Urgency, Interval, Hope." *Sociological Review* 65, no. 3 (2017): 463–77.

Antonio, Robert J., and Alessandro Bonanno. "A New Global Capitalism? From 'Americanism and Fordism' to 'Americanization-Globalization.' " *American Studies* 41, nos. 2–3 (2000): 33–77.

Armitstead, Claire. "War Baby: The Amazing Story of Ocean Vuong, Former Refugee and Prize-Winning Poet." *The Guardian,* October 3, 2017.

Arrington, Nathan T. *Ashes, Images, and Memories: The Presence of the War Dead in Fifth-Century Athens.* New York: Oxford University Press, 2015.

Associated Press. "After Complaints, Rockefeller Center Drapes Sept. 11 Statue." *New York Times,* September 19, 2002.

Auletta, Ken. "Battle Stations." *New Yorker,* December 10, 2001, 60–67.

Babington, Charles. "Some GOP Legislators Hit Jarring Notes in Addressing Katrina." *Washington Post,* September 10, 2005.

Bahng, Aimee. *Migrant Futures: Decolonizing Speculation in Financial Times.* Durham, NC: Duke University Press, 2018.

Balzer, David. "Eric Fischl Interviewed: Art's Bad Boy Looks Back." *Canadian Art,* September 28, 2015.

Barbour, Haley. "Remarks of Governor Haley Barbour to a Special Session of the Mississippi Legislature." September 28, 2005. https://da.mdah.ms.gov/series/governor/barbour/s2809/detail/256019.

Barnard, John Levi. *Empire of Ruin: Black Classicism and American Imperial Culture.* New York: Oxford University Press, 2018.

Barrett, Lindon. *Blackness and Value: Seeing Double.* Cambridge: Cambridge University Press, 1999.

Baym, Geoffrey. "Infotainment." In *The International Encyclopedia of Communication,* ed. W. Donsbach. New York: Wiley, 2008.

Baynton, Douglas C. "Disability and the Justification of Inequality in American History." In *The New Disability History: American Perspectives,* ed. Paul K. Longmore and Lauri Umansky, 33–57. New York: NYU Press, 2001.

Bear, Laura. "Doubt, Conflict, Mediation: The Anthropology of Modern Time." *Journal of the Royal Anthropological Institute* 20 (2014): 3–30.

———. "Time As Technique." *Annual Review of Anthropology* 45 (2016): 487–502.

Bellini, Federico. "Samuel Butler's *Life and Habit* and the Modernist Literary Character: Rethinking the Subject through the Everyday." *The Comparatist* 40 (2016): 111–27.

Berkow, Ira. "Sports of The Times; Bronze Guy Stands Tall Sans Towel."*New York Times,* September 7, 2001.

Berlant, Lauren. "Citizenship." In *Keywords for American Cultural Studies,* 2d ed., ed. Bruce Burgett and Glenn Hendler, 37–41. New York: New York University Press, 2020.

———. *Cruel Optimism.* Durham, NC: Duke University Press, 2011.

———. *The Female Complaint.* Durham, NC: Duke University Press, 2008.

———. *The Queen of America Goes to Washington City: Essays on Sex and Citizenship.* Durham, NC: Duke University Press, 1997.

Berlant, Lauren and Greenwald, Jordan. "Affect in the End Times: A Conversation with Lauren Berlant." *Qui Parle* 20, no. 2 (2012): 71–89.

Berlin, Ira, Joseph P. Reidy, and Leslie S. Rowland. *Freedom's Soldiers: The Black Military Experience in the Civil War*. Cambridge; Cambridge University Press, 1998.

Bibler, Michael P. "Always the Tragic Jezebel: New Orleans, Katrina, and the Layered Discourse of a Doomed Southern City." *Southern Cultures* 14, no. 2 (2008): 6–28.

Biden, Joseph R. "Remarks by President Biden at Signing of the Juneteenth National Independence Day Act." June 17, 2021. https://www.whitehouse.gov/briefing-room/speeches-remarks/2021/06/17/remarks-by-president-biden-at-signing-of-the-juneteenth-national-independence-day-act/.

Bird, S. Elizabeth. "Converging into Irrelevance? Supermarket Tabloids in the Post-9/11 World." In *Journalism after September 11,* ed. Barbie Zelizer and Stuart Allan), 191–211. 2d ed. New York: Routledge, 2011 .

Blumenfeld, Laura. "Spurred by Gratitude, 'Bomb Lady' Develops Better Weapons for US." *Washington Post,* December 1, 2007.

Boisseron, Bénédicte. *Afro-Dog: Blackness and the Animal Question.* New York: Columbia University Press, 2018.

Borgwardt, Elizabeth. *A New Deal for the World: America's Vision for Human Rights.* Cambridge, MA: Harvard University Press, 2007.

Bostick, Dani. "Not for All: Nostalgic Distortions as a Weapon of Segregation in Secondary Classics." *American Journal of Philology* 141, no. 2 (2020): 283–306.

Boyle, A. J. *Seneca* Medea. Oxford: Oxford University Press, 2014.

Boyle, Brenda. "Naturalizing War: The Stories We Tell about the Vietnam War." In *Looking Back on the Vietnam War: Twenty-first-Century Perspectives,* ed. Brenda M. Boyle and Lim Jeehyun, 175–92. New Brunswick, NJ: Rutgers University Press, 2016.

Boyle, Brenda M., and Lim Jeehyun, eds. *Looking Back on the Vietnam War: Twenty-first-Century Perspectives.* New Brunswick, NJ: Rutgers University Press, 2016.

Bray, Patrick M. "Aesthetics in the Shadow of No Towers: Reading Virilio in the Twenty-First Century." *Yale French Studies* 114 (2008): 4–17.

Brill, Susan B. "The Radical Syntactical Forms of Language Poetry." *South Central Review* 7, no. 2 (1990): 54–65.

Brockill, Gillian. "She Was the Only Member of Congress to Vote against War in Afghanistan. Some Called Her a Traitor." *Washington Post,* August 17, 2021.

Brokaw, Tom. "Two Dates Which Will Live in Infamy." Op-ed. *San Diego Union-Tribune,* December 7, 2001.

Brown, Sterling K. "Suzan-Lori Parks." In "The 100 Most Influential People of 2023." *Time,* April 13, 2023.

Burke, Tarana. *Unbound: My Story of Liberation and the Birth of the Me-Too Movement.* New York: Flatiron, 2021.

Busch, Andreas. "The Changing Architecture of the National Security State." In *The Oxford Handbook of Transformations of the State,* ed. Stephan Leibfried et al., 547–64. Oxford: Oxford University Press, 2015.

Bush, George W. "President Bush Delivers Graduation Speech at West Point United States Military Academy." June 1, 2002. https://georgewbush-whitehouse.archives.gov/news/releases/ 2002/06/20020601-3.html.

———. "Presidential Address to the Nation." October 7, 2001. https://georgewbush-whitehouse.archives.gov/news/releases/2001/10/20011007-8.html.

———. "President's Remarks at National Day of Prayer and Remembrance." September 14, 2001. https://georgewbush-whitehouse.archives.gov/news/releases/2001/09/print/20010914-2.html.

———. "A Proclamation, National Day of Prayer and Remembrance for the Victims of the Terrorist Attacks on September 11, 2001." September 13, 2001. https://georgewbush-whitehouse.archives.gov/news/releases/2001/09/20010913-7.html.

———. "Statement by the President in His Address to the Nation." September 11, 2001. https://georgewbush-whitehouse.archives.gov/news/releases/2001/09/20010911-16.html.

Butts, Jodi, and Eric Fischl. "@Risk: Risk for Art's and America's Sake." November 2020. https://soundcloud.com/canada2020/risk-for-arts-and-americas-sake.

Byre, Calvin S. "The Killing of Apsyrtus in Apollonius Rhodius' *Argonautica*" *Phoenix* 50, no. 1 (1996): 3–16.

Carey, James W. "American Journalism on, before, and after September 11." In *Journalism after September* 11, ed. Barbie Zelizer and Stuart Allan, 85–103. London: Routledge, 2002.

Carson Anne. *If Not, Winter: Fragments of Sappho.* New York: Knopf, 2009.

Carter, Bill. "ABC to End 'Politically Incorrect.' " *New York Times,* May 14, 2002.

Catanese, Brandi Wilkins. "Remembering Saartjie Baartman." *Atlantic Studies* 7, no. 1 (2010): 47–62.

Chakrabarty, Dipesh. *Provincializing Europe: Postcolonial Thought and Historical Difference.* Princeton: Princeton University Press, 2000.

Centers for Disease Control and Prevention. "End of the Federal COVID-19 Public Health Emergency (PHE) Declaration." May 5, 2023. https://www.cdc.gov/coronavirus/2019-ncov/your-health/end-of-phe.html.

———. *Health Effects of 9/11: An Online Exhibition.* World Trade Center Health Program. https://www.cdc.gov/wtc/exhibition/.

Churchill, Laurie J. "Is There a Woman in This Textbook? Feminist Pedagogy and Elementary Latin." In *When Dead Tongues Speak: Teaching Beginning Greek and Latin,* ed. John Gruber-Miller, 86–109. Oxford: Oxford University Press, 2006.

Cite Black Women Collective. "Cite Black Women: A Critical Praxis." https://www.citeblackwomencollective.org/our-praxis.html. December 21, 2018.

Conner, Robert E., Sr., and Robert E. Conner Jr. "Review: *The Greatest Generation* by Tom Brokaw." *Armed Forces & Society* 26, no. 2 (2000): 335–37.

Cosgrove-Mather, Bootie. "Commercial Free 9/11 TV Coverage." *CBS News,* July 31, 2002. https://www.cbsnews.com/news/commercial-free-9-11-tv-coverage/.

Costley, Drew. "15 Years after Katrina, a Fight against 'the Jim Crow of Climate Change' Rages on in the Gulf Coast." Black in the Time of Climate Change. One Zero. January 15, 2020. https://onezero.medium.com/15-years-after-katrina-a-fight-against-the-jim-crow-of-climate-change-rages-on-in-the-gulf-coast-d2690bc1cbab.

Culler, Jonathan. *Theory of the Lyric.* Cambridge, MA: Harvard University Press, 2015.

Curtis, Lauren. "Explaining Exile: The Aetiological Poetics of Ovid, *Tristia* 3." *TAPA* 145, no. 2 (2015): 411–44.

Curtis, Paulette G. "Stewarding a Living Collection: The National Park Service and the Vietnam Veterans Memorial Collection." *Museum Anthropology* 33 (2010): 49–61.

Dao, Vy Thuc. "The Vietnamese in Mississippi." In *Ethnic Heritage in Mississippi: The Twentieth Century,* ed. Shana Walton and Barbara Carpenter, 263–81. Jackson: University Press of Mississippi and Mississippi Humanities Council, 2012.

Davis, Lawrence-Minh Bùi, Cathy J. Schlund-Vials, Ocean Vuong, Lan Duong, Monica Sok, and Catzie Vilayphonh. "On the Center for Refugee Poetics." *Verge: Studies in Global Asias* 6, no. 1 (2020): 103–17.

Demeyer, Hans, and Sven Vitse. "The Affective Dominant: Affective Crisis and Contemporary Fiction." *Poetics Today* 42, no. 4 (2021): 541–74.

Doss, Erika. *Memorial Mania: Public Feeling in America.* Chicago: University of Chicago Press, 2010.

Dougherty, Carol. *The Raft of Odysseus: The Ethnographic Imagination of Homer's* Odyssey. New York: Oxford University Press, 2001.

Douglass, Frederick. " 'What to the Slave Is the Fourth of July?' An Address Delivered in Rochester, New York, 5 July 1852." In *The Speeches of Frederick Douglass: A Critical Edition,* ed. John R. McKivigan and Julie Husband, 55–92. New Haven: Yale University Press, 2018.

Douglass, Frederick, edited by Philip Sheldon Foner and Yuval Taylor. *Frederick Douglass: Selected Speeches and Writings*. 1st ed. Chicago: Lawrence Hill Books, 2000.

Dower, J. W. *Cultures of War: Pearl Harbor, Hiroshima, 9-11, Iraq*. New York: W. W. Norton, 2010.

Dugan, Kelly P. "The 'Happy Slave' Narrative and Classics Pedagogy: A Verbal and Visual Analysis of Beginning Greek and Latin Textbooks." *New England Classical Journal* 46, no. 1 (2019): 62–87.

Dunlap, David. "A Memorial Inscription's Grim Origins," *New York Times*, April 3, 2014.

———. "Scholarly Perspectives on Inscription at the 9/11 Memorial Museum." *New York Times* City Room Blog, April 2, 2014. https://nyti.ms/2jEuOVE.

Dunmire, P. L. *Projecting the Future through Political Discourse: The Case of the Bush Doctrine*. Philadelphia: John Benjamins, 2011.

Dwyer, Eugene. "The First Plaster Casts of the Pompeian Victims." In *Sculpture and Archaeology*, ed. Paul Bonaventura and Andrew Jones, 45–60. Farnham, Surrey, UK: Ashgate, 2011.

———. *Pompeii's Living Statues*. Ann Arbor: University of Michigan Press, 2011.

Eccleston, Sasha-Mae. "Cyrus Console's *The Odicy* and Epic Ecology." *Classical Receptions Journal* 11, no. 1 (2019): 23–43.

———. "Enemies, Foreign and Domestic: Villainy and Terrorism in *Thor*." In *Assembling the Marvel Cinematic Universe: Essays on the Social, Cultural and Geopolitical Domains*, ed. Julian Chambliss and William Svitavitsky, 168–84. Jefferson, NC: McFarland, 2018.

———. "Medals and Metals: Speculating Freedom in Suzan-Lori Parks' *Father Comes Home from the Wars*" (Parts 1, 2,& 3) (2015)." Modern Drama 64, no. 1 (2021): 24–46.

———. "Metal and Mettle: Odyssean Elements of the Racialized Body and Oddsee's Hybridity in Suzan-Lori Parks' *Father Comes Home from the Wars* (Parts 1, 2 & 3) (2015)." *American Journal of Philology* 143, no. 4 (2022): 539–66.

Eccleston, Sasha-Mae, and Dan-El Padilla Peralta. "Racing the Classics: Ethos and Praxis." *American Journal of Philology* 143, no. 2 (2022): 199–218.

Eckstein, Barbara J. *Sustaining New Orleans: Literature, Local Memory, and the Fate of a City*. New York: Routledge, 2006.

Edelman, Lee. *No Future: Queer Theory and the Death Drive*. Durham, NC: Duke University Press, 2004.

Edkins, Jenny. *Missing: Persons and Politics*. Ithaca, NY: Cornell University Press, 2011.

Edwards, Richard. "African Americans and the Southern Homestead Act." *Great Plains Quarterly* 39, no.2 (2019): 105–18.

———. "The Homestead Act and the Struggle for African American Rights." *Great Plains Quarterly* 41, nos. 3–4 (2021): 175–94.

Eidinow, Esther, and Lisa Maurizio. "Introduction." In *Narratives of Time and Gender in Antiquity*, ed. Esther Eidinow and Lisa Maurizio, 1–12. Abingdon, UK: Routledge, 2020

Eng, David L. *Racial Castration: Managing Masculinity in Asian America*. Durham, NC: Duke University Press, 2001.

Epstein, Rebecca, Jamilia Blake, and Thalia González. "Girlhood Interrupted: The Erasure of Black Girls' Childhood." Center on Poverty and Inequality, Georgetown Law School. June 27, 2017. https://ssrn.com/abstract=3000695.

Ericson, Richard V. "The State of Preemption: Managing Terrorism through Counter Law." In *Risk and the War on Terror,* ed. Louise Amoore and Marieke de Goede, 73–92. New York: Routledge, 2007.

Espiritu, Yen Le. *Body Counts: The Vietnam War and Militarized Refugees.* Berkeley: University of California Press, 2014.

———. "The 'We-Win-Even-When-We-Lose' Syndrome: U.S. Press Coverage of the Twenty-Fifth Anniversary of the 'Fall of Saigon.'" *American Quarterly* 58, no. 2 (2006): 329–52.

Fabian, Johannes. *Time and the Other.* New York: Columbia University Press, 1983.

Fagles, Robert, trans. *Homer:* The Odyssey. New York: Viking, 1996.

Fasolt, Constantin. "Breaking Up Time—Escaping from Time: Self-Assertion and Knowledge of the Past." In *Breaking Up Time: Negotiating the Borders between Present, Past and Future,* ed. Chris Lorenz and Berber Bevernage, 176–96. Göttingen: Vandenhoeck & Ruprecht, 2013.

Feeney, Denis. *Caesar's Calendar: Ancient Time and the Beginnings of History.* Berkeley: University of California Press, 2007.

———. "Time." In *The Cambridge Companion to the Roman Historians,* ed. Andrew Feldherr, 139–51. Cambridge: Cambridge University Press, 2009.

Ferguson, Niall. "The Unconscious Colossus: Limits of (& Alternatives to) American Empire." *Daedalus* 134, no. 2 (2005): 18–33.

Feyeric, Deborah. "Nude 'Ashe' Raises Racket at U.S. Open." *Los Angeles Times,* September 9, 2000.

Fischer, Mia. "Commemorating 9/11 NFL-style: Insights into America's Culture of Militarism." *Journal of Sport and Social Issues* 38, no. 3 (2014): 199–221.

Fischl, Eric, and A. M. Homes. "BombLive!" October 26, 2005. https://bombmagazine.org/articles/eric-fischl-1/.

Fitzgerald, Robert, and Jeff Clark. "Remembering A. J. Holloway, the Mayor Who Made History and Got Biloxi through 'Our Tsunami.'" *Sun Herald,* June 5, 2018.

Florida State Legislature. Individual Freedom Act (HB 7). April 2, 2022. https://www.flsenate.gov/Session/Bill/2022/7/BillText/er/PDF.

Fortier, Anne-Marie. "Afterword: Acts of Affective Citizenship? Possibilities and Limitations." *Citizenship Studies* 20, no. 8 (2016): 1038–44.

———. "Proximity by Design? Affective Citizenship and the Management of Unease." *Citizenship Studies* 14, no. 1 (2010): 17–30.

Fowler, Robert L. "Mythos and Logos." *Journal of Hellenic Studies* 131 (2011): 45–66.

Franco, Cristiana. *Shameless: The Canine and the Feminine in Ancient Greece.* Berkeley: University of California Press, 2014.

Franklin, John Hope, and Loren Schweninger. *Runaway Slaves: Rebels on the Plantation.* New York: Oxford University Press, 2000.

Freehling, William. *The South vs. the South: How Anti-Confederate Southerners Shaped the Course of the Civil War.* New York: Oxford University Press, 2001.

Freeman, Elizabeth. "Synchronic/Anachronic." In *Time,* ed. Joel Burges and Amy Elias, 129–43. New York: NYU Press, 2016.

———. *Time Binds: Queer Temporalities, Queer Histories.* Durham, NC: Duke University Press, 2010.

Frieze, James. "*Imperceptible Mutabilities in the Third Kingdom:* Suzan-Lori Parks and the Shared Struggle to Perceive." *Modern Drama* 41 (1998): 523–32.

Fulkerson, Laurel. "Epic Ways of Killing a Woman: Gender and Transgression" in *Odyssey* 22.465-72." *The Classical Journal* 97, no. 4 (2002): 335–50.

Gaonkar, Dilip Parameshwar. *Alternative Modernities.* Durham, NC: Duke University Press, 2001.

Gardinier, Suzanne. " 'A World That Will Hold All the People': On Muriel Rukeyser." *Kenyon Review* 14, no. 3 (1992): 88–105.

Garman, David. Prepared Statement. Hearing before the Committee on Energy and Commerce in the House of Representatives. 109th Congress. September 7, 2005. https://www.govinfo.gov/content/pkg/CHRG-109hhrg24246/html/CHRG-109hhrg24246.htm.

Garrett-Scott, Shennette. *Banking on Freedom: Black Women in U.S. Finance before the New Deal.* New York: Columbia University Press, 2019.

Garrett-Scott, Shennette, Rebecca Cummings Richardson, and Venita Dillard-Allen. " 'When Peace Come': Teaching the Significance of Juneteenth." *Black History Bulletin* 76, no. 2 (2013): 19–25.

Garsd, Jasmine. "Families of Undocumented Immigrants Lost on 9/11 Continue to Search for Closure." *NPR News,* September 10, 2021. https://www.npr.org/2021/09/10/1036116224/families-of-undocumented-immigrants-lost-on-9-11-continue-to-search-for-closure/.

Gates, Henry Louis. *The Signifying Monkey.* New York: Oxford University Press, 1988.

Gelpi, Albert. "The Transfiguration of the Body: Adrienne Rich's Witness." *Wallace Stevens Journal* 25, no. 1 (2001): 7–18.

Gershkoff, Amy, and Shana Kushner. "Shaping Public Opinion: The 9/11-Iraq Connection in the Bush Administration's Rhetoric." *Perspectives on Politics* 3 (2005): 525–37.

Goebel, Taylor. "Vietnam Refugee, Restaurant Owner Thanks Veterans." *Daily Times,* November 8, 2018. https://www.delmarvanow.com/story/entertainment/dining/2018/11/08/vietnam-refugee-and-rehoboth-restaurant-owner-thanks-veterans/1837688002/.

Goldhill, Simon. "Idealism in the *Odyssey* and the Meaning of *Mounos* in *Odyssey* 16." In *Allusion, Authority, and Truth,* ed. Phillip Mitsis and Christos Tsagalis, 115–28. Berlin: De Gruyter, 2010.

———. *The Poet's Voice: Essays on Poetics and Greek Literature.* Cambridge: Cambridge University Press, 1991.

Gonzáles, Rigoberto. "Be Bold: A Profile of Ocean Vuong." *Poets & Writers,* July 7, 2019.

Goold, Michael, and Andrew Campbell. "Desperately Seeking Synergy." *Harvard Business Review,* September–October 1998.

Greenwood, Emily. "Reception Studies: The Cultural Mobility of Classics." *Daedalus* 145, no. 2 (2016): 41–49.

Grethlein, Jonas, and Christopher B. Krebs. *Time and Narrative in Ancient Historiography: The "Plupast" from Herodotus to Appian.* Cambridge: Cambridge University Press, 2010.

Gwiazda, Piotr. " 'Nothing Else Left to Read': Poetry and Audience in Adrienne Rich's 'An Atlas of the Difficult World.' " *Journal of Modern Literature* 28, no. 2 (2005): 165–88.

———. *US Poetry in the Age of Empire,* 1979–2012. New York: Palgrave Macmillan, 2014.

Haiven, Max. *Cultures of Financialization: Fictitious Capital in Popular Culture and Everyday Life.* Basingstoke, UK: Palgrave Macmillan, 2014.

Haley, Shelley P. "Self-Definition, Community, and Resistance: Euripides' 'Medea' and Toni Morrison's 'Beloved.'" *Thamyris* 2, no. 2 (1995): 177–206.

Hall, John Barrie. *P. Ovidi Nasonis Tristia*. Stuttgart: Teubner, 1995.

Hamilton, Edith. *The Greek Way.* New York: W. W. Norton, 1930.

———. *Mythology.* New York: W. W. Norton, 1942.

Hanink, Johanna. "It's Time to Embrace Critical Classical Reception." *Eidolon*, May 1, 2017. https://eidolon.pub/its-time-to-embrace-critical-classical-reception-d3491a40eec3.

———. "Not All Classicists." *TLS: The Times Literary Supplement*, July 2, 2020.

Hannah-Jones, Nikole. *The 1619 Project: A New Origin Story.* New York: One World, 2021.

Hannah-Jones, Nikole, et al. "The 1619 Project." *New York Times Magazine*, August 14, 2019. https://www.nytimes.com/interactive/2019/08/14/magazine/1619-america-slavery.html.

Harrison, Paul Carter. "*Father Comes Home from the Wars:* An Arrested Development." *Black Renaissance* 15 (2015): 32–39.

Hartman, Saidiya. *Scenes of Subjection: Terror, Slavery, and Self-Making in Nineteenth-Century America.* New York: Oxford University Press, 1997.

Hartnell, Anna. *After Katrina: Race, Neoliberalism, and the End of the American Century.* Albany: SUNY Press, 2017.

———. "Domesticating Katrina: Eliding the International Coordinates of a 'Natural' Disaster." In *Challenging US Foreign Policy: America and the World in the Long Twentieth Century*, ed. Bevan Sewell and Scott Lucas, 244–59. London: Palgrave Macmillan, 2011.

———. "Katrina Tourism and a Tale of Two Cities: Visualizing Race and Class in New Orleans." *American Quarterly* 61, no. 3 (2009): 723–47.

———. "When Cars Become Churches: Jesmyn Ward's Disenchanted America: An Interview." *Journal of American Studies* 50, no. 1 (2016): 205–18.

Herring, George C. "Reflecting the Last War: The Persian Gulf and the 'Vietnam Syndrome.'" *Journal of Third World Studies* 10, no. 1 (1993): 37–51.

———. "The Vietnam Syndrome." In *The Columbia History of the Vietnam War*, 409–29. New York: Columbia University Press, 2011.

Hill, Anita. *Reimagining Equality: Stories of Gender, Race, and Finding Home.* Boston: Beacon Press, 2011.

Hirsch, Marianne. *The Generation of Postmemory: Writing and Visual Culture after the Holocaust.* New York: Columbia University Press, 2012.

Hirschman, Charles, Samuel Preston, and Vu Manh Loi. "Vietnamese Casualties during the American War: A New Estimate." *Population and Development Review* 21, no. 4 (1995): 783–812.

Ho, Rosemarie. "Love, Cruelty, and Grace: Ocean Vuong's *On Earth We're Briefly Gorgeous.*" *The Nation*, December 19, 2019.

Holleran, Samuel, and Max Holleran. "Relic Steel." *Places Journal*, September 2021. https://placesjournal.org/.

Holmes, Brooke. "At the End of the Line: On Kairological History." *Classical Receptions Journal* 12, no. 1 (2020): 62–90.

Hong, Christine. *A Violent Peace: Race, U.S. Militarism, and Cultures of Democratization in Cold War Asia and the Pacific.* Redwood City, CA: Stanford University Press, 2020.

Hong, Mai-Linh K. "Reframing the Archive: Vietnamese Refugee Narratives in the Post-9/11 Period." *MELUS* 41, no. 3 (2016): 18–41.

Huber, Sam. "Muriel Rukeyser 'Among Wars': Feminist Internationalism in the Second Wave." *American Literature* 93, no. 4 (2021): 655–83.

Hunter, Tera. *Bound in Wedlock: Slave and Free Black Marriage in the Nineteenth Century.* Cambridge, MA: Harvard University Press, 2017.

Huyssen, Andreas. *Present Pasts: Urban Palimpsests and the Politics of Memory.* Redwood City, CA: Stanford University Press, 2003.

Ikoniadou, Eleni. *The Rhythmic Event: Art, Media, and the Sonic.* Cambridge, MA: MIT Press, 2014.

Jacobs, Joshua S. " 'An Atlas of the Difficult World': Adrienne Rich's Countermonument." *Contemporary Literature* 42, no. 4 (2001): 727–49.

Jaffe, Sarah. "The Collective Power of #MeToo." *Dissent* 65, no. 2 (2018): 80–87.

Jamieson, Kathleen Hall, and Paul Waldman. *The Press Effect: Politicians, Journalists, and the Stories That Shape the Political World.* Oxford: Oxford University Press, 2003.

Jaramillo, Deborah Lynn. *Ugly War, Pretty Package: How CNN and Fox News Made the Invasion of Iraq High Concept.* Bloomington: Indiana University Press, 2009.

Jeon, Joseph Jonghyun. *Racial Things, Racial Forms: Objecthood in Avant-Garde Asian American Poetry.* Iowa City: University of Iowa Press, 2012.

Jessop, Robert. "Fordism and Post-Fordism: A Critical Reformulation." In *Pathways to Regionalism and Industrial Development,* ed. A. J. Scott and M. J. Storper, 43–65. London: Routledge, 1992.

de Jong, Irene. *A Narratological Commentary on the* Odyssey. Cambridge: Cambridge University Press, 2001.

Jordan, June. "The Bombing of Baghdad." In *The Essential June Jordan,* ed. Jan Heller Levi and Christoph Keller, 50–53. Port Townsend, WA: Copper Canyon Press, 2021.

Junod, Tom. "The Falling Man." *Women & Performance: A Journal of Feminist Theory* 14, no. 1 (2004): 216–27.

Juslin, Patrik N. *Unlocking the Secrets of Musical Affect.* New York: Oxford University Press, 2019.

Kalb, Marvin. "It's Called the Vietnam Syndrome, and It's Back." Blog post. Brookings Institution, January 22, 2013. https://www.brookings.edu/blog/up-front/2013/01/22/its-called-the-vietnam-syndrome-and-its-back/.

Kamin, Debra. "Discrimination Seeps into Every Aspect of Home Buying for Black Americans." *New York Times,* November 29, 2022.

Kaplan, Amy. "Homeland Insecurities: Reflections on Language and Space." *Radical History Review* 85 (2003): 82–93.

Kapp, Matt. "Of Stone and Steel: The Story behind the 9/11 Memorial." *Vanity Fair,* September 9, 2016.

Keeble, Arin. *Narratives of Hurricane Katrina in Context: Literature, Film, and Television.* Cham, Switzerland: Springer International, 2019.

———. "Siblings, Kinship and Allegory in Jesmyn Ward's Fiction and Nonfiction." *Critique: Studies in Contemporary Fiction* 61, no. 1 (2002): 40–51.

Kelman, Ari. *A River and Its City: The Nature of Landscape in New Orleans.* Berkeley: University of California Press, 2003.

Kendi, Ibram X. *Stamped from the Beginning: The Definitive History of Racist Ideas in America.* New York: Nation, 2016.

Kennedy, D. M. *Freedom from Fear: The American People in Depression and War, 1929–1945.* New York: Oxford University Press, 2001.

Khalid, Maryam. "Gender, Orientalism and Representations of the 'Other' in the War on Terror." *Global Change, Peace & Security* 23, no. 1 (2011): 15–29.

Kim, Catherine. "The Battle over Extending the September 11th Victim Compensation Fund, Explained." *Vox*, July 19, 2019. https://www.vox.com/2019/6/20/18691670/jon-stewart-9-11-september-11th-victim-compensation-fund-explained.

Klooster, Jacqueline. "Apollonius of Rhodes." In *Characterization in Ancient Greek Literature: Studies in Ancient Greek Narrative*, ed. K. De Temmerman and E. van Emde Boas, 80-99. Leiden: Brill, 2018.

Kolin, Philip. *Suzan-Lori Parks: Essays on the Plays and Other Works.* Jefferson, NC: McFarland, 2010.

Kurke, Leslie. "Sappho and Genre." In *The Cambridge Companion to Sappho,* ed. P. J. Finglass and Adrian Kelly, 93-106. Cambridge: Cambridge University Press, 2021.

———. "The Value of Chorality in Ancient Greece." In *The Construction of Value in the Ancient World,* ed. John K. Papadopoulos and Gary Urton, 218–35. Los Angeles: Cotsen Institute of Archaeology Press, 2012.

———. *Coins, Bodies, Games, and Gold: The Politics of Meaning in Archaic Greece.* Princeton, NJ: Princeton University Press, 1999.

Kurtz, Howard. "Journalism's Surreal Reality Check." *Washington Post,* September 17, 2001.

———. "The Line between Journalism and Sensationalism." CNN Community Chat, September 26, 2001. http://www.cnn.com/2001/COMMUNITY/09/26/kurtz/index.html.

Lang, Karen. "Eric Fischl's *Tumbling Woman,* 9/11, and Timeless Time." *Future Anterior* 8, no. 2 (2011): 20–35.

Lattimore, Richmond, trans. *Homer:* The Iliad. Chicago: University of Chicago Press, 1951.

Lawson, Mark. "Interview: Suzan-Lori Parks: 'People in America Are Often Encouraged Not to Think.' " *The Guardian.* September 21, 2016.

Lerner, Ben. *Angle of Yaw.* Port Townsend, WA: Copper Canyon Press, 2006.

Lin, Maya. "Making the Memorial." *New York Review of Books.* November 2, 2000.

———. "Maya Lin on the Challenges and Triumphs of Designing the Vietnam Veterans Memorial." Conversations at the 92nd Street Y, October 24, 2018. https://www.youtube.com/ watch?v=ImYdfEe 5xhk.

Liu, Tim. "Looking for Parnassus in America." In *A Sense of Regard,* ed. Laura McCullough, 88–90. Athens: University of Georgia Press, 2015.

Liveley, Genevieve. "Orpheus and Eurydice." In *A Handbook to the Reception of Classical Mythology,* ed. Vanda Zajko and Helena Hoyle, 287–98. Hoboken, NJ: John Wiley & Sons, 2017.

Logan, William. "Old Wounds." *New Criterion* 36, no. 10 (June 2018).

Loraux, Nicole. *The Invention of Athens: The Funeral Oration in the Classical City.* Cambridge, MA: Harvard University Press, 1986.

Lorenzini, Daniele. "Biopolitics in the Time of Coronavirus." *Critical Inquiry* 47, no. S2 (2021): S40–45.

Low, Setha M. "The Memorialization of September 11: Dominant and Local Discourses on the Rebuilding of the World Trade Center Site." *American Ethnologist* 31, no. 3 (2004): 326–39.

Lowenstam, Steven. "The Shroud of Laërtes and Penelope's Guile." *Classical Journal* 95, no. 4 (2000): 333–48.

Luciano, Dana. *Arranging Grief: Sacred Time and the Body in Nineteenth-Century America.* New York: NYU Press, 2007.

Mackie, C. J. "The Earliest Jason: What's in a Name?" *Greece & Rome* 48, no. 1 (2001): 1–17.

Malisch, Jessica L., Breanna N. Harris, et al. "In the Wake of COVID-19, Academia Needs New Solutions to Ensure Gender Equity." *Proceedings of the National Academy of Sciences* 117, no. 27 (2020): 15378–81.

Manuwald, Gesine. "Medea: Transformations of a Greek Figure in Latin Literature." *Greece & Rome* 60, no. 1 (2013): 114–35.

Martin, Richard P. *The Language of Heroes: Speech and Peformance in the* Iliad. Ithaca, NY: Cornell University Press, 1989.

———. "Telemachus and the Last Hero Song." *Colby Quarterly* 29 (1993): 222–40.

Mastronarde, Donald J. *Euripides:* Medea. Cambridge: Cambridge University Press, 2002.

McAlister, Joan Faber. "Domesticating Citizenship: The Kairotopics of America's Post-9/11 Home Makeover." *Critical Studies in Media Communication* 27, no. 1 (2010): 84–104.

McAlister, Melani. *Epic Encounters: Culture, Media, and U.S. Interests in the Middle East since 1945.* 2d ed. Berkeley: University of California Press, 2005.

McKeown, J. C. "The 9/11 Memorial and the *Aeneid:* Misappropriation or Sincere Sentiment?" Blog post. Oxford University Press, May 2, 2014. http://blog.oup.com/2014/05/911-memorial-and-aeneid/.

Medford, Edna G. *Lincoln and Emancipation.* Southern Illinois University Press, 2015.

Metres, Philip. *Behind the Lines: War Resistance Poetry on the American Home Front since 1941.* Iowa City: University of Iowa Press, 2007.

Mignolo, Walter. *The Darker Side of Western Modernity: Global Futures, Decolonial Options.* Durham, NC: Duke University Press, 2011.

Mills, C. W. "The Chronopolitics of Racial Time." *Time & Society* 29, no. 2 (2020): 297–317.

Monteiro, Lyra. "Power Structures: White Columns, White Marble, White Supremacy." Medium, October 27, 2020. https://intersectionist.medium.com/american-power-structures-white-columns-white-marble-white-supremacy-d43aa091b5f9.

Moore, Frazier. "Tom Brokaw's 'Greatest Generation' honors WWII's heroes." *Chicago Tribune,* December 28, 1998.

Mori, Anatole. *The Politics of Apollonius Rhodius' Argonautica.* Cambridge: Cambridge University Press, 2008.

Morris, Ian. "The Use and Abuse of Homer." *Classical Antiquity* 5, no. 1 (1986): 81–138.

Mueller, Marissa. "Recognition and the Forgotten Senses in the *Odyssey.*" *Helios* 43 (2016): 1–20.

Murnaghan, Sheila. "Myths of the Greeks: The Origins of Mythology in the Works of Edith Hamilton and Robert Graves." *Classical Bulletin* 84, no. 1 (2009): 81–89.

Musquelier, Adeline. "Why Katrina's Victims Aren't Refugees: Musings on a 'Dirty' Word." *American Anthropologist* 108, no. 4 (2006): 735–43.

Myers, Michelle. "Quote of the Day: 'Looks like Hiroshima.' " CNET News, August 31, 2015. https://www.cnet.com/news/quote-of-the-day-looks-like-hiroshima/.

Nagy, Gregory. "Lyric and Greek Myth." In *The Cambridge Companion to Greek Mythology*, ed. R. Woodard, 1–33. Cambridge: Cambridge University Press, 2007.

Nájera, Marcos. "Creating Roads: A Conversation with Playwright Suzan-Lori Parks." Blog post. Center Theatre Group, April 4, 2016. https://www.centertheatregroup.org/news-and-blogs/news/2016/april/creating-roads-a-conversation-with-playwright-suzan-lori-parks.

National Centers for Environmental Information. "Costliest U.S. Tropical Cyclones." https://www.ncei.noaa.gov/access/billions/. July 11, 2023.

National Park Service. Vietnam Veterans Memorial. https://www.nps.gov/orgs/1802/vive.htm.

"National Security Strategy of the United States." September 17, 2002. http://nssarchive.us/national-security-strategy-2002/.

National Women's Law Center. Time's Up Legal Defense Fund. https://nwlc.org/times-up-legal-defense-fund-/.

Nayak, Meghana. "Orientalism and 'Saving' US State Identity after 9/11." *International Feminist Journal of Politics* 8, no. 2 (2006): 42–61.

Newlands, Carole Elizabeth. *Playing with Time: Ovid and the Fasti.* Ithaca, NY: Cornell University Press, 1995.

Nguyen, Kelly. "Queering Telemachus: Ocean Vuong, Postmemories, and the Vietnam War." *International Journal of the Classical Tradition* 29, no. 4 (2022): 430–48.

Nguyen, Mimi Thi. *The Gift of Freedom: War, Debt, and Other Refugee Passages.* Durham, NC: Duke University Press, 2012.

Nguyen, Tan Hoang. *A View from the Bottom: Asian American Masculinity and Sexual Representation.* Durham, NC: Duke University Press, 2014.

Nguyen, Viet Thanh. "Seeing Double: The Films of R. Hong-an Truong." *Postmodern Culture* 17, no. 1 (2006).

———. "What Is Vietnamese American Literature?" In *Looking Back on the Vietnam War: Twenty-first-Century Perspectives,* ed. Brenda M. Boyle and Lim Jeehyun, 50–63. New Brunswick, NJ: Rutgers University Press, 2016.

Nguyen, Vinh. "Refugeetude: When Does a Refugee Stop Being a Refugee?" *Social Text* 37, no. 2 (2019): 109–31.

Nickels, Joel. *Poetry of the Possible: Spontaneity, Modernism, and the Multitude.* Minneapolis: University of Minnesota Press, 2012.

Nilges, Mathias. "The Realism of Speculation: Contemporary Speculative Fiction as Immanent Critique of Finance Capitalism." *CR: The New Centennial Review* 19, no. 1 (2019): 37–60.

Nixon, Rob. *Slow Violence and the Environmentalism of the Poor.* Cambridge, MA: Harvard University Press, 2011.

Nora, Pierre. "Between Memory and History: Les Lieux de Mémoire." *Representations* 26 (1989): 7–24.

Norris, Michele. "Suzan-Lori Parks' New Play." NPR, December 5, 2014. https://www.npr.org/2014/12/05/368640540/suzan-lori-parks-new-play-father-comes-home-from-the-wars.

Nyong'o, Tavia. *The Amalgamation Waltz: Race, Performance, and the Ruses of Memory.* Minneapolis: University of Minnesota Press, 2009.

———. "No Halvsies!" *American Quarterly* 59, no. 2 (2007): 459–66.

Obama, Barack. "Presidential Proclamation. Commemoration of the 50th Anniversary of the Vietnam War." May 25, 2012. https://obamawhitehouse.archives.gov/the-press-office/2012/05/25/presidential-proclamation-commemoration-50th-anniversary-vietnam-war.

———. "Remarks by the President at the National Defense University." National Defense University, Fort McNair, Washington, DC, May 23, 2013. https://obamawhitehouse.archives.gov/the-press-office/2013/05/23/remarks-president-national-defense-university.

———. "Remarks by the President at Presentation of the Presidential Medal of Freedom." November 22, 2016. https://obamawhitehouse.archives.gov/the-press-office/2016/11/22/remarks-president-presentation-presidential-medal-freedom.

Olick, Jeffrey K. "Collective Memory: The Two Cultures." *Sociological Theory* 17, no. 3 (1999): 333–48.

Oliensis, Ellen. "Return to Sender: The Rhetoric of *Nomina* in Ovid's *Tristia*." *Ramus* 26, no. 2 (1997): 172–93.

Olsen, Sarah. "Sappho's Kinesthetic Turn: Agency and Embodiment in Archaic Greek Poetry." In *The Routledge Handbook of Classics and Cognitive Theory,* ed. Peter Meineck, William Michael Short, and Jennifer Devereaux, 281–96. London: Routledge, 2018.

O'Malley, Michael. *Face Value: The Entwined Histories of Money and Race in America.* Chicago: University of Chicago Press, 2012.

———. "Specie and Species: Race and the Money Question in Nineteenth-Century America." *American Historical Review* 99, no. 2 (1994): 369–95.

Omi, Michael and Howard Winant. *Racial Formation in the United States.* 3d ed. New York: Routledge. 2015 .

Owen, Sidney George. *P. Ovidi Nasonis: Tristium libri quinque ibis ex ponto libri quattuor halieutica fragmenta.* Oxford: Oxford University Press, 1915.

Park, Yoosun, Joshua Miller, and Bao Chau Van. "Everything Has Changed: Narratives of the Vietnamese American Community in Post-Katrina Mississippi." *Journal of Sociology and Social Welfare* 37, no. 3 (September 2010): 79–106.

Parks, Suzan-Lori. *The America Play and Other Works.* New York: Theatre Communications Group, 1995.

———. *Father Comes Home from the Wars: Parts 1, 2 &3.* New York: Theatre Communications Group, 2015.

———. "Tradition and the Individual Talent." *Theater* 29, no. 2 (1999): 26–31.

———. *Venus: A Play.* New York: Theatre Communications Group, 1997.

Pasco-Pranger, Molly. *Founding the Year: Ovid's Fasti and the Poetics of the Roman Calendar.* Leiden: Brill, 2006.

Patman, Robert G. "Out of Sync: Bush's Expanded National Security State and the War on Terror." *International Politics* 46, no. 2 (2009): 210–33.

Pease, Donald E. *The New American Exceptionalism.* Minneapolis: University of Minnesota Press, 2009.

Peyser, Andrea. "Time to Let People Decide If 9/11 Sculpture Is Art or Exploitation." *New York Post,* September 8, 2016.

Pham, Tony. "ICE Leadership." Immigration and Customs Enforcement. https://www.ice.gov/leadership.

Polack, Peter. "George Washington: The Guerrilla King." *American Intelligence Journal* 36, no. 1 (2019): 167–70.

Pope, Kyle. "NBC Boosts Brokaw Book and Gets Boost Back." *Wall Street Journal,* January 25, 1999.

Postclassicisms Collective. *Postclassicisms.* Chicago: University of Chicago Press, 2019.

Power, Timothy. "Sappho's Parachoral Monody." In *Genre in Archaic and Classical Greek Poetry: Theories and Models,* ed. Margaret Foster, Leslie Kurke, and Naomi Weiss, 82–108. Leiden: Brill, 2019.

President's Advisory 1776 Commission. *The 1776 Report.* January 2021. https://trumpwhitehouse.archives.gov.

Purves, Alex. *Space and Time in Ancient Greek Narrative.* Cambridge: Cambridge University Press, 2010.

Ralli, Tania. "Who's a Looter? In Storm's Aftermath, Pictures Kick Up a Different Kind of Tempest." *New York Times,* September 5, 2005.

Rankine, Patrice. "The Classics, Race, and Community-Engaged or Public Scholarship." *American Journal of Philology* 140, no. 2 (2019): 345–59.

———. *Ulysses in Black: Ralph Ellison, Classicism, and African American Literature.* Madison: University of Wisconsin Press, 2006.

Reagan, Ronald. "Peace: Restoring the Margin of Safety." Address at Veterans of Foreign Wars Convention, Chicago, August 18, 1980. https://www.reaganlibrary.gov/archives/speech/peace-restoring-margin-safety.

Redfield, James M. *Nature and Culture in the* Iliad: *The Tragedy of Hector.* Durham, NC: Duke University Press, 1994.

Reed, Anthony. *Freedom Time: The Poetics and Politics of Black Experimental Writing.* Baltimore: Johns Hopkins University Press, 2014.

Reidy, Joseph P. *Illusions of Emancipation: The Pursuit of Freedom and Equality in the Twilight of Slavery.* Chapel Hill: University of North Carolina Press, 2019.

Rekdal, Paisley. *Nightingale.* Port Townsend, WA: Copper Canyon Press, 2019.

———. "Wounded Elders: On Racial Identity and Reviewing." "The Margins," Asian American Writer's Workshop, July 2018. https://aaww.org/ocean-vuong-immigrant-poetry/.

Rich, Adrienne. *An Atlas of the Difficult World*: 1988–1991. Ann Arbor, MI: Bell & Howell Information and Learning, 2000.

———. *Poetry and Commitment.* New York: W. W. Norton, 2007.

———. *The School among the Ruins*: *Poems,* 2000–2004. New York: W. W. Norton, 2004.

———. *Telephone Ringing in the Labyrinth* : *Poems* 2004–2006. New York: W. W. Norton, 2007.

———. *Time's Power.* Ann Arbor, MI: Bell & Howell Information and Learning, 1989.

———. *Tonight No Poetry Will Serve*: *Poems,* 2007–2010. New York: W. W. Norton, 2011.

Ricks, Thomas. "The Roman Character." *Mount Vernon* (Spring 2022). https://magazine.mountvernon.org/2022/Spring/the-roman-character/.

Rifkin, Mark. *Beyond Settler Time: Temporal Sovereignty and Indigenous Self-Determination.* Durham, NC: Duke University Press, 2017.

Rilke, Rainer Maria. "Orpheus. Eurydice. Hermes." Trans. Peter Joseph Belfiore. *Literary Imagination* 9, no. 3 (2007): 351–53.

Rimell, Victoria. "The Labour of Empire: Womb and World in Seneca's *Medea.*" *Studi italiani di filologia classica* 10, no. 2 (2012): 211–34.

Rood, Tim Carol Atack, and Tom Phillips. *Anachronism and Antiquity.* London: Bloomsbury, 2020.

Rowe, John Carlos. "The 'Vietnam Effect' in the Persian Gulf War." *Cultural Critique* 19 (1991): 121–39.

Roosevelt, Franklin Delano. "Four Freedoms." Annual Message to Congress, January 6, 1941. https://www.fdrlibrary.org/documents.

———. "Message to the Conference on Economic Conditions of the South." July 4, 1938. https://www.presidency.ucsb.edu/documents/message-the-conference-economic-conditions-the-south.

Rose, Jeff. "Biopolitics, Essential Labor, and the Political-Economic Crises of COVID-19." *Leisure Sciences* 43, no. 1–2 (2021): 211–17.

Rose, Kenneth D. *Myth and the Greatest Generation: A Social History of Americans in World War II.* New York: Routledge, 2008.

Rosenfeld, Megan. "Brokaw's 'Generation' Veneration; Documentary on WWII Singles Out the Vets, Leaves Out the Rest." *Washington Post,* January 15, 1999.

Rukeyser, Muriel. *The Collected Poems of Muriel Rukeyser,* ed. Janet E. Kaufman and Anne F. Herzog. Pittsburgh: University of Pittsburgh Press, 2006.

Rumsfeld, Donald. Department of Defense News Briefing. February 12, 2002. https://transcripts.cnn.com/show/se/date/2002-02-12/segment/04.

Saal, Ilka. "Of Diggin' and Fakin': Historiopoiesis in Suzan-Lori Parks and Contemporary African American Culture." In *African American Culture and Society after Rodney King,* ed. Josephine Metcalf and Carina Spaulding, 67–81. New York: Routledge, 2019.

Said, Edward W. *Orientalism.* 25th anniversary ed. New York: Vintage, 2003.

Sammons, Benjamin. "The Space of the Epigone in Early Greek Epic." *Yearbook of Ancient Greek Epic Online* 3, no. 1 (2019): 48–66.

Sanders, Mary. "A Mighty Fortress Is Our Battle Hymn of the Republic: Episcopal Liturgy and American Civil Religion in the National Prayer Service on 14 September 2001." *Anglican and Episcopal History* 85, no. 1 (2016): 63–86.

Scanlon, Jennifer. " 'Your Flag Decal Won't Get You into Heaven Anymore': U.S. Consumers, Wal-Mart, and the Commodification of Patriotism." In *The Selling of 9/11,* ed. Dana Heller, 174–99. New York: Palgrave Macmillan, 2005.

Scheible, Jeffrey Paul. "What's Mr. Pregnant Pregnant with? Prepositioning Katrina Online." In *Old and New Media after Katrina,* ed. Dianne Negra, 203–29. New York: Palgrave Macmillan, 2010.

Schmidt, Aimée. "Down around Biloxi: An Overview of Ethnic and Occupational Identity in a Coastal Town." In *Ethnic Heritage in Mississippi: The Twentieth Century,* ed. Shana Walton and Barbara Carpenter, 122–41. Jackson: University Press of Mississippi and Mississippi Humanities Council, 2012.

Schneider, William. “The Vietnam Syndrome Mutates: An ‘Iraq Syndrome’ May Be Emerging as Disillusionment with the Iraq War Intensifies.” *The Atlantic,* April 25 2006.

Schubert, W. “Zu Ovid, *Trist.* 3.9.” *Gymnasium* 97 (1990): 154–64.

Schwartz, Claire. “Review of *Night Sky with Exit Wounds* by Ocean Vuong.” *Georgia Review* 70, no. 3 (2016): 647–51.

Scodel, Ruth. “The Suitors’ Games.” *American Journal of Philology* 122, no. 3 (2001): 307–27.

Seider, Aaron. “Allure without Allusion: Quoting a Virgilian Epitaph in a 9/11 Memorial.” *Interfaces: Image Texte Language* 38 (2017): 173–94.

Senie, Harriet. *Memorials to Shattered Myths: Vietnam to 9/11.* New York: Oxford University Press, 2016.

Shalev, Eran. “Ancient Masks, American Fathers: Classical Pseudonyms during the American Revolution and Early Republic.” *Journal of the Early Republic* 23, no. 2 (2003): 151–72.

Shapiro, Gideon Fink. “Rebuilding Confidence: The Design, Safety, and Security of One World Trade Center.” *Architect Magazine: The Journal of the American Institute of Architects* (October 2018).

Sharma, Sarah. “Critical Time.” *Communication and Critical/Cultural Studies* 10, nos. 2–3 (2013): 312–18.

———. *In the Meantime: Temporality and Cultural Politics.* Durham, NC: Duke University Press, 2014.

———. “Temporality.” In *Keywords for Media Studies,* ed. Laurie Ouellette and Jonathan Gray, 194–96. New York: NYU Press, 2017.

Sharpe, Christina. *In the Wake: On Blackness and Being.* Durham, NC: Duke University Press, 2016.

Silva, Cynthia. “Tony Pham, Interim Director of Immigration and Customs Enforcement, to Step Down.” NBC News, December 14, 2020. https://www.nbcnews.com/news/asian-america/tony-pham-interim-director-immigration-customs-enforcement-step-down-n1251159.

Silvermintz, Daniel. “Unravelling the Shroud for Laërtes and Weaving the Fabric of the City: Kingship and Politics in Homer’s *Odyssey.*” *Polis: The Journal for Ancient Greek and Roman Political Thought* 21, nos. 1–2 (2004): 26–42.

Smith, Paul Chaat. *Everything You Know about Indians Is Wrong.* Minneapolis: University of Minnesota Press, 2009.

Snepp, Frank. “The Vietnam Syndrome; Are We Telling Ourselves—and Believing—the Same False Story We Told in 1975?” *Los Angeles Times,* May 5, 2013.

Sodaro, Amy. *Exhibiting Atrocity: Memorial Museums and the Politics of Past Violence.* New Brunswick, NJ: Rutgers University Press, 2018.

Spahr, Juliana. *The Connection between Everything with Lungs: Poems.* Berkeley: University of California Press, 2005.

———. “Introduction.” In *American Women Poets in the 21st Century: Where Lyric Meets Language,* ed. Claudia Rankine and Juliana Spahr (Middletown, CT: Wesleyan University Press, 2002), 1–17.

———. “ ‘Love Scattered, Not Concentrated Love’: Bernadette Mayer’s *Sonnets.*” *differences* 12, no. 2 (2001): 98–120.

———. "Poetry in a Time of Crisis." *Poetry Project Newsletter* 188 (February–March 2002).

Spigel, Lynn. *Make Room for TV: Television and the Family Ideal in Postwar America.* Chicago: University of Chicago Press, 1992.

Stahl, Roger. "A Clockwork War: Rhetorics of Time in a Time of Terror." *Quarterly Journal of Speech* 94, no. 1 (2008): 73–99.

Stanley, Kate. "Habits of Modernism." *Criticism* 56, no. 4 (2014): 853–60.

Stavrinaki, Maria. "Fossil." In *Liquid Antiquity*, ed. Brooke Holmes and Karin Marta, 174–77. Athens: Deste Foundation, 2017.

Stevens, Benjamin Eldon. "Medea in Jesmyn Ward's *Salvage the Bones*." *International Journal of the Classical Tradition* 25, no. 2 (2018): 158–77.

Students for Fair Admission, Inc. v. Presidents and Fellows of Harvard College. 600 U.S. 20–1199 (2023). Thomas, J., concurring. https://www.supremecourt.gov/opinions.

Sturken, Marita. "The 9/11 Memorial Museum and the Remaking of Ground Zero." *American Quarterly* 67, no. 2 (2015): 471–90.

———. *Tangled Memories: The Vietnam War, the AIDS Epidemic, and the Politics of Remembering.* Berkeley: University of California Press, 1997.

———. "Weather Media and Homeland Security: Selling Preparedness in a Volatile World." Social Science Research Council Web Forum. *Understanding Katrina: Perspectives from the Social Sciences*, 2005. https://items.ssrc.org/understanding-katrina/weather-media-and-homeland-security-selling-preparedness-in-a-volatile-world/.

Suckert, Lisa. "The Coronavirus and the Temporal Order of Capitalism: Sociological Observations and the Wisdom of a Children's Book." *Sociological Review* 69, no. 6 (2021): 1162–78.

Sullivan, Nikki. *A Critical Introduction to Queer Theory.* New York: NYU Press, 2003.

Taylor, Keeyanga-Yamatta. *Race for Profit: How Banks and the Real Estate Industry Undermined Black Homeownership.* Chapel Hill: University of North Carolina Press, 2019.

TenHouten, Warren. "The Emotions of Hope: From Optimism to Sanguinity, from Pessimism to Despair." *American Sociologist* 54, no. 1 (2023): 76–100.

Trethewey, Natasha. "Our Loss, through the Eye of the Storm." *New York Times*, August 28, 2010.

Trinacty, Christopher. "*Imago Res Mortua Est:* Senecan Intertextuality." In *Brill's Companion to the Reception of Senecan Tragedy*, ed. Eric Dodson Robinson, 11–33. Leiden: Brill, 2016.

Tulip, Madeleine. "From Ancient to Modern Myth: Storytelling in Jesmyn Ward's *Salvage the Bones*." In *Adaptation in Young Adult Novels: Critically Engaging Past and Present*, ed. Dana E. Lawrence and Amy L. Montz, 213–27. New York: Bloomsbury, 2020.

Van Schepen, Randall. "Falling/Failing 9/11: Eric Fischl's *Tumbling Woman* Debacle." *Aurora: The Journal of the History of Art* 9 (2008): 116–43.

Varon, Elizabeth. *Armies of Deliverance: A New History of the Civil War.* New York: Oxford University Press, 2019.

Vernant, Jean-Pierre. *Mortals and Immortals: Collected Essays.* Princeton: Princeton University Press, 1991.

Vietnam Veterans Memorial Fund. "Items at the Wall." https://www.vvmf.org/items/.

Virilio, Paul. *Desert Screen: War at the Speed of Light.* London: Continuum, 2002.

Voigt, Eva-Maria. *Sappho et Alcaeus. Fragmenta.* Amsterdam: Athenaeum, 1971.

Vout, Caroline. "Rodin's Complicated Relationship with Classical Art." *Apollo: The International Art Magazine,* May 22, 2018.

Voyce, Stephen, Juliana Spahr, Joshua Clover, and Jasper Bernes. "Poetry and Other Antagonisms: An Interview with Commune Editions." *Iowa Review* 47, no. 1 (2017): 176–87.

Vuong, Ocean. *Night Sky with Exit Wounds.* Port Townsend, WA: Copper Canyon Press, 2016.

———. *On Earth We're Briefly Gorgeous.* New York: Penguin, 2019.

———. *Time Is a Mother.* New York: Penguin, 2022.

de Waal, Alex. "An Imperfect Storm: Narratives of Calamity in a Liberal-Technocratic Age." Social Science Research Council Web Forum. *Understanding Katrina: Perspectives from the Social Sciences,* 2006. https://items.ssrc.org/understanding-katrina/an-imperfect-storm-narratives-of-calamity-in-a-liberal-technocratic-age/.

Waldman, Kate. "Adrienne Rich on *Tonight No Poetry Will Serve.*" Blog post. *Paris Review,* March 2, 2011. https://www.theparisreview.org/blog/2011/03/02/adrienne-rich-on-%E2%80%98tonight-no-poetry-will-serve%E2%80%99/.

Wallace, Jennifer. *Tragedy since 9/11: Reading a World Out of Joint.* New York: Bloomsbury, 2020.

Walsh, Lisl. "The Metamorphoses of Seneca's *Medea.*" *Ramus* 41, nos. 1–2 (2012): 71–93.

Walton, Shana, and Barbara Carpenter. *Ethnic Heritage in Mississippi: The Twentieth Century.* Jackson: University Press of Mississippi and Mississippi Humanities Council, 2012.

Wang, Claire. "Interim ICE Director, a Vietnamese refugee, Draws Fire from Asian Groups." NBC News, August 28, 2020. https://www.nbcnews.com/news/asian-america/tony-pham-new-interim-ice-director-vietnamese-refugee-draws-criticism-n1238755.

Ward, Jesmyn. *Salvage the Bones.* New York: Bloomsbury, 2011.

———. *Sing, Unburied, Sing.* New York: Scribner, 2017.

Ward, Marchella, and Mathura Umachandran. *Critical Ancient World Studies: The Case for Forgetting Classics.* London: Routledge, 2023.

Weil, Simone. "*The Iliad,* or, The Poem of Force." Trans. Mary McCarthy. *Chicago Review* 18, no. 2 (1965): 5–30.

Weiss, Naomi A. "Ancient Greek *Choreia.*" In *A Companion to Ancient Greek and Roman Music,* ed. T. A. C. Lynch and E. Rocconi, 161–72. London: Wiley-Blackwell, 2020.

West, M. L. *Iambi et Elegi Graeci ante Alexandrum Cantati.* Oxford: Oxford University Press, 1989.

Will, George F. "Anh Duong, Out of Debt." *Newsweek,* December 17, 2007, 84.

William, Bruce Alan, and Michael X. Delli Carpini. *After Broadcast News: Media Regimes, Democracy, and the New Information Environment.* New York: Cambridge University Press, 2011.

Williams, Raymond. *Marxism and Literature.* Oxford: Oxford University Press, 1977.

Woodard, R. *The Cambridge Companion to Greek Mythology.* Cambridge: Cambridge University Press, 2007.

Wright, Gavin. "The New Deal and the Modernization of the South." *Federal History* 10 (2010): 70–73.

Wright, Katharine, Toni Haastrup, and Roberta Guerrina. "Equalities in Freefall? Ontological Insecurity and the Long-term Impact of COVID-19 in the Academy." *Gender, Work & Organization* 28 (2021): 163–66.

Wright, Matthew. "Making Medea Medea." In *Female Characters in Fragmentary Greek Tragedy*, ed. P. J. Finglass and Lyndsay Coo, 216–43. Cambridge: Cambridge University Press, 2020.

Wyke, Maria. *Caesar in the USA.* Berkeley: University of California Press, 2012.

Wyly, Elvin. "The Subprime State of Race." In *The Blackwell Companion to the Economics of Housing: The Housing Wealth of Nations*, ed. Susan J. Smith and Beverley A. Searle, 381–413. New York: Blackwell Wiley, 2010.

Young, Elizabeth Marie. "Inscribing Orpheus: Ovid and the Invention of a Greco-Roman Corpus." *Representations* 101, no. 1 (2008): 1–31.

Young, James E. "Memory and Counter-Memory: The End of the Monument in Germany." *Harvard Design Magazine* 9 (1999).

Yu, Timothy. *Race and the Avant-Garde: Experimental and Asian American Poetry since 1965.* Redwood City, CA: Stanford University Press, 2005.

Zelizer, Barbie, and Stuart Allan. *Journalism after September 11.* London: Routledge, 2002.

Zerubavel, Eviatar. "The Sociology of Time." In *Time, Temporality, and History in Process Organization Studies*, ed. Juliane Reinecke et al., 44–49. Oxford: Oxford University Press, 2020.

Credits

This page constitutes a continuation of page iv.

Index

Figures are indicated by italicized page numbers.